LONDON ARCHITECTURE

by Marianne Butler

London Architecture

Written by Marianne Butler
Edited by Abigail Willis
Design by Lesley Gilmour & Susi Koch
Illustrations by Lesley Gilmour
Photography see image credits p.410
Front cover Tate Modern © Andy Stagg
Inside cover Bloomberg Offices © Nigel Young/Foster + Partners

All rights reserved. No part of this publication may be reproduced, stored in a retrieval system or transmitted in any form or by any means electronic, mechanical, photocopying, recording or otherwise without the prior consent of the publishers and copyright owners. Every effort has been made to ensure the accuracy of this book; however, due to the nature of the subject the publishers cannot accept responsibility for any errors which occur, or their consequences.

Third edition published in 2019 by
Metro Publications Ltd
www.metropublications.com

Metro® is a registered trade mark of Associated Newspapers Limited.
The METRO mark is under licence from Associated Newspapers Limited.

Printed and bound in China.
This book is produced using paper from registered sustainable
and managed sources.

© 2019 Marianne Butler
British Library Cataloguing in Publication Data. A catalogue record for
this book is available from the British Library.

ISBN 978-1-902910-64-2

For William and Joseph
with love

Acknowledgements

I would firstly like to thank Andrew Kershman and Susi Koch from Metro Publications for giving me the opportunity to write this book. My gratitude also goes to Abigail Willis for her patient, insightful editing, Lesley Gilmour for her careful design work and Maxwell Hutchinson for having been such a first-class teacher. My thanks and apologies go to my long-suffering friends and family, and especially my husband, all of whom have shared my enthusiasm for London's architecture, whether they wanted to or not.

This book was written in memory of my brother Daniel.

About the Author

Marianne Butler has a Masters degree in ancient history from the University of London and works as a freelance researcher and writer. She has worked with the architect and broadcaster Maxwell Hutchinson on the book, published by Headline, of the much acclaimed Channel 4 series 'No 57 – The History of a House'. Marianne divides her time between her old house and garden in the Scottish borders and the architectural delights of London.

Contents

Introduction 1
Area Maps 2
01 In the Beginning 11
02 London Before Wren 21
03 Wren and the Rebuilding of the City 59
04 From Restoration to Georgian London 87
05 Victorian London... 135
06 Edwardian London and the Rise of Modernism 171
07 1945 to the 21st Century... 199
08 Walking London's Architecture:
    Bartholomew Walk.. 281
    Fleet Street and Beyond Walk 290
    Greenwich Walk.. 298
    John Nash Walk 308
    South Bank Walk 322
    Strand Walk 336
    Whitehall Walk 344
09 Eat and Drink Architecture.. 357
10 Shopping and Architecture.. 379
11 Architecture with a View 389
Appendix (Timeline, Glossary, Bibliography, Websites) 398
Index... 403

Former Commonwealth Institute (1958-1962), now The Design Museum (John Pawson 2010-2016)

Introduction

Having been brought up in an architecturally soulless New Town, what I remember most about childhood were the trips to London. There was the annual visit to see 'Father Christmas' at the splendid Selfridges store, and occasional films in Leicester Square. But, good as 'Father Christmas' or the film may have been, my imagination was captured by the buildings. The Leicester Square cinema was the largest, plushest interior I had ever encountered and whilst, of course, I didn't know it was 'Art Deco', I just knew the place oozed glamour. What I loved was the fact that a simple stroll down any London street could reveal buildings of startling contrast in age, form and function. I still find London and its architecture exciting and, fortunately, I am not alone in my enthusiasm.

These are exciting times with architects of international renown making their mark on the capital, such as Renzo Piano with the soaring glass Shard transforming the London skyline. Some of London's more established buildings have also been transformed. David Chipperfield has worked his magic at the Royal Academy of Arts in Piccadilly, exposing and utilising forgotten areas, while Amanda Levete has created a welcoming, spacious alternative entrance to the somewhat fusty Victoria and Albert Museum.

The wholesale revamping of areas such as Covent Garden, Paddington Basin, the South Bank and the Kings Cross area, has transformed once rather forbidding places into vibrant public spaces, often revealing architectural gems such as the German Gymnasium. It would seem that we, the public, are being encouraged to take an interest in London's built environment. Visit the capital during the annual 'Open House Weekend' (see p.402) and not only will you be able to experience architectural treasures such as the Daily Express building in Fleet Street and the Foreign Office in Whitehall, but you will also witness the huge, enthusiastic and good-humoured crowds this event attracts.

This guide is essentially a hop, skip and jump through the history of London's built environment. Each chapter begins with a brief description of a particular period and offers a selection of buildings that are representative of that era which, taken together, will, I hope, give the reader an insight into the architectural forces that have shaped this great city.

The principal aim of this guide is to forge or further an interest in London's architecture. I have tried to avoid jargon, for whilst it is one thing to know a spandrel from a spangle, a beautiful building can be admired and understood without recourse to technical language. With this book to hand, and some comfortable shoes the best of London's architecture awaits you.

I have greatly appreciated the correspondence generated from the previous editions of this book. Please e-mail your thoughts to londonarchitecture@yahoo.co.uk.

Marianne Butler

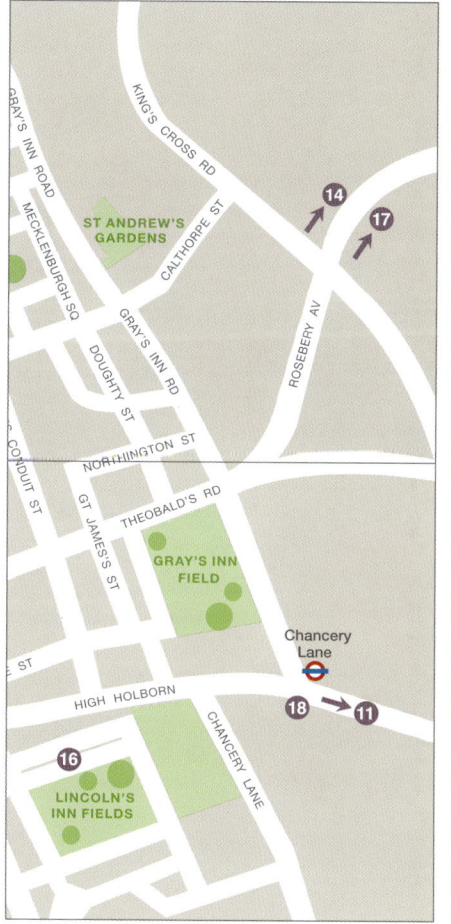

1) British Library B:2 (p.360)
2) BT Tower A:1 (p.223)
3) Centre Point B:1 (p.224)
4) British Museum B:1 (p.183)
5) Daimler Car Hire Garage B:2 (p.195)
6) Euston Fire Station A:2 (p.177)
7) Fitzroy Square A:2 (p.119)
8) Freemasons' Hall B:1 (p.189)
9) Imagination A:1 (p.204)
10) The Midland Grand Hotel B:2 (p.156)
11) St Andrew, Holborn C:1 (p.68)
12) St George's, Bloomsbury B:1 (p.100)
13) St Pancras Station B:2 (p.156)
14) Sadler's Wells C:2 (p.205)
15) Senate House, University of London B:1 (p.197)
16) Sir John Soane's Museum C:1 (p.127)
17) Spa Green Estate C:2 (p.210)
18) Staple Inn, Holborn C:1 (p.43)

Bloomsbury Area Map

1) 17, 21 & 23 Portland Place C:1 (p.314)
2) 27-47 Portland Place C:1 (p.314)
3) All Saints Church, Margaret St C:1 (p.146)
4) All Souls Church C:1 (p.317)
5) BBC Broadcasting House C:1 (p.316)
6) Chester Gate C:2 (p.312)
7) Chester Terrace B:2 (p.313)
8) Cornwall Terrace B:2 (p.313)
9) Cumberland Terrace C:3 (p.310)
10) Fitzrovia Chapel C:1 (p.168)
11) Gloucester Lodge & Gloucester Gate B:3 (p.310)
12) Hanover Gate A:2 (p.313)
13) Hanover Terrace A:2 (p.313)
14) Holy Trinity Church, Marylebone B:2 (p.127)
15) Home House B:1 (p.118)
16) Langham Hotel C:1 (p.314)
17) London Central Mosque A:2 (p.313)
18) Park Crescent B:2 (p.314)
19) Royal College of Physicians C:2 (p.228)
20) Royal Institute of British Architects C:1 (p.314)
21) Rudolf Steiner House B:2 (p.192)
22) St Peter, Vere Street C:1 (p.107)
23) Selfridges B:1 (p.386)
24) Sussex Place B:2 (p.313)
25) Ulster Place B:2 (p.314)
26) Wellcome Trust & Collection C:2 (p.251)
27) Regent's Park Zoo B:3 (p.310)

Regent's Park & Marylebone Area Map

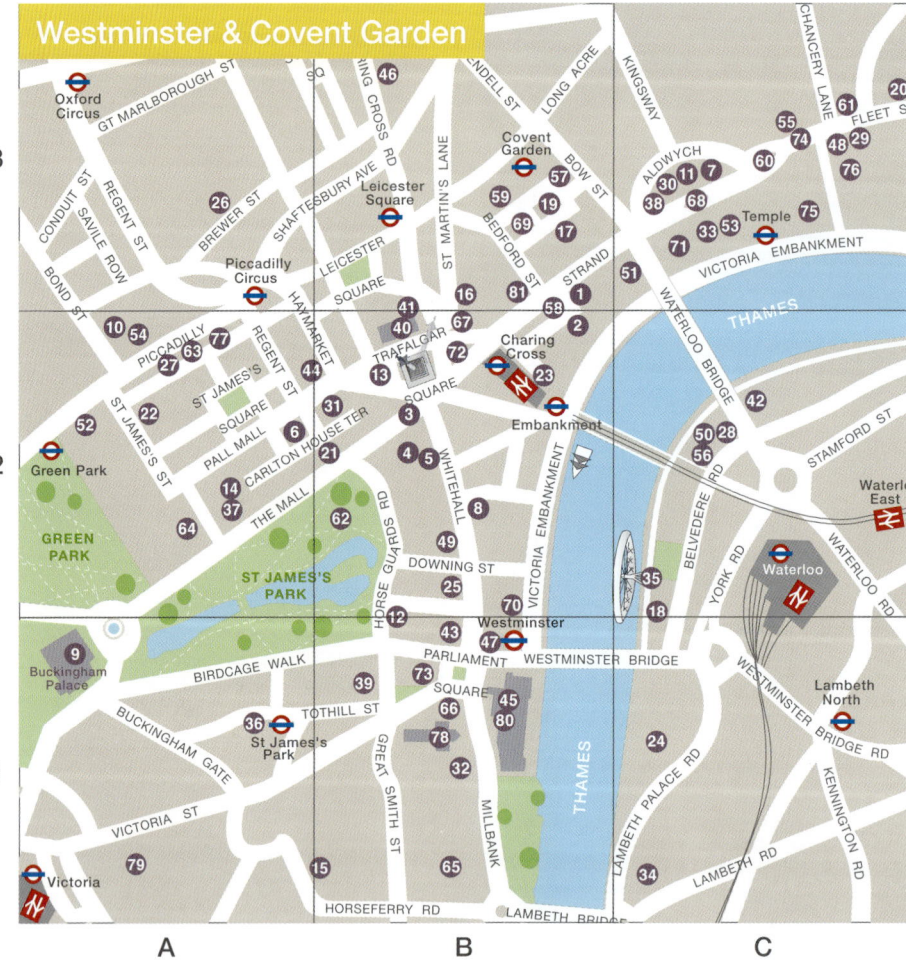

1) 6-10 Adam Street B:3 (p.343)
2) Adelphi B:2 (p.118)
3) Admiralty Arch B:2 (p.349)
4) Admiralty House B:2 (p.349)
5) Admiralty Screen B:2 (p.349)
6) The Athenaeum A:2 (p.318)
7) Australia House C:3 (p.341)
8) Banqueting House B:2 (p.47)
9) Buckingham Palace A:1 (p.320)
10) Burlington Arcade A:2 (p.381)
11) Bush House C:3 (p.341)
12) Cabinet War Rooms B:2 (p.353)
13) Canada House B:2 (p.347)
14) Carlton House Terrace A:2 (p.319)
15) Channel 4 Headquarters B:1 (p.234)
16) Coliseum Theatre B:3 (p.180)
17) Country Life Offices (Former) B:3 (p.181)
18) County Hall (Former) C:2 (p.186)
19) The Piazza, Covent Garden B:3 (p.48)
20) Daily Telegraph building C:3 (p.292)
21) Duke of York's Column B:2 (p.319)
22) The Economist Building A:2 (p.233)
23) Embankment Place B:2 (p.256)
24) Evelina London Children's Hospital C:1 (p.250)
25) Foreign and Commonwealth Office B:2 (p.352)
26) Former Lex Garage A:3 (p.192)
27) Fortnum & Mason A:2 (p.381)
28) Hayward Gallery C:2 (p.219)
29) Hoare's Bank C:3 (p.293)
30) India House C:3 (p.342)
31) The Institute of Directors B:2 (p.318)
32) Jewel Tower B:1 (p.33)
33) King's College C:3 (p.340)
34) Lambeth Palace C:1 (p.55)
35) London Eye C:2 (p.393)
36) London Transport Headquarters A:1 (p.191)
37) Marlborough House A:2 (p.96)
38) ME London C:3 (p.342)
39) Methodist Central Hall B:1 (p.184)
40) National Gallery B:2 (p.346)
41) National Portrait Gallery B:3 (p.369)
42) National Theatre C:2 (p.227)
43) New Government Offices B:1 (p.353)
44) New Zealand House A:2 (p.222)
45) Palace of Westminster/
    Houses of Parliament B:1 (p.143)
46) Phoenix Theatre B:3 (p.193)
47) Portcullis House B:1 (p.353)
48) Prince Henry's Room C:3 (p.294)
49) Privy Council Chambers B:2 (p.352)
50) Queen Elizabeth Hall C:2 (p.219)
51) Queen's Chapel of Savoy C:3 (p.342)
52) The Ritz A:2 (p.370)
53) Roman Bath C:3 (p.338)
54) Royal Academy of Arts A:2 (p.271)
55) Royal Courts of Justice C:3 (p.337)
56) Royal Festival Hall C:2 (p.217)
57) Royal Opera House B:3 (p.22)
58) Royal Society of Arts B:3 (p.118)
59) Russell House, Covent Garden B:3 (p.105)
60) St Clement Danes C:3 (p.338)
61) St Dunstan in the West C:3 (p.293)
62) St James's Café B:2 (p.372)
63) St James's, Piccadilly A:2 (p.92)
64) St James's Palace A:2 (p.42)
65) St John's, Smith Square B:1 (p.372)
66) St Margaret's, Westminster B:1 (p.41)
67) St Martin-in-the-Fields B:2 (p.347)
68) St Mary-le-Strand C:3 (p.106)
69) St Paul's Church B:3 (p.48)
70) Scotland Yard House B:2 (p.353)
71) Somerset House C:3 (p.340)
72) South Africa House B:2 (p.349)
73) Supreme Court B:1 (p.354)
74) The Temple Bar C:3 (p.296)
75) Two Temple Place C:3 (p.169)
76) Temple Church C:3 (p.52)
77) Waterstones, Piccadilly A:2 (p.387)
78) Westminster Abbey B:1 (p.27)
79) Westminster Cathedral A:1 (p.178)
80) Westminster Hall B:1 (p.32)
81) Zimbabwe House B:3 (p.183)

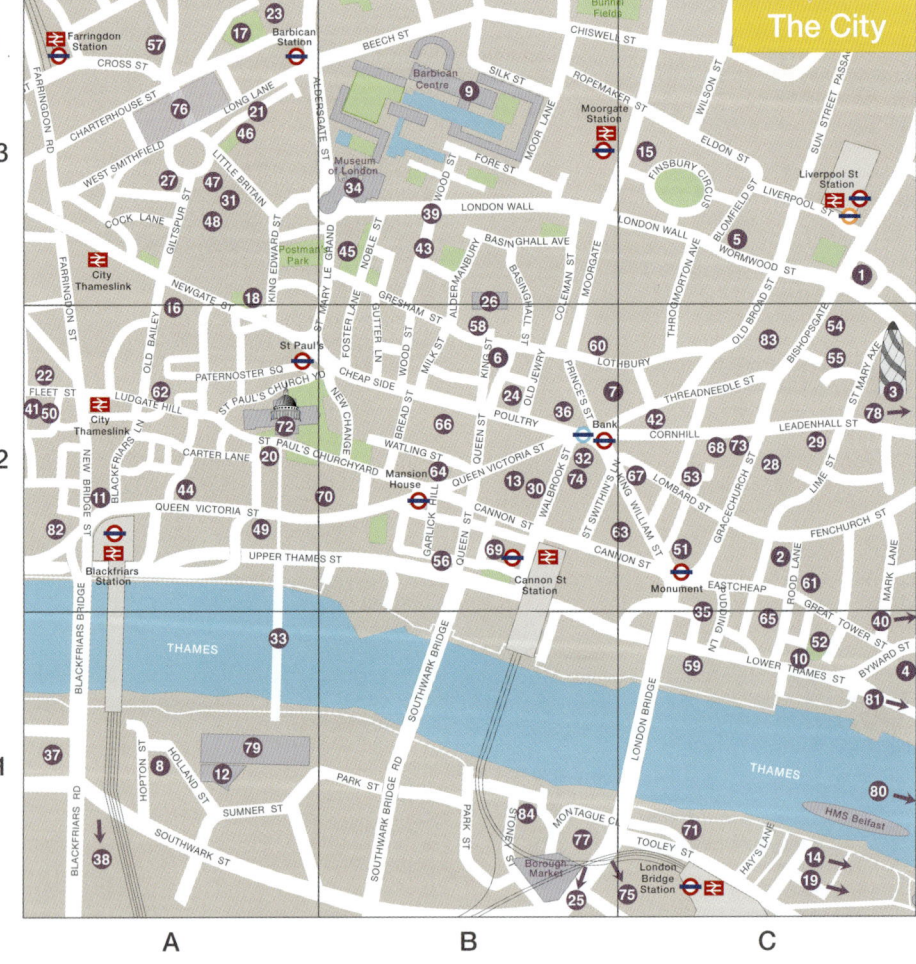

1) 110 Bishopsgate (Heron Tower) C:3 (p.363)
2) 20 Fenchurch Street (Walkie Talkie) C:2 (p.374)
3) 30 St Mary Axe (Gherkin) C:2 (p.244)
4) All Hallows by the Tower C:1 (p.30)
5) All Hallows Church C:3 (p.122)
6) Banco Commerciale Italiana B:2 (p.145)
7) Bank of England B:2 (p.125)
8) Bankside Lofts A:1 (p.332)
9) Barbican Estate B:3 (p.230)
10) Billingsgate Roman House and Bath C:1 (p.17)
11) Black Friar Public House A:2 (p.359)
12) Blavatnik Building (Switch House) A:1 (p.397)
13) Bloomberg European Headquarters B:2 (p.246)
14) Bridge Theatre C:1 (p.324)
15) Britannic House C:3 (p.187)
16) Central Criminal Court, Old Bailey A:2 (p.182)
17) Charterhouse Square A:3 (p.56)
18) Christ Church, Newgate A:3 (p.66)
19) City Hall C:1 (p.242)
20) City of London Information Centre A:2 (p.269)
21) Cloth Fair A:3 (p.282)
22) Daily Express building A:2 (p.292)
23) Florin Court A:3 (p.282)
24) Frederick's Place B:2 (p.119)
25) George Inn B:1 (p.364)
26) Guildhall B:3 (p.18)
27) Haberdashers' Hall A:3 (p.285)
28) Leadenhall Market C:2 (p.384)
29) Lloyd's of London C:2 (p.235)
30) London Mithraeum B:2 (p.18)
31) Maggie's Barts A:3 (p.277)
32) Mansion House B:2 (p.122)
33) Millennium Bridge A:1 (p.331)
34) Museum of London B:3 (p.19)
35) The Monument C:2 (p.394)
36) The Ned B:2 (p.367)
37) One Blackfriars A:1 (p.332)
38) Palestra A:1 (p.260)
39) Pizza Express, Alban Gate B:3 (p.368)
40) Port of London Authority (former) C:1 (p.376)
41) Reuters Building A:2 (p.291)
42) Royal Exchange C:2 (p.383)
43) St Alban B:3 (p.67)
44) St Andrew by the Wardrobe A:2 (p.68)
45) St Anne & St Agnes B:3 (p.69)
46) St Bartholomew the Great A:3 (p.34)
47) St Bartholomew the Less A:3 (p.284)
48) St Bartholomew's Hospital A:3 (p.283)
49) St Benet, Paul's Wharf A:2 (p.70)
50) St Bride, Fleet St A:2 (p.71)
51) St Clement Eastcheap C:2 (p.72)
52) St Dunstan in the East C:1 (p.72)
53) St Edmund the King & Martyr C:2 (p.73)
54) St Ethelburga's C:2 (p.50)
55) St Helen's Bishopsgate C:2 (p.38)
56) St James Garlickhithe B:2 (p.73)
57) St John's Priory A:3 (p.36)
58) St Lawrence Jewry B:2 (p.74)
59) St Magnus the Martyr C:1 (p.74)
60) St Margaret, Lothbury B:2 (p.75)
61) St Margaret Pattens C:2 (p.76)
62) St Martin within Ludgate A:2 (p.77)
63) St Mary Abchurch C:2 (p.77)
64) St Mary Aldermary B:2 (p.78)
65) St Mary at Hill C:1 (p.79)
66) St Mary-le-Bow B:2 (p.79)
67) St Mary Woolnoth C:2 (p.100)
68) St Michael Cornhill C:2 (p.80)
69) St Michael Paternoster Royal B:2 (p.81)
70) St Nicholas Cole Abbey B:2 (p.83)
71) St Olaf House C:1 (p.196)
72) St Paul's Cathedral A:2 (p.63)
73) St Peter upon Cornhill C:2 (p.82)
74) St Stephen Walbrook B:2 (p.85)
75) The Shard C:1 (p.255)
76) Smithfield Market A:3 (p.286)
77) Southwark Cathedral B:1 (p.33)
78) Spanish & Portuguese Synagogue, Bevis Marks C:2 (p.51)
79) Tate Modern A:1 (p.263)
80) Tower Bridge C:1 (p.395)
81) Tower of London C:1 (p.31)
82) Unilever House A:2 (p.194)
83) Vertigo, Tower 42 C:2 (p.377)
84) Winchester House B:1 (p.329)

The City Area Map

Roman Wall and 19th-century statue of Trajan, Tower Hill

01

IN THE BEGINNING

IN THE BEGINNING

There is little evidence of pre-Roman habitation in the London area, just a few small settlements along the river Thames west of Whitehall. One explanation for this is that the river acted as a natural barrier and border between tribes of Britons – the Atrebates, Regni and Cantiaci, who lived south of the Thames, and the powerful Catuvellauni tribe, who lived to the north.

For at least six centuries before the Roman occupation of Britain, the country had enjoyed substantial links with a trade network that stretched from the western Mediterranean, Spain, southern Gaul to northern Germany and the Baltic Islands. The Thames acted as a super highway transporting raw materials and goods from Britain's abundant natural resources, copper from Wales, tin from Cornwall.

Archaeologists tell us that conditions in the area settled by the Romans were idyllic with the land almost entirely covered by a mix of open oak and hazel woodland. Small clean and clear flowing rivers, such as the Fleet and the Walbrook, poured into the Thames, wider than it is today and with small boggy islands at various points. The impetus for bridging the Thames, at a point not far from where London Bridge is today, may have been a military one, but it also made for an attractive and convenient place to settle and trade.

Almost within living memory of the Roman conquest of 43 CE the southern half of Britain was a hive of activity: road building, setting up trading posts and establishing towns. Londinium, as Roman London was to become known, with its establishment as a major port, was central to this activity as at high tide the area could be reached by merchant ships that sailed up the Thames laden with goods from all parts of the Empire.

Founded in about 50 CE on the north bank of the Thames, early Londinium must have resembled a frontier town of the Wild West filled with pioneering merchants and dealers. Settlement began in the area that is today the City of London. Flimsy, wooden dwellings, warehouses and a small fort were hurriedly constructed and the town rapidly expanded, becoming the largest town in Britain in just ten years.

However, this fledgling town was destroyed in 60 CE by the Iceni tribe, from the area known today as East Anglia, led by their queen Boudicca. She also razed Colchester and St Albans to the ground in her revolt against Roman rule. But by 70 CE Londinium was once again a boomtown with a programme of public works in place and within 30 years prestigious buildings such as the amphitheatre, the governor's palace and public baths, now built from durable stone and tile, were gracing its streets. Domestic dwellings and shops were still made from wood, closely packed together and generally situated on the busier, noisier streets.

The central, and perhaps most characteristic feature of any Roman town was the forum, of which Londinium could boast the largest example in the northern Roman provinces, about 600 feet square in total. Situated approximately at modern Cornhill, such a complex consisted of a large central open space surrounded by buildings which housed the town hall and legal centre. The open space was used by the populace as a venue for conducting religious and official business, as well as serving as a market place.

This was a period of great prosperity for the town and for builders and planners this meant that new problems required new solutions. Continuous supplies of food and goods needed to be brought in from outside and it is about this time that the wooden landing stage that had passed as the town's port facility was superseded by a well-built quay, with warehouses of commercial proportions.

Such was its importance Londinium received a visit from Emperor Hadrian in 122 CE and by 200 CE a defensive wall surrounded the city. This wall, almost two miles in length, anywhere between 9 and 15 feet thick, was made from Kentish ragstone, a hard limestone from the Medway valley. The whole of Londinium was enclosed within about 330 acres in total. Gateways controlled access and allowed the passage of the major Roman roads.

During the 3rd century CE the population of Londinium began to shrink considerably, due in large part to an economic downturn. Nevertheless, the citizens of the town were notably wealthier than ever before, with homes made from stone, or at least only half-timbered. Interiors were brightened with mosaics and wall paintings and possibly one or two rooms had the luxury of a hypocaust central heating system.

The end of the 4th century saw the decline of the Roman Empire as a whole and by the mid-5th century Londinium was abandoned and its once grand public buildings and busy streets were left to fall into decay.

There is virtually nothing left to see of Roman London. Although archaeology can confirm the existence and position of buildings, what size they were and what materials they were made of, there is not much in the way of written evidence to tell us what the buildings actually looked like. To bridge this gap we have to consider what Roman architecture was like generally and apply this to London's remains in order to get some sort of picture of Londinium's principal buildings.

Many of the outward forms of Roman architecture are clearly taken from the Greek. In colonising Greece during the 2nd century BCE the blossoming Roman Empire was able to exploit the skill of Greek builders who had perfected a standard post and lintel type of construction. Greek buildings were composed entirely of horizontal blocks supported by columns and walls – this was a style of architecture characterised by straight lines and a complete absence of arches or curves.

However, such construction had its constraints. The span between columns was limited, as was the weight bearing capacity, and therefore buildings could be no more than two storeys high. This was not enough for the Romans who wanted the architecture of their empire to make a strong statement of authority, which was very important to an acquisitive empire. The solution to the need for taller, more lavish buildings was found through the ingenious combination of the column and the rounded arch – a system that allows for a much higher load-bearing capacity.

The rounded arch is a distinctive feature of Roman architecture, as are the orders, or columns. The Romans had five different styles of columns, (see opposite page) three of which were copies of Greek orders – Doric, plain with no fancy carving; Ionic, with fluted or scrolled capitals (that is the uppermost part of the column); and Corinthian with a capital decorated with carved acanthus leaves. All three Greek orders had fluted shafts. To this the Romans added the Tuscan order, like the Greek Doric but even plainer in appearance as the shaft was not fluted, and the Composite, similar to the Corinthian, but with more elaborate carving on the capital.

The influence of Greco-Roman buildings cannot be overestimated, with many of their forms becoming part of the common language of western architecture. Indeed the very word 'architecture' is derived from the Latin and one of the most widely read and respected works on the subject is Vitruvius's *De architectura libri decem* (Ten Books of Architecture). Written sometime between 31 BCE and 14 CE, Vitruvius' treatise highlighted the affinity between architecture and engineering and his work went on to influence a succession of architects over the ages, including Inigo Jones whose work in the 17th century is discussed in the following chapter.

Although there are few Roman remains to be seen in London today, archaeologists continue to turn up interesting finds and the remains of Londonium's amphitheatre can be seen in-situ in the undercroft of All Hallows by the Tower on Byford Street (see p.30). More recently, a reconstruction of the Roman Temple of Mithras, located within the new Bloomberg European Headquarters and featuring interactive displays, has opened to the public. The remains of a Roman house and baths can also be viewed in Billingsgate, but with very limited access, see p.17

In addition, the British Museum and the Museum of London have extensive Roman displays, helping us to imagine what Londinium would have been like.

Tuscan

Doric

Ionic

Modern Ionic

Corinthian

Composite

Above: Capitals of the Five Classical Orders and of the Modern Ionic Order

WHAT THERE IS TO SEE OF LONDINIUM?

Billingsgate Roman House & Baths

101 Lower Thames Street, EC3R 6DL • Nearest transport Monument or Tower Hill LU

Dating from the late 2nd century CE, the remains of this Roman house and bath were first discovered in 1848 during construction of the London Coal Exchange on Lower Thames Street. Further excavations were carried out when the site was redeveloped during the 1960s, when it was found that the building had north and east wings with a hypocaust system (underfloor heating) around a central courtyard. By the 3rd century, a bath house had been added in the courtyard, comprising a frigidarium (cold room), tepidarium (warm room) and a caldarium (hot room).

Visits to this site are limited to pre-booked tours, please visit www.cityoflondon.gov.uk for more details. *Area Map p.8, C:1*

British Museum

Great Russell Street, WC1B 3DG • Tel 0207 323 8299 • www.thebritishmuseum.ac.uk • Nearest transport Holborn LU and Russell Square LU • Admission free except for major exhibitions • See website for opening times

The Weston Gallery of Roman Britain has an extensive display of artefacts from the Roman occupation, although not necessarily from Londinium. The museum also houses a fascinating collection of Greek and Roman architectural remains, offering an excellent insight into how the various orders were used and the role of elements such as capitals, cornices and friczes. *Area Map p.8, C:1*

Left: Ruins of the Roman wall in front of Richard Rogers' Wood Street office

Guildhall

Guildhall Yard, EC2P 2EJ • Tel 020 7332 3700 • www.guildhall-art-gallery.org.uk • Nearest transport Bank LU • See website for opening times and admission charges

During the 1988 preparation work for an extension to the Guildhall in the heart of the City, short stretches of Roman wall were discovered. Much excitement ensued when it was realised that what had been found was the site and remains of Londinium's amphitheatre – which would have been used for gladiatorial combat, animal fighting, public executions and religious ceremonies.

A line set into the paving in the square in front of the Guildhall indicates the location of the amphitheatre. Centuries of subsequent building mean that the site is now below street level, but can be accessed via the Guildhall Art Gallery. Here you can also see archaeological finds relating to the site which provide a good evocation of Roman life. *Area Map p.8, B:3*

London Mithraeum

12 Walbrook, London, EC4N 8AA • www. londonmithraeum.com • Nearest transport Bank or Cannon Street LU • Visits are free of charge but must be booked in advance, see website for opening times

In approximately 240CE, the Romans built a temple next to the Walbrook river to one of their most mysterious cult figures, Mithras. The site was first identified in 1954 when archaeologists, quite by accident, unearthed the carved head of a handsome young god within the remains a small rectangular building. This ignited the imagination of post-war Londoners, who queued for hours to catch a glimpse of the muddy foundations of this exciting Roman discovery at the heart of the City.

Unfortunately, office building took precedence over preserving ancient sites and artefacts at that time. When Bloomberg acquired the site in 2010 to build their European headquarters (see p.246), further excavations were undertaken, and plans were made to incorporate a reconstruction of the temple that reflected its original location, appearance and importance. Bloomberg worked closely with Museum of London Archaeology to create the new London Mithraeum, set at the original depth of the 1954 discovery and located close to the original site.

Visits to the Mithraeum can be made by prior booking only, see above. There is plenty to interest the visitor - at the ground floor there is a display of some 600 artefacts found during the excavations. At Mezzanine level there are interactive information boards about the cult of Mithras and the discovery of the temple. On the floor below is the reconstructed temple, which offers a multisensory experience of sound and light to show how this place of worship would have been used in Roman times. *Area Map p.8, B:2*

Museum of London

London Wall, EC2Y 5HN • Tel 020 7001 9844 • www.museumoflondon.org.uk • Nearest transport Barbican LU and St Paul's LU • Admission free • See website for opening times

A wonderful resource in the heart of the City of London. Archaeological finds and atmospheric room reconstructions show how Roman Londoners would have lived and worked. There is also a section of old Roman city wall which can be glimpsed from the museum. The museum is due to relocate in 2022 to new, larger premises in the Smithfield area - see the Bartholomew Walk on p. 281 for further information. *Area Map p.8, B:3*

Rose window with stained glass designed by Sir James Thornhill in 1722, north transept, Westminster Abbey

02

LONDON BEFORE WREN

LONDON BEFORE WREN

"Go where we may, rest where we will, Eternal London haunts us still" Thomas More

The monk and historian The Venerable Bede (672-735) tells us that even after the end of Roman rule London was a 'mart of many nations'. For many years archaeologists and historians were baffled as to where the latest settlers in London, the Saxons and the Angles – Germanic tribes from Northern Europe who settled in Britain from the late 4th and 5th centuries onwards – actually lived. The first St Paul's, a wooden structure, was in place on the site of the present Cathedral by the early 7th century, but there is no evidence of other early settlement within the abandoned Roman city. It would appear that, initially at least, the Saxons avoided the site of Londinium and settled along the Thames valley at places such as Croydon, Mitcham, Rainham, Hanwell, and Twickenham.

However, during the building of an extension to the Royal Opera House in Covent Garden in the 1980s, remains were found of the elusive Saxon town of 'Lundenwic'. They had settled a mile or so to the west of the ruined Roman city, underlying what is today the West End and the Aldwych, the name which may refer to the 'old town'. It was not until the later Saxon period, from the expulsion of invading Danes by King Alfred in 886 until the Norman invasion of 1066, that the area within the old Roman walls was used again.

There is nothing left standing of the Saxon period, save a few traces at All Hallows by the Tower (see p.30), due mainly to their preference for building timber structures, with no permanent presence above ground, or for re-using Roman brick from the City area, thereby usually confusing matters. Because it is regarded as a time of cultural unenlightenment, the period of about 400 years between the departure of the Romans and the arrival of the Normans is often referred to as the 'Dark Age', although this is a little unfair given the beautifully crafted articles produced in this period, examples of which can be seen in the British Museum.

However, one very important Saxon architectural legacy is the concept of the 'Hall' dwelling – one large room, open to the rafters, constructed of whole or split logs, with a fire for cooking and warmth at the centre. The size of the construction depended upon how many people had to be accommodated. This simple structure was the basis of later 'Halls' for meetings and dining such as at Westminster, the City (Guildhall see p.40) and was central to communal living in institutions such as the Inns of Court (see Section Two 'Walking London's Architecture' p.290) and the colleges of Oxford and Cambridge.

The Norman invaders were prolific castle and church builders, the finest examples of which in London are to be found at the White Tower and St John's Chapel (see Tower of London p.31). The Tower was one of three castles built in the area, the others being Baynard's Castle and Montfitchet Castle, both of which perished in the Great Fire of 1666.

There are two notable characteristics of Norman architecture. The first is the use of enduring materials such as stone, or re-used Roman bricks. The second is the rounded arch, borrowed from Roman builders and the reason why Norman architecture is often called 'Romanesque'. The rounded arch was found to be extremely strong and experimentation with the pointed arch did not come until much later. The ground plan of a Norman church is always in the shape of a Latin cross, with the altar, almost without exception, at the east end of the building – in the direction of Jerusalem – with the main entrance at the west end.

Many Norman French words have been absorbed into our everyday language such as lodge, grange, vale and forest, and place names from this period still resound in London – Barbican, Savoy, Old Bailey, Charterhouse.

The term 'Gothic' is a Renaissance term of abuse – describing a style humanists found barbaric and anti-classical, but which embraced several changes in architectural thought and application between the 12th and 16th centuries.

The Gothic style is generally held to have begun with the rebuilding of St Denis in France in the 1140s, under the auspices of Abbot Suger (1081-1151) who clearly understood the impact architecture could make. He wanted a large building with plenty of room for the perambulation of pilgrims on feast days and, as he firmly believed in the transcendental power of light and colour, he demanded large stained glass windows.

On entering a Gothic church the impression is of great height. This is created by the actual height of the building and by the optical illusion created by the columns, arches and ribs all pointing upwards. An exterior feature of Gothic church building is the flying buttress, the function of which is to counterbalance the outward thrust exerted on the seemingly impossibly tall, thin walls. The best example of Gothic architecture in London is the nave of Westminster Abbey (see p.27).

Medieval London had a rich and sophisticated government and, by virtue of its wealth and size, was more independent than other cities. Some individuals became so rich they were able to lend vast sums to the crown if the king was in need of extra cash. One such wealthy individual was Richard Whittington, businessman, entrepreneur and philanthropist, who died in 1423. He financed the first public toilets in the City, and was three times Lord Mayor of London. Whittington had financial dealings with three monarchs, Richard II, Henry IV and Henry V and was the same person loosely portrayed in the apocryphal story of young 'Dick Whittington and his Cat', retold every year in pantomime.

Despite the proliferation of rich and powerful individuals, London was a place of extremes of wealth and poverty. The livery companies, some dating from the early 12th century, not only looked after the interests of their members but also built enduring premises. The great churches and monasteries of this period are impressive, so too are the Inns of Courts and the houses of noblemen, but the back streets, dark and overhung, would have contained rough dwellings. Whilst the main thoroughfares would have been kept relatively clean, other lesser streets were dank, smelly places, littered with animal dung and industrial waste, such as animal parts discarded by leatherworkers.

The average life expectancy for Londoners during this period was just over thirty years with an infant mortality rate of 30%, with bubonic plague regularly afflicting rich and poor alike. Attempts were made to 'zone' activity in order to contain dirt and pollution, such as having specific areas for butchers on the edge of the City. Others took the view that health terrors were caused by immorality – a moral city was a healthy one – so prostitutes, beggars and lepers were subject to regular summary expulsions. However, rich citizens were able to invest in their spiritual wellbeing by financing monasteries, setting up alms houses or providing wards for unmarried mothers, as a way of avoiding divine retribution.

The start of the 15th century saw London, along with the rest of Europe, emerging from a century of trauma – the 'Hundred Years War' and the Black Death had devastated the population and the accompanying economic recession affected many. Industry, farming and business recovered gradually, and by the end of the century a new confidence and a revival in international trade was being felt, in part due to improvements in navigation and the acquisition of new empires.

By the early 16th century, Henry VIII was changing the face of London with the construction of palaces in Whitehall, St James and Greenwich and projects such as the royal dockyards at Deptford and Woolwich, bringing relief to the overcrowded City docks. The once dominant monasteries were now no longer the most impressive buildings in London. After the Dissolution of the Monasteries, which took place between 1535 and 1540, confiscated monastic land and buildings were sold to friends and supporters of the King, but not many of them could afford lavish new buildings, so adaptation was the order of the day.

It was Cardinal Wolsey who acknowledged the Renaissance fashions emanating from Italy. He commissioned an Italian sculptor to produce roundels of the Roman emperors for his fabulous new Hampton Court, architecturally every inch a late medieval castle.

The Reformation had driven a wedge between England and Catholic Italy and so trade and political ties were established with the protestant Low Countries, and England's ideas of the Renaissance were initially imported via Antwerp rather than Rome or Florence. The reigns of Mary and of Elizabeth saw little in the way of royal building. Elizabeth chose to encourage her courtiers, the new men who rose up in wealth and influence under the Tudor monarchy, to build for her. The queen preferred to be entertained in such 'prodigy houses' rather than at court, and spent much of her reign going from one house to another, along with her colossal entourage. Such a house would be built with a range of state apartments – a great chamber, withdrawing chamber and bedroom fit for a monarch – all financed by the host.

It was under Elizabeth's successor James I, who came to the throne in 1603, that Renaissance architecture was embraced and the first building to be started in this new style was the Queen's House at Greenwich by Inigo Jones (see p.44).

What was so new about the Renaissance style? The architect now had to be mindful of the ideals of proportion and symmetry, using Classical inspiration and mathematical precision to create unified, balanced structures. Inigo Jones (1573-1652) was the first in England to implement these ideals. Despite his humble background, Jones had travelled extensively in Italy, studying its Roman remains a full century before it became de rigeur for every fashionable young man of means to do so. He became Surveyor of the King's works in 1615 and in the following year received the commission from Queen Anne, wife of James, to design a new pavilion at Greenwich.

Jones' first role at the Royal Household was as a masque designer, working in collaboration with the dramatist Ben Jonson, when they turned traditional court entertainment into a theatrical and intellectual display of excellence. Masques combined music, drama, dance and art and Jonson and Jones were the European masters of the genre – until they quarrelled and the partnership was ended in 1632. However, by this time, Jones was well established as an architect, responsible for England's first truly Renaissance buildings – the Banqueting House, the Queen's House, the first protestant church and the first London square at Covent Garden (see p.48).

However, with the execution of Charles I in 1649 and inauguration of the Commonwealth under Oliver Cromwell all such work was stopped and Jones's services were no longer required. Inigo Jones died in 1652, eight years before the Restoration that would witness the rise of the architectural genius Christopher Wren.

Westminster Abbey

Westminster Abbey

Dean's Yard, SW1 • Tel 020 7222 5897 • www.westminster-abbey.org • Nearest transport St James's Park or Westminster LU • See website for opening times and admission charges

Westminster Abbey, or more correctly The Collegiate Church of St Peter, Westminster, is a living, breathing place of Anglican worship with regular daily and Sunday services throughout the year as well as a host of special services.

Since William the Conqueror's coronation here on Christmas Day 1066, most English monarchs have been crowned at the Abbey. The building has become the focus for national sorrow, such as the funeral of Princess Diana in 1997, and celebration – services of thanksgiving and royal weddings, most recently that of Prince William and Catherine Middleton, the Duke and Duchess of Cambridge.

The royal couple made their vows standing on the newly restored Cosmati pavement in front of the High Altar. Unlike Roman or medieval mosaics, Cosmati work consists of geometrical patterns built up from pieces of stone, purple porphyry, green serpentine, yellow limestone, as well as opaque coloured glass, cut into a variety of shapes: triangles, squares, circles, rectangles etc. The pavement covers an area of 24 feet 10 inches (7m 58cm) square and had been covered by carpet for the past 150 years until the restoration work was completed in 2010.

A Benedictine monastery had been established on the site by the Saxons from as early as the 7th or 8th century. Sacked by the invading Danes, and restored by King Edgar (944-75) the abbey subsequently fell into disrepair.

It was the Saxon King Edward the Confessor who decided to build a magnificent church on the site, regardless of cost. Between 1045-50 he built what was in reality a classic Norman church – years before the Norman invasion of 1066. Edward had spent 25 years in exile in Normandy and had not only admired its architecture but understood the impact a church building could have as a unifying force within the kingdom. Edward's church was to be larger than any in Normandy. He also had his residence built alongside, thus establishing the site of the Palace of Westminster. Very soon the medieval town grew around this 'west minster'.

Little is left of Edward's Norman church as subsequent monarchs have left their mark on the Abbey. There is a depiction of the building stitched into the Bayeux Tapestry – how accurate is open to debate.

After the Confessor's founding of the Abbey, the monarch who has made the greatest architectural contribution to the place is Henry III. During his long reign in the 13th century, Henry, with far more ambitious good taste than cash, undertook many major building projects. At Westminster he added the Lady Chapel to the east side of the existing Abbey (1220 to 1245) and as soon as this was completed he had the Norman church demolished to make way for a magnificent new construction. The full extent of this new building was never fully realised and its plan has been lost to us, but nevertheless Henry's legacy is, in the words of Nikolaus Pevsner, 'the most French of all English Gothic churches'.

The building and repair of the Abbey was paid for by the Crown until 1698 when an annual payment for upkeep was granted by Parliament. The names of the masons and architects associated with the Abbey include Henry Yevele, Sir Christopher Wren, Nicholas Hawksmoor, John James, James Wyatt, Edward Blore and Sir George Gilbert Scott.

The available space in this little book only allows the briefest outline of some of the highlights of this magnificent building:

The Exterior. Well worth taking the time to have a closer look – even if time does not allow a visit to the inside of the Abbey. Of particular note is the North Transept, this is the 'short arm' of the Latin cross that faces Parliament Square. Indeed for many years this served as the state entrance from the Palace of Westminster – three porches under pointed gables are reminiscent of work at Chartres, with beautifully carved figures, a splendid rose window and two-tiered flying buttresses.

Visitors to the Abbey today are admitted via the West Front, an architectural mix of the 12th, 14th, 15th and 16th centuries. The most iconic part of this building, the twin towers, are a strange but pleasing mix of Gothic and Classical detail. They date from the early 18th century (designed 1734, built 1735-45) and were the last project of Nicholas Hawksmoor and completed after his death.

Great Cloister. A reminder that this building was once a monastery for this is where the monks of the Abbey would live and study. The visitor has to imagine glass in the windows, rushes on the floor, chairs, tables and log fires keeping the whole area warm. Surprisingly large, each cloister is approximately 100 feet in length, but there is very little of the 11th-century building remaining since much of it was destroyed in a fire in 1298. Most of the building dates from the 13th to the 15th centuries.

Pyx Chamber. The word 'pyx' means box – in this case a box for money. This room derives its name from the fact that it was at one time the site of the crown treasury. Part of the Undercroft, and sometimes referred to as the Chapel of the Pyx, this vaulted chamber retains its original medieval tiled floor.

The Nave. Only 35 feet wide but the tallest in England at 102 feet (31 metres); Salisbury

Cathedral, the next in height, is 84 feet (25.5 metres). It was begun in 1246, making it the first example of High French Gothic architecture to be built in England. The tall, thin walls only stand upright with the aid of the massive external flying buttresses, which are a work of art in themselves.

Chapter House. Begun in 1246, this octagonal vaulted room of eight bays, supported on a single pier, has a spectacular tent-like appearance. The huge windows with heraldic crests and the beautifully tiled floor date from 1259. From about 1400 to 1547 this room was used for Parliamentary meetings.

Chapel of Henry VII (also known as the Lady Chapel). Built between circa 1503-15, when it replaced the Lady Chapel of 1220-45. The superb pendant fan vaulting makes this arguably the most spectacular surviving ceiling of its time.

Feretory – Chapel of St Edward the Confessor. This Chapel, containing the shrine of St. Edward the Confessor, lies east of the Sanctuary at the heart of the Abbey. It is closed off from the west by a stone screen, probably dating from the 15th century, carved with scenes from the Confessor's life. Many past kings and queens are buried here, and the chapel has been a place of pilgrimage – particularly for the sick who would come to the shrine on their knees seeking a cure. Of particular note is the Cosmati work on the base of the Confessor's shrine – red and green porphyry and glass mosaics set into Purbeck stone.

There are many works of art and monuments to see within the Abbey – over 450 if the grave–slabs are included. Poets' Corner, located in the South Transept, is almost a 'Who's Who' of English literature, and always popular with visitors. Geoffrey Chaucer, author of *The Canterbury Tales*, was the first poet to be buried here in 1400. He held the post of Clerk of the King's Works at the nearby Palace of Westminster for a short time, and would have been very familiar with the Abbey. In March 2018 the remains of Professor Stephen Hawking were interred near the graves of Isaac Newton and Charles Darwin.

In June 2018 the Queen's Diamond Jubilee Galleries were opened to the public. The museum galleries, set more than 16 metres above the Abbey's floor in the medieval Triforium, explain the history of the building and display treasures from the Abbey's collection. The poet and church lover, Sir John Betjeman. described the Triforium as having 'the best view in Europe'. Access to this space is through the Weston Tower, a new construction, housing a staircase and lift. The tower is the first major addition to the Abbey church since Hawksmoor's twin towers of 1745, and was designed by Ptolemy Dean, the Abbey's Surveyor of the Fabric, who took inspiration from a star shape pattern throughout found in the Abbey.
Area Map p.6, B:1

All Hallows by the Tower

Byward Street, EC3R 5BJ • Tel 020 7481 2928 • www.ahbtt.org.uk • Nearest transport Tower Hill LU • See website for opening times

This interesting church, located very close to the Tower of London in the City, was built as a daughter church of Barking Abbey, Essex and first mentioned in documents dating from 1086. All Hallows can claim to be the only City church with standing fabric from the Anglo-Saxon period; a section of the south-west wall and part of the north-west corner of the nave. Two sections of Roman tessellated pavement are also to be seen, one still in situ between the Saxon foundations of the tower, the other recently re-laid as part of the crypt flooring.

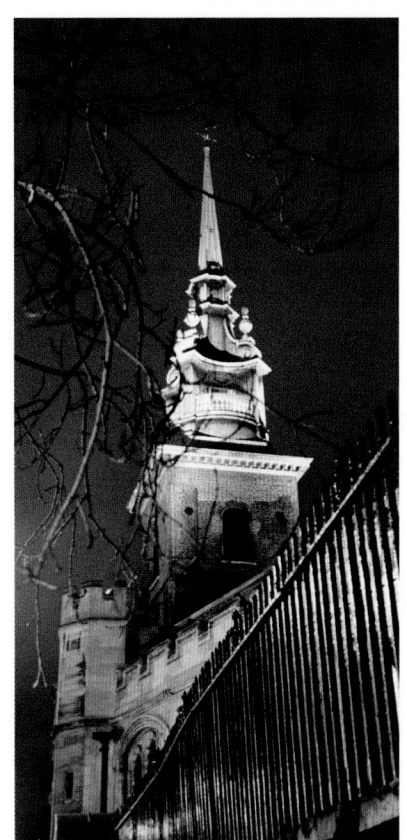

Most of the pre 17th century fabric of the church was destroyed in a fire in 1650 and the church was rebuilt between 1658-59 making it the only London church to have work carried out during the Commonwealth. The church again suffered extensive damage from enemy bombing during the Second World War and drastic reconstruction was undertaken by Lord Mottistone of Seely and Paget architects. The same firm were commissioned to add the spire to the brick tower during the 1950s.

Do not miss the exquisite font cover dated 1682 and attributed to Grinling Gibbons – a feast of carved leaves, cherubs, fir cones and flowers. Many historical figures are associated with this church – William Penn, Quaker and founder of Pennsylvania was baptised here and John Quincy Adams, 6th President of the USA, married here in 1797.
Area Map p.8, C:1

Tower of London

Tower Hill, EC3 • Tel 0870 756 606 (information line) • www.hrp.org.uk • Nearest transport Tower Hill LU & Tower Gateway DLR • See website for opening times & admission charges

The Tower of London, built by William the Conqueror in the south-east angle of the existing Roman wall sometime after 1077, has been a royal palace, fortress, prison, place of execution, jewel house, mint, arsenal and royal zoo. Successive monarchs have added various buildings thereby bequeathing a complex mix of architecture from various periods, such as the Cradle Tower (1348-1355), New Armouries (1663) and the Waterloo Barracks (1845). However, as at Westminster Abbey, Henry III made a significant mark.

The oldest and most familiar building within the walled 12 acre site is the central keep, the White Tower. It was a bold statement by the conquering Normans, and initially served as a stronghold as well as a palace. The Tower walls, in parts 12 feet thick, were originally made from Kentish ragstone with Caen stone dressings, specially shipped over from Normandy, now replaced with Portland stone. Originally the walls were whitewashed, hence the name. The White Tower is a roughly square building with turrets on each of the four corners. The whole roofline was crenellated until the mid-16th century when ogee caps were added.

One of the architectural highlights of the Tower is St John's Chapel on the second floor. This is perhaps one of the finest early Norman structures remaining anywhere. It is massive and solid with a tunnel-vaulted nave – a feature almost unique in England. With its two-level arcade, powerful round piers below and dramatic arches it certainly is one of the most impressive spaces in London. Pleasingly unadorned, to the modern eye at least, the Chapel lost its screens and stalls during the Reformation. *Area Map p.8, C:1*

Westminster Hall

Houses of Parliament, Palace of Westminster, SW1 • www.parliament.uk/visiting • Nearest transport Westminster LU • Entrance by ticket – please apply to your local MP, paid guided tours are also available during the Summer Opening, see website for more details

The Hall was originally a Norman addition incorporated into the old Palace of Westminster built by Edward the Confessor as the principal residence of the monarch and remaining so until the reign of Henry VIII. Thereafter it was used mainly as a meeting place for Parliament, a use it has retained through to the present day. The Hall and the Jewel Tower are the only surviving parts of the old Palace. Built by William II (also known as William Rufus) in 1099, some of the original masonry still survives but the Hall was heavily renovated during the reign of Richard II when the magnificent hammerbeam roof was added.

This renovation of the Hall was needed to create a setting appropriate for royal ceremonies on a grand scale and was the work of royal mason/architect Henry Yevele, who also oversaw the building of the nave at Westminster Abbey. However, it was master carpenter Hugh Herland who was the genius responsible for the hammerbeam roof. It had already been decided to use the Hall's existing walls, so the new roof needed to span the whole space without the use of aisle posts, which by the 14th century, as a rule, were not included in British halls. This had never been achieved before on such a large scale and Herland's solution was to apply an arched brace to each bay, intersecting the hammerbeam construction. The roof timbers of Westminster Hall are entirely of oak, and nearly all are cases of Sussex oak, felled from the royal forests. The whole roof weighs in the region of 660 tons and is a magnificent sight.
Area Map p.6 B:1

Jewel Tower

Abingdon Street • SW1 3JY • Tel 020 7222 2219 • www.english-heritage.org.uk • Nearest transport Westminster LU • See website for opening times and admission charges

The Jewel Tower was built in the south-west corner of the old Palace of Westminster grounds in 1365/66 to house the personal treasure of King Edward III. The Tower had been moated as an effective additional form of security, the remains of which can still be seen.

The building is L-shaped, has three floors each consisting of just one large room, with a fireplace and a smaller inner-room. The polygonal turret contains the stone staircase. The ground floor rooms are a little grander than the upper floors, with an interesting vaulted ceiling and three bosses depicting comical faces. It is believed that this building was constructed by the great mason Henry Yevele, who was responsible for work on the nave at Westminster Abbey next door. The only jarring note of the Tower is the size and shape of the windows. These were enlarged and dressed with Portland stone in the early 18th century when the building was used as a record repository for the Parliament Office.

The Tower now houses a small museum containing items relating to the old Palace of Westminster. *Area Map p.6, B:1*

Southwark Cathedral

Montague Close, SE1 9DT • Tel 020 7367 6700 • www.southwarkcathedral.org.uk • Nearest transport London Bridge LU & Rail • See website for opening times

Amid the railway tracks, roads, blocks of flats and offices and in the shadow of the approach to London Bridge stands Southwark Cathedral. Built on the site of a much earlier church this former Augustinian Priory of St Mary Overie (meaning St Mary 'over the river') has its Norman and medieval plan still pretty much intact. This is despite serious fires in 1212 and 1390 which destroyed most of the fabric of the building. Subsequent rebuilding and renovation have nonetheless left the choir and retro-choir undisturbed and for this reason the Cathedral can lay claim to being the 'oldest Gothic building in London'.

The addition of ancillary accommodation, including a theological library, shop and refectory was completed in 2001. The old and new parts of the building marry perfectly, which is due to the careful use of materials: limestone and Norfolk flint under a Westmorland slate roof. *Area Map p.8, B:1*

02 London Before Wren

St Bartholomew the Great

West Smithfield, EC1A 7JQ • Tel 020 7606 5171 • www.greatbarts.org • Nearest transport Farringdon or Barbican LU • See website for opening times & admission charges

The church was founded in 1123 as an Augustinian priory by Rahere (a compassionate and enterprising monk). He established the kernel of the now world famous St Bartholomew's Hospital and in 1133 received royal permission to hold an annual fair, which raised a considerable sum of money for his work – see Bartholomew Walk p.281.

Very little of the 12th-century church remains, however what survives is one of the most beautiful buildings in London. Originally a modest structure of a choir, ambulatory and Lady Chapel, enlargement took place during the next 100 years with the addition of transepts and crossing, as well as a lengthening of the nave which gives the whole building the feel of a classic Norman church.

The part of the priory serving as a hospital survived the Reformation but the monastery itself was closed, the church sold off to the parish and part of the nave demolished. The splendid gateway of 1595 marks where the original nave finished. The crypt was used as a wine and coal store; the Lady Chapel became private dwellings and a print works (Benjamin Franklin worked here during 1725); horses were stabled in the cloisters; a blacksmith operated in the north transept and a carpenter set up a workshop in the sacristy. The building was also used as a non-conformist meeting place and a school at various times throughout its history. It is a small miracle there was any fabric left to work with but the eminent architect Aston Webb spent from 1884-96 restoring the building to what we see today.

The church contains many notable features including an oriel window, installed in 1517, overlooking the choir (probably to act as a watch tower to keep an eye on the gifts left at Rahere's tomb). The crossing has splendid, solid Romanesque pillars and the earliest pointed arches in London dating from 1145-60. The medieval font dates from around 1405, and served in the baptism of painter William Hogarth in 1697. The interior has often been used for filming, such as 'Four Weddings and a Funeral' (1994) and 'Shakespeare in Love' (1998). *Area Map p.8, A:3*

Right: The Norman choir of St Bartholomew the Great

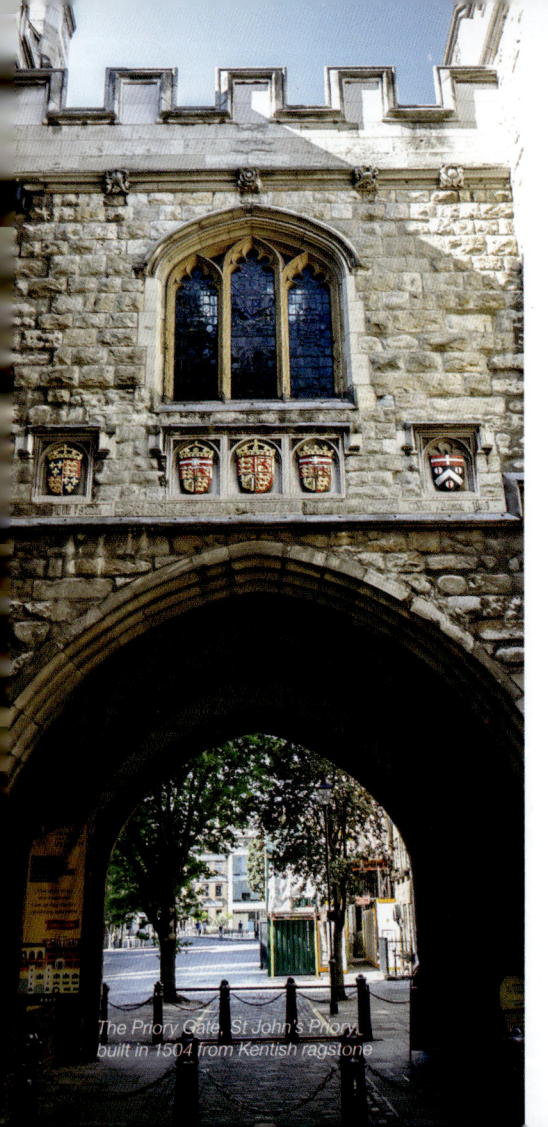
The Priory Gate, St John's Priory, built in 1504 from Kentish ragstone

St John's Priory

St John's Gate, St John's Lane, Clerkenwell, EC1M 4DA • Tel 020 7324 4070 • www.museumstjohn.org.uk • Nearest transport Farringdon LU & Rail • See website for opening times

Established in about 1140, the Knights Hospitallers' Priory of St John covered about six acres in Clerkenwell and was the English headquarters of the Order of St John. The Order was founded to give succour to pilgrims and crusaders, and in 1877 became the St John Ambulance Brigade.

After the dissolution of the monasteries during the reign of Henry VIII, the Priory buildings were put to various uses, the residence of Queen Elizabeth I's Master of Revels; a pub; a coffee shop, reputedly run by the father of the painter William Hogarth; offices of 'The Gentlemen's Magazine'. Today St John Ambulance have their head office on the premises, thus bringing the story full circle.

What is left of architectural interest is a fine 12th-century crypt over which a Georgian parish church was built; the original church having been circular, similar to Temple Church (see p. 52). Also of note is the large and impressive St John's Gate, built in 1504, its grand size denoting the importance of the Priory and now home to a museum containing many items of interest such as illustrated manuscripts and items relating to the history of the Order.
Area Map p.8, A:3

St Pancras Old Church

Pancras Road, NW1 1UL • Tel 020 7387 4193 • www.posp.co.uk • Nearest transport King's Cross LU & Rail • See website for details

Amid the redevelopment in the King's Cross area, sits St Pancras Old Church. Given its present surroundings, it is difficult to believe that this little church was once encircled by fields, serving a country parish that stretched from what is now the Russell Square area all the way to Hampstead.

The church is named after Pancratius, an orphaned boy living in the household of the Emperor of Rome who, on refusing to relinquish his Christian beliefs, was martyred in 304 CE; a basilica was later built in his honour on the Aurelian Way. During the time of the Roman occupation of London the River Fleet was navigable to just beyond where the church is sited today. Legend tells us that an encampment here raised the first place of worship in the name of St Pancras, the anglicised version of his name. What form this building took can only be guessed at as no trace of it remains. However a carved altar stone dating from the 6th or 7th century and an entry in the Doomsday Book of 1086 confirm the church's earlier existence making it one of the oldest sites of continuous Christian worship in London.

The fairly substantial Norman church had been reworked during the 12th century and

Above: The Soane Mausoleum in the churchyard is one of only two Grade I listed monuments in London. The design was a direct influence on Giles Gilbert Scott's design for the red telephone box

dramatically remodelled during the 19th century, with mixed success. It is a pity that during this latter work the medieval tower was removed in order to extend the church west and add a south facing entrance porch and tower. There are many fine monuments in the churchyard including that of the eminent architect Sir John Soane and his family (illustrated here).

St Helen's Bishopsgate

Great St Helen's, EC3A 6AT • Tel 020 7283 2231 • www.st-helens.org.uk • Nearest transport Liverpool Street LU & Rail • See website for opening times

An interesting church that escaped damage in the Great Fire of 1666 and World War II, only to sustain serious damage by IRA bombing in 1992 and 1993. Architect Quinlan Terry restored and reworked the interior between 1993-95 to provide a more flexible space for worship. This little church, now almost hidden amid a thicket of tall, shiny office blocks, started life circa 1200-1215 as a Benedictine nunnery. However there was already a parish church on the site, possibly 11th or early 12th century, and the nun's new church was built alongside the existing building. This has given the church its odd appearance of having two 'main' entrances almost side by side, one for the nuns, and one for the parish. The naves are now one, but it is possible to trace their original configuration.

The church has a number of noteworthy features, not least of which is the Shakespeare window which dates from 1884 (he is believed to have lived nearby); a richly decorated pulpit dating from circa 1633 and a superb collection of pre-1666 monuments. *Area Map p.8, C:2*

Eltham Palace

Eltham Palace

Court Yard, Eltham, SE9 5QE • Tel 0208 294 2548 • www.elthampalace.org.uk • Nearest transport Eltham Rail • See website for opening times & admission charges

Eltham Palace was built on a site that has been occupied by substantial houses since Saxon times. In 1275 it was owned by the Bishop of Durham who presented it to the first Prince of Wales, the future King Edward II. It was a favourite royal palace until Henry VIII's reign, when Greenwich was preferred. Eltham was sold off during the Commonwealth and was subject to an inglorious history until 1931 when the exceedingly wealthy Stephen Courtauld purchased the lease and embarked on a six-year restoration programme of the old Hall. He also built an entirely new adjoining house. Within a mere eight years the lease was sold to the Army Education Corps and in 1995 the property was acquired by English Heritage.

The Great Hall dates from 1475, measures 100 feet by 36 feet, and still has its superb original hammerbeam ceiling the only survival of the Palace's medieval splendour. The house built during the 1930s is Art Deco in style which, whilst not pleasing the purists, does provide a terrific contrast to the Hall. Of particular note is the entrance hall where the glass dome illuminates some extremely elegant period furniture and a circular carpet beneath. Both buildings are set in romantic, moated gardens.

Guildhall

Gresham Street, London, EC2V 7HH • Tel 020 7606 3030 • www.guildhall.cityoflondon.gov.uk • Nearest transport Bank LU • The Guildhall is open to the public when not in use, see website for details

There had been a guildhall (from the Anglo Saxon 'gild' meaning payment – a place where citizens paid their taxes) on this site for many years. Apart from the East Crypt which dates from 1042, this building begun in 1411, is one of the best examples of architecture from this period. Enemy bombing in 1940 destroyed the complex of the City's medieval buildings, the Guildhall being the only survivor. Post-war restoration was carried out by Sir Giles Gilbert Scott who also added new office accommodation on the north wall. Further work during the 1960s added more offices as well as a new L-shaped library. The building of the art gallery during the 1990s was delayed by the exciting discovery of remains of a Roman amphitheatre (see previous chapter). The art gallery, designed by Richard Gilbert Scott, was opened in 1999.

The Guildhall is the City's largest secular building and is still an important focus of official ceremonies and celebrations. Much of its 15th-century perpendicular architecture is still in evidence – with its characteristic lightness of stonework and splendid windows with notably accomplished tracery.

Another interesting feature of the Guildhall is the 1788/89 porch by George Dance the Younger. Made mainly from Portland stone, it is arguably the earliest example of Indian influence in English architecture; a form which went on to be labelled 'Hindoo-Gothic'. At this time there was much debate amongst architects and intellectuals as to the origins and nature of 'the Gothic', and here Dance is experimenting with these forms. Another theory is that the inclusion of such eastern motifs and echoes may well have been a nod of recognition towards the City's vital trading links with the Orient. *Area Map p.8, B:2*

St Margaret's Church

Westminster, Parliament Square, SW1P 3PA • Tel 020 7222 5152 • www.westminster-abbey.org • Nearest transport St James's Park or Westminster LU • Admission free • See website for opening times and details of services

In the shadow of the magnificent Westminster Abbey, this lovely building is easily overlooked. Built 1482-1523, but with a much earlier, perhaps late 11th-century foundation, it is the only surviving pre-Reformation church in Westminster. Built in a Perpendicular style, the final flowering of the Gothic style, the interior was heavily restored during the 18th and 19th centuries, notably by George Gilbert Scott in 1877. The church exterior is somewhat dominated by a tower built in 1734-5.

St Margaret's has been the official parish church of Parliament since April 1614 and is where Samuel Pepys, John Milton and Winston Churchill were married.

This church has an interesting selection of stained glass windows ranging from the very early 16th century to a fabulous example of John Piper's work – an abstract titled 'Spring in London' and dated 1968. *Area Map p.6, B:1*

St James's Palace

Cleveland Row, Marlborough Gate, SW1A 1BH • www.royal.gov.uk • Nearest transport Green Park LU • No public entry apart from service attendance, services are held in the Chapel Royal on Sundays throughout the year, except for August and September and after Easter and Christmas

Although not open to the public (apart from the chapel) there is plenty of St James's Palace to see from the street. The complex of buildings includes Clarence House, latterly the home of the late Queen Mother and now Prince Charles's London residence.

The Palace was built by Henry VIII between 1531-40, at the same time Whitehall was under construction and would appear to have been intended to house the monarch's heir rather than the king himself. When Whitehall burned to the ground in 1698 St James's became the focus of the Royal court in London. This association however was relatively short-lived as George III thought St James's unsuitable and eventually moved to Buckingham House (later Palace).

When a fire in 1809 destroyed much of St James's Palace, restoration work was carried out by John Nash almost immediately. The wall and gatehouse which face onto Cleveland Row were the oldest parts of the Palace to survive, with the Tudor brickwork (red brick with blue brick diapering) dating from 1531-40 with later alterations. The gatehouse is typical of early Tudor design with its octagonal turrets. The ogee topped cupola and clock face were added in 1832.

The Chapel Royal is also part of the original range of buildings but was heavily renovated by Robert Smirke in 1836/37. The beautiful decorative ceiling dates from 1540 and is still very much intact. It was in this remarkable chapel that King Charles I took communion on the morning of his execution and in which Queen Victoria and Prince Albert were married in November 1840.

Close by is St James's Park, which at one time was a swamp but which Henry VIII had drained in 1533 and stocked with deer for the royal hunt. *Area Map p.6, A:2*

Staple Inn

High Holborn, WC1V 7PX • Nearest transport Chancery Lane LU • No public access – apart from shops on ground floor

This is a rare survivor of Elizabethan architecture in Central London and despite extensive restoration it is still a very impressive building. The front of this half-timbered building is in two halves – the slightly shorter section is probably just the older of the two, dating from 1586. Both parts have two overhanging storeys and the shops on the ground floor are just one room apiece, as they were originally planned. Staple Inn gives us a tantalising glimpse of what London looked like prior to the Great Fire of 1666.
Area Map p.2-3, C:1

Charlton House

Charlton Road, SE7 8RE • Tel 0208 856 3951 • www.greenwich.gov.uk • Nearest transport Charlton Rail • See website for access details

The last remaining example in London of a truly Jacobean house. It was built for Sir Adam Newton, tutor to the eldest son of James I, who died as a teenager before he could become King Henry IX. Instead his younger brother was to become the ill-fated King Charles I. Constructed in the E-plan favoured at the time, as this allowed more light into the core of a building, Charlton House is a massive three-storey mansion with four symmetrical bay windows. It was built between 1607 and 1617 of red brick with stone dressing and each of the four towers that grace the corners is topped with an ogee roof. The interior contains a hall of double height, much fine panelling (mostly, alas, not original), interesting stone and marble fireplaces and a superb carved staircase. The House sits in very pleasant gardens and parkland.

It is interesting to compare the bulkiness of this house with the work of Inigo Jones as his Queen's House (see following page) was designed a mere four or so years later. Inigo Jones may well have been familiar with Charlton as he, like Sir Adam Newton, was in the employ of the Royal Household.

02

London Before Wren

The Queen's House, Greenwich

National Maritime Museum, Greenwich, E10 9NF • Tel 020 8858 4422
• www.nmm.ac.uk • Nearest transport Cutty Sark DLR, Greenwich & Maze Hill Rail • Admission free • See website for opening times

This riverside location was once the site of the Palace of Placentia, the birthplace of Henry VIII and his daughters Mary and Elizabeth. It was a favourite royal residence with an armoury and a tiltyard complete with romantic medieval towers and was conveniently close to the Royal Naval yards at Deptford and Woolwich.

In 1616 work began on the Queen's House, commissioned for the wife of James I, Anne of Denmark, who unfortunately died three years later, when work stopped on the House. The half-completed construction was covered in thatch and only finished in 1635 for Henrietta Maria, Charles I's queen.

The Queen's House was the first wholly classical building in England and is considered to be one of the most important buildings in British architectural history; there simply had been nothing like it before. Inigo Jones built what was effectively a small (just 110 by 120 feet) two-storey Italian villa. Built in brick, with rusticated stone facings up to the first floor level on its north and south sides and plastered elsewhere, it was a pure white house contrasting with the heavy-looking piebald Tudor and Jacobean buildings of the time. The central loggia on the second floor overlooking Greenwich Park is pure Palladio, with a balustrade and Ionic columns with intricately carved capitals.

The interior contains many gems such as the royal apartments and the Great Hall, a 40-foot cube which Jones designed in accordance with Palladio's rules of proportion. The beautiful 'Tulip' staircase, so-called because of the flower motifs on the finely crafted wrought-iron balustrade, was the first cantilevered spiral staircase in Britain. One of the most significant works of architecture in London and now housing an important collection of art, including works by Canaletto, Lowry, Stubbs, and the iconic Armada portrait of queen Elizabeth I.

Tulip Staircase, The Queen's House

The Banqueting House

61 Whitehall, SW1A 2ET • Tel 020 7839 8918 • www.hrp.org.uk • Nearest transport Westminster LU and Embankment LU • See website for opening times and admission charges

On its completion the Banqueting House drew the comment from a contemporary observer that the building was 'too handsome for the rest of the palace'. Built 1619-22 as part of the Whitehall Palace complex, really a collection of buildings of varying quality and style, Inigo Jones's Banqueting House was not only a more than satisfactory provision of a new reception hall and masquing house, but also a momentous triumph in the history of English architecture.

Begun after Jones's Queen's House at Greenwich, but completed first, the Banqueting House also incorporated elements of Palladio's Vicenzan architecture.

The Banqueting House is approximately 110 feet in length and 55 feet in height, being a double cube; its seven bays are divided by Ionic pillars with Corinthian pilasters above. Externally the two main elevations match. The three middle bays have attached columns whereas the outer bays have pilasters doubled at the outer edge of the building for emphasis. To add further interest to the façade different coloured masonry was used; Oxfordshire stone at the lower level with Northamptonshire stone above and Portland stone for all the main architectural detailing and the parapet, which runs the length of the building, both front and back. However, only Portland stone was used during subsequent renovation, principally by Sir William Chambers during the late 18th century and by Sir John Soane in the early 19th.

Seeing inside this building is very rewarding. The brick groin-vaulted undercroft, which originally sported a grotto and fountain, was the venue for Charles I's notorious drinking parties. The vast ceiling of the main room is particularly memorable. Divided into cornices and enriched with gilded carvings, it is more in keeping with classical Italian style than the rather fussy English fashion of the time. The whole building and its decoration, all coolly Classical, contrast with the ceiling panels, painted by Rubens, from which tumble colour and vigour. In place by 1635, the nine paintings proclaim the blessings of the reign of James I and glorify the Stuart dynasty. Commissioned by Charles I in honour of his father, one wonders whether he may have glanced upwards to take a last look at them as he was led through this room to his execution outside in the cold on 30 January 1649. *Area Map p.6, B:2*

The Piazza & St Paul's Church, Covent Garden

Covent Garden Piazza, Covent Garden, WC2E 8HB • Nearest Transport Covent Garden LU

St Paul's, Bedford Street, WC2E 9ED • Tel 020 7836 5221 • www.actorschurch.org • Nearest transport Covent Garden LU

It is hard to imagine when walking through the now bustling Piazza that this land was once used for growing provisions for Westminster Abbey. When Henry VIII closed the monasteries the whole area was given to Sir John Russell, the first Earl of Bedford and it was the 4th Earl who decided to develop the land. Between 1629-37 what emerged was London's first residential square, designed by the most fashionable architect of the day, Inigo Jones.

Influenced by recent Parisian and Italian building, Jones produced a plan of individual houses behind a continuous façade in a Classical design. The development attracted wealthy residents who enjoyed the novelty of living in the grand terraced housing. Jones's church of St Paul sat to the south of the square. However, within two decades the 5th Earl wanted a larger return on the investment and had a fruit and vegetable market built at the centre of the square. The smarter residents promptly decamped to newer squares in town and less desirable occupants moved in. Jones's houses had all been demolished by 1890. What remains is the Georgian central market place, considered the best preserved in England, built for the 6th Earl in 1828 and restored and renovated after 1974 when the market moved to larger premises in south London. The three terraces of market buildings now house small shops and restaurants. To get a flavour of what Jones's houses were like we can look at Bedford Chambers in the locality. Built 1877-79 by the eminent architect Henry Clutton and in a slightly larger scale, they do nonetheless resemble Jones's design especially in terms of proportion.

The Church of St Paul was the first parish church to be built in London since before the reign of Queen Elizabeth. Jones's challenge was to build a church appropriate for the Protestant Church of England. His plans gave concern to his patron that the building would be likened to a barn to which Jones replied 'Then you shall have the handsomest barn in England'. The main body of the church feels wide for there are no side chapels or altar screen and the fittings are simple, with a notable carved wreath by Grinling Gibbons, who is buried in the churchyard. Externally, the most striking feature of the church is the portico with two square piers, one at each corner of the porch-front with two Tuscan columns between.

St Paul's is known as the 'actors' church' due to its proximity to Drury Lane and 'Theatreland'.
Area Map p.6, B:3

Fulham Palace

Fulham Palace and Museum, Bishop's Avenue, SW6 6EA • Tel 020 7736 3233 • www.fulhampalace.org • Nearest transport Putney Bridge LU • See website for opening times and admission charges

Architectural historian Nicholas Pevsner called this 'one of the best medieval domestic sites in London'. Set in thirteen acres of beautiful grounds by the Thames, this was the country residence of the Bishop of London from 704 until 1973, having been acquired by the Saxon Bishop Waldhere. Archaeological evidence shows that the site has been occupied since the Neolithic period.

Fulham Palace is an interesting mix of building styles – the earliest surviving part being the great hall which dates from about 1480 with 16th-century additions. The hall underwent changes in decoration as well as function, from chapel to drawing room, as each incumbent Bishop endeavoured to make his mark on the Palace. The rest of the building is mostly Tudor and of particular note is the exquisite brickwork which makes an interesting contrast with the machine made bricks of the Victorian era.

Since 1973 the Palace has been leased to the Borough of Fulham and is now a museum. Among the exhibits is a fascinating model of the building – colour coded to help visitors identify the various architectural styles.

Above: West Courtyard, Fulham Palace

St Ethelburga's, Bishopsgate

St Ethelburga's Centre for Reconciliation and Peace, 78 Bishopsgate, EC2N 4AG • Tel 020 7496 1610 • www.stethelburgas.org • Nearest transport Liverpool Street LU & Rail • See website for opening times

It is hard to imagine that during the medieval period this was the largest building in the area – now it is one of the smallest. Miraculously untouched by the Great Fire of London in 1666 and enemy bombing during the Blitz, this beautiful little church was extensively damaged by an IRA bomb in 1993. Building insurance does not, as a rule, cover acts of terrorism and so much debate ensued regarding the possibility of fundraising before it was decided to rebuild as a Centre for Reconciliation and Peace.

Following restoration by the architectural firm of Purcell Miller Tritton, who specialise in church and cathedral work, in November 2002 St Ethelburga's was reconsecrated and started a new phase of its life.

The earliest evidence of a place of worship on this site is from about 1200. The present church fabric dates from the late 14th century with much of the shattered remains of this building being re-used – including much of the main tower and the 1671 weather vane, both of which were spared in the blast. The main entrance on to Bishopsgate was restored to look as it did originally, the collapsed roof has been replaced by a new steel structure and the Portland stone mullioned windows are new. Of particular note is the east window depicting St Ethelburga gathering up the fragments from the previous shattered window, made by Helen Whittaker. The new altar and lectern, is also worthy of attention and is made from the remains of the old organ loft.

In the tiny garden at the east end of the church sits a tent, opened in May 2006 as a place for the meeting of all faiths. The tent was designed by Professor Keith Critchlow, a world expert in sacred geometry, using the universal languages of geometry, algebra, astronomy and harmony. Made using traditional Bedouin techniques, it is a 16-sided structure covered in woven goat's hair and is a place of extraordinary peace.

Area Map p.8, C:2

Right: St Ethelburga's, Bishopsgate. Now dwarfed by its neighbours, St Ethelburga's was once the largest building in Bishopsgate

Bevis Marks Synagogue

4 Heneage Lane, EC3A 5DQ • Tel 020 7626 1274 • www.bevismarks.org.uk • Nearest transport Aldgate LU • See website for opening times and tour details

Dating from 1699-1701, this is the oldest surviving synagogue in England and it is still a thriving place of Jewish worship. It was built by Joseph Avis, a Quaker carpenter, in a style reminiscent of the simpler Wren churches that were being built elsewhere in the City, mixed with elements from the Great Synagogue of Amsterdam built in 1675. There are many highlights, including twelve Corinthian columns, one for each of the tribes of Israel, supporting the gallery and the seven superb brass chandeliers that hang low – representing the days of the week.

The building is often open to visitors. Regular tours are available, and highly recommended.
Area Map p.8, C:2

Temple Church

Temple Lane, EC4Y 7BB • Tel 020 7353 3470 • www.templechurch.com • Nearest transport Blackfriars LU/Rail, Chancery Lane LU • See website for opening times & admission charges

This church was built for the Knights Templar, an organisation formed at the end of the 11th century for the protection of Christian pilgrims journeying to and from the Holy Land. The churches they built throughout Europe were based on the circular design of the Church of the Holy Sepulchre in Jerusalem. Temple Church is one of the last surviving examples of such a church in England. The building was consecrated in 1185 in the presence of King Henry II and was dedicated to St Mary. The church is associated with many historic events, such as the mediation between King John and the barons in 1215. The Knights Templar fell out of favour at the beginning of the 14th century and on confiscation of their church by the Crown is was leased to lawyers of the Middle and Inner Temples.

The circular nave of the Temple Church is a very fine example of the Transitional phase of architecture between the Norman and Gothic, indeed probably one of the first buildings to incorporate Gothic themes in England. The main piers in the nave are of Purbeck marble, its first use as a building material in London.

Many famous architects – Wren, George Gilbert Scott, Robert and Sidney Smirke, Decimus Burton among them – have supervised restoration of the church at one time or another and their involvement is a testament to its architectural significance. With superb acoustics this is a popular venue for concerts and is very much a thriving, working church as well as an immensely interesting building to visit. Visitors should not miss the life-size Purbeck marble effigies of knights dating from the 13th century. *Area Map p.6, C:3*

For other buildings in the area of 'The Temple' see Fleet Street & Beyond Walk, p.290.

Temple Church, a building in transition, with revolutionary pointed Gothic arches beneath a blind arcade of intersecting round arches of the old Norman style

Crosby Hall

Crosby Hall, at junction of Cheyne Walk and Danvers Street, SW3 5AZ • Nearest transport South Kensington, Gloucester Road and Sloane Square LU

Although this is one of the oldest buildings in Chelsea it originally stood in Bishopsgate in the City, where it was the Great Hall of the 15th-century Crosby Place. Built between 1466 and 1475 by an unnamed mason for Sir John Crosby, a wealthy merchant, this former city mansion was familiar to Shakespeare who makes mention of it in 'Richard III' as the scene of Gloucester's plotting. Indeed the building was occupied by Richard when he was Duke of Gloucester. The Hall was moved stone by stone from Bishopsgate to Chelsea in 1910 in order to rescue it from proposed demolition and a plaque on the side of a modern banking house marks its original position. It was then incorporated into the buildings of the British Federation of University Women and used as a dining hall, but is now a private residence and not open to the public. The Hall was owned by Sir Thomas More for a period after 1523, and it is perhaps fitting that it now sits in what was once More's orchard.

There is no public access to this building, but it can be readily viewed from the street.

All Saints (Chelsea Old Church)

Cheyne Row, SW3 5LT • Tel 020 7795 1019 • www.chelseaoldchurch.org.uk • Nearest transport South Kensington, Gloucester Road and Sloane Square LU• See website for opening times & services

The chancel of this church dates from the 13th century, with two chapels dating from the early 14th century. The More chapel on the south side was built in 1528 for Sir Thomas following the death of his first wife and the nave and tower were built in about 1670. Some beautifully carved capitals and a little 17th-century Flemish stained glass survived the terrible bomb damage that the church sustained during the Second World War. The many interesting monuments and the calm atmosphere make this church interior a very special space.

Lambeth Palace

Lambeth Palace Road, SE1 7JU • Nearest transport Lambeth North LU • Lambeth Palace is not open to the public but tours can be arranged by writing to the Booking Department at the above address

The palace and official London residence of the Archbishop of Canterbury, the most senior cleric of the Church of England, has occupied this site since 1207. This is the last remaining bishopric palace of any size along either bank of the Thames; the others all disappeared with the Reformation.

The simple but beautifully constructed undercroft of the Palace chapel dates from before 1240. The west doorway with its notable trefoiled opening are all that remain of the original building, the rest of which was damaged by Second World War enemy bombing and now restored. The water tower, also called Lollards' Tower, dates from 1435 and was used as a prison in the 17th century.

The Gatehouse dates from about 1495 and is an excellent chance to see the red bricks used extensively in high quality Tudor building. The Great Hall of 1663, is also built of brick but with stone dressings and is a magnificent example of Gothic architecture with buttresses, pointed windows and a high-pitched roof with a splendid hammerbeam ceiling. Since the 19th century the Hall has been used as a library. The principal offices and residence are the work of the architect Edward Blore (1787-1879) and all, according to the novelist Walter Scott, 'in the best Gothic taste'. *Area Map p.6, C:1*

Sir Paul Pindar's House Façade

Medieval & Renaissance, Room 64b, The Simon Sainsbury Gallery, Victoria and Albert Museum, Cromwell Road, SW7 2RL • Tel 020 7942 2000 • www.vam.ac.uk • Nearest transport South Kensington and Knightsbridge LU. • See website for opening hours

An extraordinary survival of the façade of a house that once sat in Bishopsgate Without in the City and built in about 1600 for Sir Paul Pindar (1566-1650), a wealthy merchant. The house was much larger than even this 9.5 metre (over 30 feet) fragment suggests as the ground floor frontage was altered in succeeding centuries so only the original upper two storeys were brought to the Museum when the building, by now a public house named The Sir Paul Pindar, was demolished in 1890 to make way for an extension to Liverpool Street Station.

The Charterhouse

Charterhouse Square, EC1M 6AN • Tel 0203 818 8873 • www.thecharterhouse.org • Nearest transport Farringdon and Barbican stations • See website for opening hours and admission charges

One of London's best kept secrets opened its doors to the public in 2017. The Charterhouse is perhaps the most interesting building in a city filled with interesting buildings, recalling the story of London, if not England, in its very fabric.

The story begins in the plague year of 1348 when the grounds hereabouts, being just outside the walls of the City, were consecrated as a burial field and an estimated 45,000 Londoners were interred. A small chapel was erected shortly after this time where masses for the dead were celebrated and this was no doubt the root from which the Carthusian monastery grew.

Founded in 1371 by Sir Walter de Manny, senior adviser to King Edward III, the monastery was just one of many religious houses in London of this period. Manny clearly had great ambition for this project, envisaging a space for 24 monks and a prior, a large community by Carthusian standards, and engaging the most celebrated mason, or architect as we would describe his role today, Henry Yevele (c1320-1400), to design the cloister and the first monks' cells. Yevele, also in the employment of the King and a colleague and close friend of Geoffrey Chaucer, is also associated with work at Westminster Hall and Canterbury Cathedral. He was also in charge of rebuilding of the splendid Westminster Abbey nave as we see it today.

Following Henry VIII's Act of Supremacy in 1535, the monastery was brutally supressed and passed to the Crown. Subsequently it was granted to Sir Edward North, who constructed a fine Tudor mansion here, which can still be seen today, and later sold to the fourth Duke of Norfolk. On 23 November 1558, the day of her accession to the throne, Elizabeth I arrived at Charterhouse for a five-day stay to await her coronation at Westminster Abbey.

In 1611, Norfolk's son, Thomas Howard, first Earl of Suffolk, sold the mansion to Thomas Sutton, who used much of his wealth to endow a charitable foundation on the site to educate boys and care for elderly men, known as 'Brothers'. John Wesley, founder of the Methodist Church, was a pupil at the school as was William Makepeace Thackeray in the early nineteenth century. Although Charterhouse School moved to Godalming, Surrey, in 1872, the site is still home to approximately 40 'Brothers', both male and female.

Despite subsequent alterations and reuse, there is much to see and enjoy both historically and architecturally at this remarkable assembly of buildings. The principal historic buildings were severely damaged by enemy bombing in May 1941 but were sensitively restored in the

1950s, allowing restoration of some medieval and much 16th and 17th-century fabric that had previously been obscured.

A recent programme of development and enhancement to the buildings and gardens has opened up the site for visitors to enjoy. The small museum, with archaeological finds discovered during recent nearby excavations for the Crossrail 'Elizabeth Line', and other historical artefacts, can be visited during open hours and services in the Chapel are open to the public. However, the rest of this fascinating complex of buildings, the lovely cloisters and gardens are only accessed by guided tour, bookable in advance and highly recommended. *Area Map p.8, A:3*

See also the 'Bartholomew Walk' on p.281.

St Paul's Cathedral, see p.63

03

WREN & THE
RE-BUILDING OF THE CITY

WREN & THE RE-BUILDING OF THE CITY

"Resurgam – I shall rise again"

At certain points in its history London has been a city of ruins and with its tindery mix of thatch and timber was accustomed to conflagration, whether by act of vandalism or by accident. The spark that ignited Thomas Farriner's bakery on 2nd September 1666 in Pudding Lane started what history recalls as 'The Great Fire of London'. The fire raged for four days and nights and destroyed five-sixths of the City; 460 streets containing approximately 13,200 houses were lost, four of the seven City gates, 85 churches and 44 halls of livery companies were razed to the ground. The human misery caused by such catastrophe is incalculable but there were those who saw the sweeping away of the seething, stinking, plague-ridden streets with their mish-mash of buildings as an opportunity for urban renewal.

Even before the ashes of the fire had cooled plans for a more modern city were submitted to the Crown by, amongst others, Robert Hooke, John Evelyn and Christopher Wren. It is Wren's name that became synonymous with the re-building of the City, even though the vision he put forward was ignored.

Christopher Wren had spent the previous year, 1665, in Paris. Whether to avoid the plague that was ravaging London or to see for himself the extensive building work that was taking place under the glitteringly extravagant Louis XIV, this was the one and only time Wren ventured abroad. Paris enjoyed imposing buildings, squares, theatres and aristocratic hotels (mansions) as well as the Chateau de Versailles and its gardens, all constructed in conformity with the ideals of the Italian Renaissance. Architects of the calibre of Leonardo da Vinci and Cellini had been employed at the French court since the beginning of the century, and during the summer of 1665 the great Italian architect Gian Lorenzo Bernini (1598-1680) was also in Paris having been summoned by Louis XIV to work on the Louvre. Bernini and Wren met only briefly but the encounter must have made an impact on the younger man.

Architecture in the 17th century was not as yet a profession and Christopher Wren, without building skills and experience, was merely a gentleman-amateur. Educated at Westminster and Oxford, he was Professor of Astronomy and a scientist of outstanding reputation by the age of 29. His first venture into architecture arose when his aged uncle, who happened to be the Bishop of Ely, asked him to design the new chapel he was sponsoring at Pembroke College, Cambridge. The resulting construction was considered to be a successful, if unimaginative, example of a neo-classical building. His next buildings of note were both in Oxford, the Sheldonian Theatre and a new quad at Trinity College.

On his return from Paris in late 1665, Wren was appointed to restore St Paul's Cathedral, which shall henceforth be referred to as Old St Paul's to differentiate it from the post Great Fire building. Old St Paul's was one of the largest medieval cathedrals in England, 585 feet long and 489 feet high to the top of its spire. The main body of the cathedral was started in the 11th century and its spire renewed in 1315 after a fire. The spire was struck by lightning and rebuilt circa 1444 only to be struck again in 1561, when a decision was made not to rebuild it. Without its hapless spire the building looked like a huge, squat ship, dwarfing all around it. We owe our knowledge of what Old St Paul's, and indeed the City as a whole, looked like from the panoramic drawings and engravings of Wenceslaus Hollar who worked in London in the 1650s.

Magnificent as it must have been, the old cathedral suffered neglect after the Reformation and much abuse during the Civil War when Cromwell's men, and their horses, were housed in the nave with other parts of the building let to traders. Stained glass windows, carved woodwork, effigies, statues and an Inigo Jones porch were wantonly destroyed and the dilapidated roof finally caved in. Wren's restoration plans were rendered unnecessary when the cathedral burnt to the ground in 1666, along with most of the City.

The vision Wren and his contemporaries had for the City was for something resembling Paris or Rome, with a regular street plan. However, the survival of London as an important commercial capital depended upon its immediate reconstruction and there was simply neither the time nor the will to resolve the complicated land titles that each plot had accrued over the centuries. Rebuilding could only thus be carried out on the lines of the existing streets. In October 1666 the King appointed Wren as one of three Crown Commissioners to consider the methods of rebuilding and these were eventually encapsulated in a series of Acts of Parliament to safeguard against such a catastrophe ever happening again. These were:

i) The structural standardisation of new-build houses in three specific types, all made from brick, with specified floor-height and wall thickness; this point in fact set a trend for house building throughout the whole country. The Commissioners had no say over the actual design of what was to be built, even though the King demanded a 'much more beautiful city' to replace the old one.

ii) The provision of a Thames-side quay and conversion of part of the River Fleet into a canal.

iii) The authorisation for collection of a tax on coal imports into London to pay for a limited number of public works. This amount was subsequently found to be wholly inadequate and had to be trebled within a couple of years.

It took nearly three months to complete the demolition of the charred remains of the City and clear the rubble that lay everywhere. Labourers and skilled workers were brought in from all over the country to fulfil anticipated demand. Disputes between landowners and tenants had to be resolved and money found to cover the cost of rebuilding. At this time there was no such thing as fire insurance (although this eventually came about as a result of the Great Fire) and little or no compensation; so only those City Companies, institutions, colleges and private individuals with enough capital invested elsewhere had the means to begin rebuilding immediately. Indeed many wealthy private individuals chose not to rebuild their London houses within the City but moved west instead.

Important buildings, such as the Royal Exchange, the Custom House, the College of Arms and many of the City Livery Companies' halls were under reconstruction within three or four years of the Great Fire, having been forced to carry on their business elsewhere in the meantime.

Perhaps as compensation for not being able to implement his overall plan for the City, Christopher Wren was charged with the task of personally overseeing the rebuilding of the City churches and St Paul's Cathedral. The whole project was to be financed from the aforementioned Coal Tax, which could only barely cover the actual construction and fabric of the churches. The interior fittings and decoration were to be the responsibility of the parish, although in most cases advice was sought from Wren. Of the pre-Great Fire churches 85 out of 107 had been destroyed and it was decided to rebuild only 51 of them. However many of the churchyards and burial grounds still exist and can be visited.

Assisted by Robert Hooke and Edward Woodroffe, exactly how much input Wren had in each individual church is debatable, but he was in overall control. Many of the designs had to fit into awkward spaces and most of the churches are easy to pass by at ground level but they do display an astonishing variety of invention. This is particularly so with regard to the spires Wren added to each church, which lent the City an elegance and an element of fantasy not seen before. He understood how important such landmarks would have been to a pre *London A-Z* and 'sat-nav' citizen. Wren also gave the country a blueprint for Protestant church building.

It was not until 1675 that Wren was able to start work on St Paul's Cathedral. His first design was rejected by the clergy who were hostile to its Classical lines. What they wanted was, more or less, a straight replacement of the Gothic Old St Paul's with its high nave and lower side aisles but Wren envisaged a high dome that would act as a focal point for the City as a whole. Wren got his way by encouraging the clergy to agree to one design and then fundamentally altering it as the Cathedral was being built.

St Paul's Cathedral

Ludgate Hill, EC4 • Tel 020 7236 4128 • www.stpauls.co.uk • Nearest transport St Paul's LU • See website for opening times, admission charges and access details (Cathedral occasionally closes at short notice for special services)

The foundation stone for Wren's masterpiece, laid 21 June 1675, bears the inscription 'RESURGAM', Latin for 'I shall rise again', and was a relic from the Old St Paul's destroyed by the Great Fire of 1666. The new Cathedral, the fourth on the site, was completed in 1708, with the interior furnished by 1710. Christopher Wren personally oversaw the project from beginning to end, a unique feat for nowhere else in the world has one Cathedral had just one architect and although his plans had to be approved by the Cathedral dean and chapter, what we see today is the pure product of Wren's genius. Whereas his City churches are essays in northern Protestant order, the design of St Paul's has its roots in the grand architecture of the Renaissance and the Baroque. The Cathedral bears comparison with, and indeed in some parts arguably surpasses, Michelangelo's St Peter's in Rome.

In order to provide a visually adequate substructure on which to place the dome Wren doubled the apparent height of the building by raising false screen walls on top of the aisle walls all around the cathedral. This also enabled him to conceal the flying buttresses that support the vault of the choir as well as giving the whole building a Classical feel. The porticoes which extend from the transepts

and the much-photographed western towers were both influenced by buildings under recent construction in Rome, Rainaldi's Church of Gesù e Maria and Bernini's Santa Maria della Vittoria for example – so much inspiration from a city unvisited by Wren.

The familiar outline of St Paul's is due mostly to its great dome. It is almost hemispherical, and sits more sedately, more majestically than the elongated Roman type. However, this dome, that has dominated the London skyline for so long and is regarded by many to be the most beautiful in the world, is actually one of three structures. Such a large dome would have been fine viewed from the outside, but the observer inside the cathedral looking upwards would have had the feeling of staring into a vast cavernous hole and so, as with St Peter's in Rome, another smaller, saucer shaped dome was placed inside to solve the problem. Wren went further by placing a golden ball and cross, 23 feet high and weighing 7 tonnes, on top of the outer dome and in order to support its weight he introduced a third dome, or perhaps cone is a better description, made of brick and placed between the two others.

As wonderful as it is to view from the outside, a visit to the interior of St Paul's is a must. The crypt contains Wren's tomb; he was one of the first to be buried here when he died at the age of 91. National figures including Lord Nelson and the Duke of Wellington are also buried here. There are numerous monuments and notable statues such as the one by Flaxman of Sir Joshua Reynolds. The crypt also holds the plans and models made by Wren of the Cathedral itself.

But no visit to St Paul's would be complete without a visit to the famous dome. A mere 259 steps take one to the Whispering Gallery, so named because by a quirk in its construction a whisper against one wall can be heard on the opposite side. A further climb will take one to the Stone Gallery that encircles the outside of the dome and of course provides a fantastic view over London. However just 530 steps from ground level will take you to the highest point, the Golden Gallery. It is said Wren, in his mid-seventies, was hauled up here in a basket once a week to inspect the work in progress.

This iconic building celebrated its 300th birthday in 2010 with a £40 million-restoration with an intensive programme of external cleaning and improved access for visitors.
Area Map p.8, A:2

Left: The Dome, St Paul's Cathedral. It was Wren's intention that the interior of the dome should be decorated with mosaics, which would have been unique in England at that time. However eminent painter Sir James Thornhill was commissioned to provide monochrome depictions of the life of St Paul instead. Eventually mosaics designed by Alfred Stevens in 1864 were used in the spandrels

WREN'S CITY CHURCHES

Before the Great Fire of 1666 the City of London had 107 parish churches, all highly individual, built in different periods and in various styles. The Great Fire destroyed 85 of the 107 and a decision was made that only 51 would be rebuilt. In addition, St Andrew's Holborn, which whilst untouched by the fire and not strictly within the City, was included as its crumbling fabric made it a special case. Wren was put in charge of the whole project, with Robert Hooke as one of his assistants, with the rather restrictive brief that the churches had to be rebuilt within their existing, frequently irregular and cramped plots. However notwithstanding these limitations, Wren and Hooke designed and built an amazing variety of airy, well lit buildings. Without an English Protestant church tradition, they looked to Dutch Protestant churches for inspiration.

Of these 51 churches only 24 complete buildings and six towers remain. These are listed below in alphabetical order rather than by merit or date.

Most of these churches are open to the public Monday to Friday, unless stated. Many have regular services of worship and lunchtime concerts – please telephone the individual church for details. If you are only able to see one, St Stephen Walbrook is highly recommended.

Christ Church, Newgate Street

Newgate Street, EC1A 7BA • Nearest transport St Paul's LU • The tower can be viewed at any time

The first church on this site dated from the mid 13th century and was built by Franciscan friars (also known as Greyfriars). Rebuilt in the early 14th century, and the second largest medieval church in the City after Old St Paul's, following the Dissolution of the Monasteries in 1536, Christ Church was used as a store for wine, rumoured to have been plundered from French ships, the chancel became a parish church and the King's printer set up shop in the nave.

When Wren rebuilt the church after the Great Fire he made use of the medieval foundations and lower walls and the church therefore remained comparatively large. Enemy bombing during the Second World War destroyed the main body of the church but the tower, regarded by some as the most beautiful in London, was mercifully spared. The spire, which has been likened to a square version of the one belonging to St Mary-le-Bow, was the subject of preservation work during the 1960s and a small garden has been formed where the body of the church once stood. *Area Map p.8, A:3*

St Alban

Wood Street, EC2 • Nearest transport St Paul's LU • The exterior of the tower can be viewed any time

It is believed that the first building on the site was the chapel of King Offa, dating back to the 8th century. An 11th-century Saxon church certainly stood here and was enlarged over the centuries until it perished in 1666. Rather than design a completely new church, Wren appears to have been content to construct a fairly faithful replica of what was lost to the Great Fire. Wren worked on St Alban between 1682-6 but the church was destroyed by enemy bombing in 1940, leaving his beautiful Perpendicular Gothic tower standing forlorn and alone.

The tower was renovated during the 1960s and in 1984-85 it was converted into a private house and is now used as offices. Nothing remains of the churchyard used during the 18th and 19th centuries by the Barber-Surgeon's Company for burying the remains of executed criminals whose bodies had been used for dissection. *Area Map p.8, B:3*

Left: St Alban, Wood Street, a sacred site since the 8th century now surrounded by traffic and the 21st-century City

St Andrew, Holborn

Holborn Circus, EC4 3AB • Tel 020 7353 3544 • www.standrewholborn.org.uk • Nearest transport Chancery Lane LU or Farringdon LU & Rail • See website for opening times, services & events

There has been a church on this site since at least 959 CE which, although untouched by the Great Fire, had been pitifully neglected and Wren was charged with its rebuilding. The work started in 1684 and it took just two years to complete. Wren kept the 15th-century tower and refaced it in Portland stone. The interior is similar to St James's Piccadilly (completed 1682), also by Wren, with its barrel-vaulting, groin-vaults on Corinthian columns over the aisles and a two-storey Venetian window in the chancel. Enemy bombing during 1941 destroyed much of the building, the outer walls and tower surviving, but a faithful reconstruction was completed in 1961.

Although the original furnishings have been lost, there is much of interest. The organ is modern but sits within a case donated by the composer Handel in 1750, and the pulpit and font are from the Foundling Hospital.

On the outside wall of the west end of the church are 17th-century statues of a young boy and girl from a nearby former parish school. St Andrew's now houses the Royal College of Organists. *Area Map p.2-3, C:1*

St Andrew by the Wardrobe

St Andrew's Hill & Queen Victoria Street, EC4V 5DE • Tel 020 7329 3632 • www, standrewbythewardrobe.net • Nearest transport Blackfriars LU & Rail • See website for opening times, services & events

So named because of its proximity to the building where royal ceremonial robes and arms were stored from the mid 14th century. A church has occupied this spot since about 1170 and this unadorned red brick rectangular church with its plain tower was one of Wren's last City churches to be completed (1685-94).

Over time 'improvements' to Queen Victoria Street robbed St Andrew's of its churchyard and have somewhat elevated the building so it is now very easy to pass by without noticing it. The original furnishings were destroyed by enemy bombing in 1940, and were replaced by a collection from other Wren churches, such as the font and font cover made for St Matthew Friday Street, which was demolished during the 19th century. There is also a splendid stained glass window depicting the conversion of St Paul made for Bulstrode Park in Buckinghamshire in the early 18th century. *Area Map p.8, A:2*

St Anne and St Agnes

St Anne & St Agnes, Gresham Street, EC2V 7BX • Tel 020 7606 4986 • www.greshamcentre.com • Nearest transport St Paul's LU, Barbican LU & Rail • See website for opening times, services & events

Wren designed this small church to a cross-in-square plan, although it is believed Robert Hooke was heavily involved in its actual construction. A modest weatherboard pyramid with a square lantern tops the roof. The church sustained fire damage during World War II and the subsequent renovation did not include the original elaborate interior decoration, which suited the church's new role as a place of Lutheran worship. Services are now held in Amharic, English and Swahili.
Area Map p.8, B:3

Right: St Anne and St Agnes. Here, as with his other City churches, Wren creates a sense of light and space in a relatively small building

St Benet

Paul's Wharf, Queen Victoria Street, EC4V 4ER • Tel 020 7489 8754 • www.stbenetwelshchurch.org.uk • Nearest transport Blackfriars LU & Rail

This delightful little church of red and blue brick chequerwork is thought to be the design of Robert Hooke, rather than Wren, though it is attributed to the latter. The exterior is heavily influenced by Dutch church building and inside there is some interesting 17th-century furniture, such as a carved communion table. There has been a church on this site since at least the early 12th century and it is believed that the architect Inigo Jones was buried in the chancel on his death in 1652, but his memorial was destroyed in 1666. Much of the churchyard was lost in a road-widening scheme of 1870 and further 'improvements' left the church virtually marooned on its own small island. The nearby College of Arms uses St Benet for worship and since 1879 it has been the London Church of the Welsh Episcopalians, conducting a number of its services in Welsh.
Area Map p.8, A:2

St Bride

Fleet Street, EC4Y 8AU • Tel 020 7427 0133 • www.stbrides.com • Nearest transport St Paul's LU, City Thameslink Rail • See website for opening times, services & events

Named for St Bridgit, the daughter of a 5th-century Irish prince of Kildare, it is believed that a building of some sort has occupied this site since the Roman occupation of Britain. Many famous people are associated with this church. Wynkyn de Worde, apprentice to William Caxton who brought the first press to England in 1471, set up his printing works alongside the medieval church and thus inaugurated Fleet Street, 'the street of ink', as the centre for the printed word in England. Worde was buried in the churchyard in 1535.

Wren started work on replacing the ruined medieval church in 1671, finishing seven years later. The magnificent spire was added in 1701-03. This is the tallest of all Wren's spires at 226 feet and is said to have inspired a local baker, William Rich, to create the first tiered wedding cake. The spire is telescoped in five stages, becoming slimmer as it reaches its peak, and is similar to an unexecuted design Wren made for the steeple of the old St Paul's Cathedral. The spire is notable not only for its height and beauty but also because it defiantly withstood enemy bombing during World War II, which was severe enough to melt the bells within. However the extensive damage to the fabric of the church allowed the eminent archaeologist Professor Grimes to discover Roman and medieval remains that had lain hidden for hundreds of years. These are now on display in the Crypt along with a comprehensive and entertaining history of the church and the surrounding area.

Restoration work took place between 1955-57 and Wren's barrel-vaulted ceiling, oval clerestory windows, and five-bay nave, with paired Tuscan columns were faithfully rebuilt. It was decided not to replicate the galleries that once ran along both sides of the nave. Of particular note is the trompe l'oeil painted by Glyn Jones that creates the illusion of a half-domed apse. *Area Map p.8, A:2*

Left: St Bride, Fleet Street. Wren's tallest spire completed in 1703, it measured 236 feet (72 metres) was shortened by 10 feet (3 metres) in 1764 and has been an inspiration for wedding cakes ever since

St Clement Eastcheap

Clement's Lane, EC4N 7AE • Tel 020 7283 2711 • Nearest transport Monument LU • Please telephone for opening times

Wren built this, his plainest church, between 1683-87 to replace the earlier 11th-century church. The exterior is stuccoed brick with stone quoins and dressings, and, with neither steeple nor cupola, is considered 'too plain' for some. However there are some interesting furnishings – particularly the large pulpit and tester and a carved wooden font cover depicting a caged dove. *Area Map p.8, C:2*

St Dunstan in the East

St Dunstan's Hill, off Lower Thames Street, EC3R 5DD • Nearest transport Monument LU • The tower and remaining walls can be viewed at any time

One of two churches in London named for a Saxon Archbishop of Canterbury. The original 13th-century church was noted for its wealth and for the prosperity of its parishioners; indeed repairs undertaken after the Great Fire were paid for by a private benefactor. Wren added the steeple in 1695-1701 in a Gothic style, no doubt to match the patched-up body of the church. Enemy bombing during World War II rendered the building a shell once again, and this is how it remains today, although a garden was planted in the ruins in the early 1970s. *Area Map p.8, C:1*

St Edmund the King & Martyr

Lombard Street, EC3V 9AN • Tel 020 7626 9701 • Nearest transport Bank LU • Please telephone for opening times

There has been a place of worship on this site for almost 1,000 years and it was named after the 9th-century King of East Anglia, killed by Viking invaders. The eponymous king also gave his name to the town of Bury St Edmunds in Suffolk.

There is very strong evidence that Wren's assistant Robert Hooke was responsible for much of the work on the body of this church. Another of Wren's assistants, Nicholas Hawksmoor, is thought to have designed the spire, originally adorned with 12 decorative flaming urns and topped with a weathervane. The urns were inexplicably removed during late 19th-century renovation by William Butterfield, whose taste was for the Gothic rather than anything that even hinted at the Baroque.

The building now houses The London Centre for Spirituality. *Area Map p.8, C:2*

St James Garlickhithe

Garlick Hill, EC4V 2AL • Tel 020 7236 1719 • www.stjamesgarlickhythe.org.uk • Nearest transport Mansion House LU • See website for opening times, services & events

This is perhaps one of the unluckiest buildings in London. The original Norman church was destroyed in the Great Fire, Wren's church was subject to inappropriate restoration during the 19th century, it was bombed during World War II and then in 1991 a tall crane, working on a nearby building, fell on it! Happily it survived and what the visitor sees today is very much what Wren completed in 1674. With its interior of white walls, ceiling and columns, with just a few touches of gold, and its many windows of clear glass, this luminous building is known as 'Wren's Lantern'. *Area Map p.8, B:2*

St Lawrence Jewry

Gresham Street, EC2V 5AA • Tel 020 7600 9478 • www.stlawrencejewry.org.uk • Nearest transport Bank LU • See website for opening times, services & events

Named for a 3rd-century Roman who refused to denounce Christianity, this church has been the Corporation of London's official place of worship since the Guildhall chapel was demolished in the early 19th century. Unusually for a City church it stands quite detached at the head of King Street, one of only two new roads built in the City immediately after the Great Fire (the other being Queen Street), laid to ease the route between the Thames and the Guildhall.

The interior of St Lawrence is an essay in white Corinthian pilastered walls, gold leaf and magnificent chandeliers hanging from the richly coffered ceiling. When built in 1670-87 it was one of the largest and most expensive of Wren's churches. Gutted by enemy bombing on 29th December 1940, the church was fully restored in 1957. *Area Map p.8, B:2*

St Magnus the Martyr

Lower Thames Street, EC3R 6DN • Tel 020 7626 4481 • www.stmagnusmartyr.org.uk • Nearest transport Monument LU • See website for opening times & services

Built 1671-76 with its 185 feet steeple added in 1703, this church was named for St Magnus the Viking Earl of Orkney who lived 1080-1116. The church stood at the approach to the Old London Bridge. So busy was the route that in 1762 the approach was widened, reducing the church by two bays at its west end, and so isolating the solid square tower.

The visitor will not fail to notice that, in comparison with other Wren churches, the interior is fairly sumptuous. The furnishings for City churches were the responsibility of the parish and St Magnus is fortunate in having many of its original fittings which, unusually, are very much in continental Baroque style. Some additions were made during the 1920s when the church was embellished further for Anglo-Catholic worship.

Some fine paintings are contained within the church – Moses and Aaron on the reredos, and a Virgin and Child in the style of Van Dyck. There is also an interesting model of the Old London Bridge. On the west exterior wall is a clock dating from 1709, which was a famous London landmark for some 200 years until obscured by 20th-century buildings. *Area Map p.8, C:1*

St Margaret Lothbury

Lothbury, EC2R 7HH • Tel 020 7726 4878
• www.stml.org.uk • Nearest transport
Bank LU • See website for opening times,
services & events

The original church on this site dated from the 12th century with 15th-century additions. Wren's church was built between 1683-92, with the plain square tower completed in 1700. The tower and its distinctive fine lead spire are thought to be the work of Robert Hooke.

Entrance to the building is via the stone-clad south side, through the tower, much in the style of London medieval churches. Wren may well have kept the old foundations and building pattern here. Much of the exquisite furnishing comes from now demolished London churches such as the superb carved font which was originally at St Olave Jewry. *Area Map p.8, B:2*

Right: St Margaret Lothbury

St Margaret Pattens

Eastcheap, EC3M 1HS • Tel 020 7623 6630 • www.stmargaretpattens.org • Nearest transport Monument LU • See website for opening times, services & events

The unusual name of this church has two possible explanations; either it is named for a wealthy parishioner canon of St Paul's, Ranalf Patin or the name refers to the pattens, wooden shoe covers, which were made in the vicinity.

The original 12th-century church on this site apparently collapsed and was rebuilt in the 16th century. Wren's church was built between 1684-89 with the lead-covered spire, added 1698-1702, probably by Nicholas Hawksmoor. The exterior of the church is built mainly of Portland stone and the interior consists of a plain rectangular nave.

Many of the interior furnishings survive including now rare examples of twin canopied churchwardens' pews, an hourglass in an iron stand used for timing sermons and a punishment bench with a carved Devil's head.
Area Map p.8, C:2

Left: St Margaret Pattens. The lead-covered spire, at nearly 200 feet (61m), is the only one of the rebuilt City churches to be designed in a medieval style

St Martin within Ludgate

40 Ludgate Hill, EC4M 7DE • Tel 020 7248 6054 • www.stmartin-within-ludgate.org.uk • Nearest transport City Thameslink Rail, St Paul's LU • See website for opening times, services & events

Situated close to the west end of St Paul's Cathedral on a site near the old Lud Gate, Wren's church of 1677-86 incorporates part of the Roman city wall. The church is built on a centralised plan, a cross inside a square – the cross being defined by columns supporting the barrel vaulting. From the tower rises a lead spire, which is thought to be influenced by Dutch design.

The church of St Martin was fortunate to suffer little from 'improvements', renovations and World War II bomb damage and is therefore a relatively good example of Wren's design. However, Robert Hooke's diary tells of at least 31 visits to the site at both the design and construction stages, which might suggest St Martin is more his work than Wren's. *Area Map p.8, A:2*

St Mary Abchurch

Abchurch Lane, off King William Street, EC4N 7BA • Tel 020 7626 0306 • Nearest transport Bank LU & Cannon Street LU/Rail • Please telephone for opening times, services & events

This church was built by Wren between 1681-86 on the site of a medieval church. Constructed from dark red brick with stone quoins and with a tower on its north-west corner, which carries a slender lead-covered spire. The rather plain exterior shows Dutch influence and gives no hint of the sweetest of Wren's interiors.

The small interior has no aisles and is made to look spacious by the placement of a shallow dome on eight arches. The interior of the dome was decorated in 1708 by William Snow, colourfully depicting a heavenly choir with sun rays and clouds. Also of major interest is the very large carved reredos known to be by Grinling Gibbons, the only such example of his work on this ambitious scale in the City.

Enemy bombing during World War II caused extensive damage to the church. The dome had to be restored and the precious reredos, which had been blown into over 2,000 pieces. A seven year programme of restoration has brought St Mary back to something like its former glory. *Area Map p.8, C:2*

St Mary Aldermary

Watling Street, EC4M 9BW • Tel 020 7248 4906 • Nearest transport Mansion House LU • Please telephone for opening times

'Aldermary' denotes that this church of St Mary is the oldest in the City. At first sight one can hardly believe that this is a Wren church given that it is one of the finest examples of 17th-century Gothic revival in the country. The main body of the church was built with money from a private benefactor under the supervision of Wren and this may go some way to explain the deviation in design from other contemporary City churches. Stone refacing during the late 19th century accentuates this difference. A look inside the church reveals a unique example of a Wren fan-vaulted ceiling. *Area Map p.8, B:2*

Right: St Mary Aldermary. A fine example of Wren's Gothic Revival work

St Mary at Hill

St Mary at Hill, EC3R 8EE • Tel 020 7626 4184 • www.stmary-at-hill.org • Nearest transport Monument LU • See website for opening times, services & events

Wren was able to reuse three walls and most of the tower of the medieval church on this site first mentioned in the 12th century. But 19th-century renovations, during which 3,000 bodies were exhumed from the churchyard and re-interred at Norwood Cemetery, and a serious fire in 1988 requiring extensive repairs have left the church as a mixture of periods. Nevertheless, this is a lovely little church, being a simple brick building with stone trimmings tucked away down a small side-street. The interior is a rectangular space which has been subtly divided by the four free-standing fluted columns of the central square, on which the vaults rest, with emphasis given to Wren's central plan by the shallow dome in the middle.

With its close proximity to Billingsgate, the church is used by Guild of Fishmongers for their annual Harvest Festival service.
Area Map p.8, C:1

St Mary-le-Bow

Cheapside, EC2V 6AU • Tel 020 7248 5139 • www.stmarylebow.co.uk • Nearest transport Bank LU or St Paul's LU • See website for opening times, services & events

If a child is born within the sound of Bow Bells, so the legend tells us, he or she can declare themselves a Cockney. Cynics may point out the bells are hard to hear above the roar of the passing traffic. However, the 11th-century medieval church previously on this site had to contend with the cacophony of a medieval market outside in Cheapside.

On commencement of work on the site after the Great Fire, Wren not only found he could reuse the medieval crypt but was also delighted to find part of a gravelled Roman roadway on which to build the church tower. The steeple, made from Portland stone, cost almost as much as the rest of the building and is, at 224 feet, second only to St Bride in height and was the first to be built on a post Great Fire church (1678-80). The Basilica of Maxentius in Rome apparently inspired the square nave with its three wide arches on piers.

Enemy bombing in 1941 caused extensive damage to the steeple and bells, but the tower remained upright. The interior, however, had to be radically repaired and all the furnishings were renewed between 1956-64.

There is a great café in the crypt – see p.360
Area Map p.8, B:2

St Michael Cornhill

St. Michael's Alley, Cornhill, EC3V 9DS
• Tel 020 7248 382 • www.st-michaels.org.uk • Nearest transport Bank LU • See website for opening times, services & events

As with St Mary at Hill, St Michael's contains a mix of periods. It would appear that the body of the church was rebuilt after the Great Fire at the behest of the parish rather than Wren and his Commissioners. The original medieval tower was demolished and replaced between 1715-22 by Wren's office in a Gothic style to a design by Nicholas Hawksmoor. George Gilbert Scott carried out renovations between 1857-60 in the High Victorian Style removing most of the original furnishings but adding a superb Gothic porch on the north side. *Area Map p.80, C:2*

St Michael Paternoster Royal

College Hill, Upper Thames Street, EC4R 2RL • Tel 020 7248 5202 • Nearest transport Cannon St LU & Rail, Mansion House LU • Please telephone for opening times

There has been a church on this site since at least 1100. The building that perished in the Great Fire had been built in 1409 by the famous Lord Mayor of London, Richard (Dick) Whittington, who lived close by. Wren built its replacement between 1685-94 as a plain rectangular church with a tower, which has arched windows and a pierced parapet. To this was added a steeple (1713-17) considered to be one of the most beautiful in the City.

This was one of the last churches to be repaired (1966-68) following severe damage sustained by bombing in World War II. Fortunately most of the furnishings, such as the carved reredos from the 17th century, survived. There is also a charming modern stained glass window depicting Dick Whittington (see opposite).

The term 'paternoster' refers to the rosary makers who worked in the locality and the 'royal' in the church's name is thought to be a corruption of 'La Reole', after the area of France with which a nearby wine-importer had business dealings. *Area Map p.81, B:2*

Right: St Michael Paternoster Royal. Stained glass window depicting Dick Whittington by John Hayward, installed 1968

St Peter upon Cornhill

Cornhill, EC3V 9DS • Tel 020 7283 2231
• www.stpeterscornhill.org.uk • Nearest transport Bank LU

Wren, assisted by Robert Hooke, built this church between 1677-84. The crowded site, a place of worship since at least Saxon times, gives us a glimpse of what London was like before 19th and 20th-century road widening schemes left some churches marooned. Access to the church is through the door between the Ionic columns of the porch that protrude onto Cornhill from between the Victorian shops on either side.

An attractive feature of this small church is the brick tower and leaded dome with an obelisk-like spire of copper, topped with a weathervane in the shape of the key of St Peter.

One of this church's boasts is that Felix Mendelssohn played the newly installed organ here in 1840. He obviously enjoyed the experience as he returned for an encore two years later!

Regular services are no longer held here and the church is now under the wing of St Helen's Bishopsgate, where details of access to St Peter's may be obtained. *Area Map p.8, C:2*

St Nicholas Cole Abbey

Queen Victoria Street, EC4V 4BJ • Nearest transport Blackfriars LU & Rail • www.stnickschurch.org.uk

Not very far away from St Paul's Cathedral and the Millennium Bridge, this church has a splendid spire surmounted by a gilded ship. 'Cole Abbey' is thought to be a corruption of the term 'cold harbour', a temporary shelter for travellers.

Wren rebuilt this church slightly larger than its Medieval foundation in order to accommodate parishioners from the nearby St Nicholas Olave, which was not rebuilt after the Great Fire.

This rectangular building of Portland stone has large, arched windows, some of which contain some interesting modern (1960s) stained glass by Keith New. The north-west steeple has an inverted trumpet-shaped spire crowned by a weathervane in the shape of a ship which once sat atop the now demolished nearby St Michael's Queenhithe.

The interior is relatively plain, except for gilt Corinthian pilasters and panelling. Despite extensive bomb damage in 1941, much of the late 17th-century furnishings have been beautifully preserved – notably the font cover and pulpit.

Changing street patterns and extensive building in the City has resulted in the church finding itself amid busy roads and this has given it a somewhat isolated air. St Nicholas Cole Abbey also has a popular café called The Wren which is open throughout the week from 7am till 4pm and has helped to transform the interior of the church into a social space. *Area Map p.8, B:2*

Left: St Nicholas Cole Abbey

St Stephen Walbrook

39 Walbrook, EC4N 8BN • Tel 020 7283 4444 • www.ststephenwalbrook.net • Nearest transport Bank LU • See website for opening times, services & events

Located behind the Mansion House in close proximity to its neighbours it would be easy to dismiss this church with its dull exterior at street level, despite its magnificent spire. However, this is one of the most remarkable church interiors in London, if not the whole country. It is known for certain that Wren was closely involved in the design and construction of St Stephen and was paid a 20 guinea bonus because the finished project so delighted the parishioners. Wren may have used the building of this church as an experimental model for St Paul's Cathedral, and he certainly employed the same group of craftsmen.

This is one of the largest of the City churches of this period and what greets the visitor is a light and airy interior. Sixteen carefully spaced Corinthian columns, all of equal height, give the nave an exquisite sense of division. The beautiful coffered and moulded dome sits on eight arches supported by eight of the columns. Very little alteration took place during the 18th and 19th centuries but extensive renovation work needed to be carried out during the 1980s when the building was in imminent danger of collapse. This work, costing approximately £1.3 million, was done with great care and sensitivity, but there was controversy concerning the reordering around a new altar, an eight foot circle of Travertine marble by Henry Moore.

Another contemporary touch was the light-coloured wooden curved benches which replaced the old box pews.

The eminent 16th-century composer John Dunstable and the architect and playwright John Vanburgh (1664-1726) are buried here. It is from this church that the then rector, Chad Varah, founded The Samaritans in 1953.

Area Map p.8, B:2

Chiswick House, see p.108

04

FROM RESTORATION TO GEORGIAN LONDON

FROM RESTORATION TO GEORGIAN LONDON

"Oh bear me to the paths of fair Pell Mell! Safe are thy pavements, grateful is thy smell." John Gay

When the monarchy was restored to Britain in 1660, Charles II and his entourage brought back from their enforced exile continental ideas and tastes that were to change the face of much of London. One of the first projects the King undertook on his return was the remodelling of St James's Park and opening it to the public. The Park's main feature was a straight canal, tree lined in the French style. Pall Mall was laid out alongside the Park, this too has a continental flavour as its name refers to pell mell (pallo a maglio in Italian) a game played with a mallet and ball and popular with the Court.

The wealthy in society built their houses in the newly fashionable West End of London – St James's, Soho, Westminster, Piccadilly and Mayfair. Following Inigo Jones's example in Covent Garden of 1629, the London square became a desirable place to live as well as a golden opportunity for speculative building. Terraces of tall houses resembled one large mansion enabling those with aspirations to be vague as to how much of it they actually lived in. Squares laid out in this period were St James's (1661), Leicester (1670), Golden (1677) and Bloomsbury, which is thought to have been the first, planned in early 1661 by the Earl of Southampton.

Three sides of Bloomsbury Square contained terraced houses, whilst the fourth side was taken up with the Earl's own large abode, Southampton House, now demolished. Here, as with other schemes, the aristocratic model of development went on alongside smaller-scale speculative building. Most of the Square has been subsequently rebuilt, but numbers 9-14 retain some fabric and certainly the proportions of the original houses.

Some of the building schemes executed in the 1660s, particularly those in Soho, were shoddily constructed and needed replacement when their 60-year lease expired. Subsequent redevelopment, during the 1730-40s, was dominated by the fashion for the Palladian Revival style. The renewed interest in the work of Inigo Jones was perhaps a reaction to the Baroque architecture perfected by Wren and Vanbrugh (see Greenwich Walk p. 298). The architect Colen Campbell mooted a national architectural style over the 'affected and licentious' Baroque, which was considered to carry too many associations of foreign tyranny and absolutism. He suggested a return to the 'Antique Simplicity' found in the Queen's House, Greenwich and the Banqueting House, Whitehall.

Chiswick House

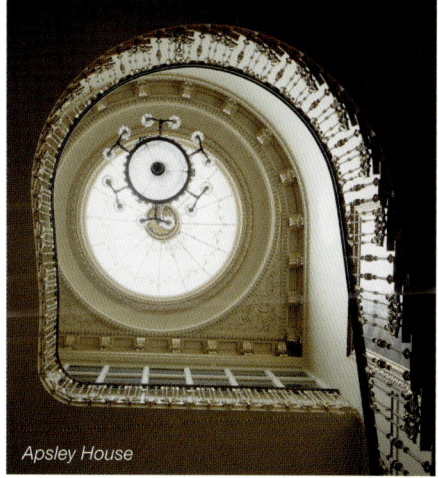
Apsley House

However, the return to the works of Jones and Palladio required a reinterpretation. Instead of being a vehicle for Stuart pretensions, Palladianism was viewed as a way of adapting the buildings of Roman antiquity to suit the governing classes. As the Roman patrician travelled from his country estate to the Senate, so the English gentleman travelled from his country estate to Parliament. The work of Burlington and Kent especially embraced Palladio's architectural philosophy (see p.91).

By 1760 Neoclassicism had become fashionable, by-passing Palladianism to return to the pure forms of Greek and Roman architecture, as practised by Robert Wood, James Stuart and Robert Adam (see p.112).

London was by far the largest city in Europe by 1700, with a population of 600,000, but most of its citizens did not enjoy the privilege of good living conditions. The writings of Smollett and the paintings of Hogarth show a world of squalor and want. Many of those flooding into London were refugees, particularly Huguenots from France after the persecution of 1685, who settled in the East End, working mainly in the textile trade. The Government became alarmed at this influx of non-conformists with unknown political allegiances and so the 1711 Building of Fifty New Churches Act was passed to reassert the primacy of the Established Church, the Church of England. This work was to be paid for from a tax on the purchase of coal with a brief to build the churches in stone with towers or steeples, no doubt influenced by Wren's City churches. Only 12 of the churches were built, the most notable being St John's Smith Square (Archer, see p.372), St Mary-le-Strand (Gibbs, see p.106) and St Mary Woolnoth, (Hawksmoor, see p.100).

The 18th-century growth in state and commerce generally led to buildings for specific official purposes, for example the Admiralty (see Whitehall Walk p.349) and Sir William Chambers' creation, of one of the first purpose-built office complexes in Europe at Somerset House (see p.343). Also built were barracks, hospitals, theatres, opera houses, coffee houses, banks and bridges. London became the first 'consumer society' in the world as shops sprang up all over the capital. Purpose-built shops with large windows were now becoming commonplace; number 34 Haymarket has probably the oldest shop front in London and numbers 165-167 Bond Street date from the 1770s.

Gentlemen's clubs were an 18th-century invention, and were often named after their original owner. Two such can still be found in St James's Street, Westminster and are, more or less, in their original form. Boodles was built in 1775-76 in the Adam style and Brooke's, dating from 1776-78 is by the architect Henry Holland.

Another 18th-century phenomenon was the emergence of the architect as an arbiter of taste and design. An architect could so designate himself by virtue of his academic training in the subject. His whole approach to design and construction was based on theoretical knowledge rather than observation and practical experience, the tools by which a master mason or master carpenter learned his trade. That is not to say a medieval mason would have been ignorant of geometry, for how else would he have been able to build the Gothic churches with their impossibly tall walls. Cooperation between master masons and other master craftsmen would have been paramount to the production of fine buildings.

The rise of the architect began in the 17th century when the tastes of many of London's patrons, principally the Royal Household and in particular the Stuart dynasty, coincided with those of Inigo Jones. Jones was well-travelled and well-versed in the work and writings of Andrea Palladio, the master of Italian Renaissance architecture. Palladio interpreted all that was elegant about Roman building and applied this vision to 16th-century villa and palazzo building with notable success. Jones used Palladio's theories in his own work at the Queen's House and the Banqueting House. He was able to do so, in part, because Palladio had set his ideas on paper in his architectural treatise *I quatro libri dell'architettura* (The Four Books of Architecture), published in 1570. Architecture was henceforth the marriage of the practical to the theoretical.

Inigo Jones paved the way for others, such as Wren, Vanbrugh and Nash who, like him, were holders of posts within the Royal Works. However, although positions within the Works were prestigious and, to a large extent, lucrative, the knowledge gained therein was not felt to have been passed on thoroughly enough. It therefore became usual from the early part of the 18th century for practising architects to take on articled clerks who learned their profession 'on the job', at the drawing board, attending lectures and, if funds were sufficient, travelling in Europe, principally to Northern Italy, Rome and Greece.

The Royal Academy of Arts, founded in 1768, incorporated architecture into its remit and appointed a Professor of Architecture. In 1791 a group of leading London architects set up 'The Architects' Club' with a mission to define the profession and qualifications of an architect. A few years later, in 1809, The London Architectural Society formed to provide lectures and a library. In 1810 the first tentative steps were taken to institute a Royal Academy of Architecture, but its first official meeting was not held until 1835.

To follow are listed, as far as possible, in date order, the 18th century's leading architects and some of their work still to be seen in London. Many were 'amateur' architects in that they did not rely on their architecture practice to earn a living, and were wealthy gentlemen in their own right. Most had travelled abroad, some extensively so having been on the 'Grand Tour', and this is where many found the inspiration to try their hands at architecture.

Opposite: Somerset House

SIR CHRISTOPHER WREN
(1632-1723)

See the previous chapter for St Paul's Cathedral and the City churches. Other buildings by Wren are:

St James's, Piccadilly

197 Piccadilly, W1J 9LL • Tel 020 7734 4511 • www.sjp.org.uk • Nearest transport Piccadilly Circus LU • See website for opening times, services & events

The area surrounding the church was granted to Henry Jermyn, Earl of St Albans in 1662 for residential development. In 1672 Wren was commissioned to design and build the new parish church, which was eventually consecrated by the Bishop of London on 13 July 1684. Built of red brick with Portland stone dressings St James's is a supremely elegant building. Its interior is wide and spacious with galleries on three sides supported by square pillars and handsome Corinthian columns carry the barrel vault of the nave.

The font and reredos are by Grinling Gibbons and are stunning examples of his work and make a visit to this charming church even more worthwhile. Sculpted in white marble the font depicts scenes from Genesis, whilst the reredos of carved limewood is of garlands of flowers and a pelican with her young. St James's is a lively place with a busy café and a popular crafts market held in the courtyard on most days. *Area Map p.6, A:2*

Royal Hospital Chelsea

Royal Hospital Road, SW3 4SR • Tel 020 7881 5209 • www.chelsea-pensioners.co.uk • Nearest transport Sloane Square LU • See website for opening hours, details of guided tours and chapel service times

Built at the behest and expense of Charles II as a home for war-wounded and elderly soldiers, the Royal Hospital was inspired by the magnificent Hôtel des Invalides in Paris. Although nothing like as grand as the French model it is considered by its residents to be a 'homely' space in which to live. Built between 1682 and 1691, 476 old soldiers had moved in by 1689.

Built of two coloured brick with some Portland stone dressings, the Hospital was Wren's largest domestic commission, built in a Dutch style but with Classical porticoes and trimmings. The buildings are arranged around three open courtyards, the longest of which fronts the road and houses both the Hall and Chapel. From the central octagonal, domed vestibule turn left into the Great Hall, which contains some superb paintings, including two by the 18th-century portraitist Allan Ramsay, as well as tattered banners from historic military campaigns. This wood panelled room, which is still used for dining, has a very plain, flat ceiling and large round-headed windows. The tunnel-vaulted Chapel has an apse with the Resurrection painted by Sebastiano Ricci.

The central courtyard, the Figure Court, is enclosed by buildings on its northern, eastern and western sides, but the southern side is open with a view to the grounds and the river. The statue of Charles II dressed as a Roman Emperor, from which the Court takes its name, is the work of Grinling Gibbons.

Visitors are welcome here and permitted to visit the Hall, Chapel and courtyards. The Long Wards are not open to the public as they are still very much in use by ex-soldiers, known as Chelsea Pensioners, whose scarlet uniforms cut quite a dash in this part of town.

Kensington Palace

Kensington Palace

Kensington Palace State Apartments, Kensington Gardens, W8 4PX • Tel 0844 482 7777 • www.hrp.org.uk • Nearest transport High Street Kensington LU, Queensway LU or Notting Hill Gate LU • See website for opening times and admission charges

In his capacity as Royal Surveyor Wren built various additions to the London residence of the monarch, Whitehall Palace, most of which have since been demolished. In 1688 James II was deposed and William and Mary were crowned. However, the new King found Whitehall damp and instructed Wren to transform the newly purchased Nottingham House, in the more salubrious area of Kensington, into a palace where they would reside.

This building became Kensington Palace, although it was not known as such until the 18th century. To save cost, Wren initially made use of the modest scale of the original house and the material used was chiefly brick. The main entrance is under the clock tower into Clock Court with the King's Staircase on the far right of the Court, which once took visitors up to the Royal Suite. The Court now serves as the private quarters for residents and modern visitors now enter through the back of the Palace.

The tastes of the Dutch King of England are clearly reflected in this building, in that it has more than a passing resemblance to his own country retreat in Holland, Het Loo, near the town of Apeldoorn, but on a much smaller scale. Remodelling and enlargement was subsequently undertaken by William Kent and Nicholas Hawksmoor.

George II was the last reigning monarch to live here, although Wren's Clock Court remains a residence of the royal family, most notably Diana Princess of Wales who lived here from her marriage until her death but since then Kensington Palace has been the London home for various members of the royal family, such as the Queen's sister, Princess Margaret, and Diana, Princess of Wales. Presently the Duke and Duchess of Cambridge live in one of the larger apartments, with some twenty rooms, whilst other members of the royal family occupy smaller suites in the Palace or cottages in the grounds.

Marlborough House

The Commonwealth Centre, Pall Mall, SW1Y 5HX • To arrange visits contact meetingrooms@commonwealth.int

When Sarah, Duchess of Marlborough, friend and confidante of Queen Anne, decided to build a London home, she chose not to engage the services of Sir John Vanbrugh, who had designed Blenheim Palace for the Duke. This was due in part to a lingering animosity between the Duchess and architect, instead she appointed Sir Christopher Wren who, in the year of the commission, 1709, would have been at the height of his skill and fame. Unfortunately, the Duchess and Wren also had a somewhat stormy relationship but, nonetheless, Marlborough House was completed within two years.

The usually extravagant Duchess courted a little thrift in her insistence in using red Dutch bricks, brought to England as ballast in the troop transports that had carried soldiers for the Duke's army in Holland. The house is somewhat plain and was originally a two-story structure with just a little carved stone decoration and top balustrade and has been enlarged several times most notably by Sir William Chambers in 1771, John Taylor in 1870 and Fielden and Mawson in 1990.

Marlborough House has not only served generations of Dukes and Duchesses, but has also been home to royalty and in the wake of the Great Exhibition it became the Government School of Design and the Department of Practical Art. In 1959 the Queen placed Marlborough House at the disposal of the British Government as a Commonwealth Centre and today it serves as the Commonwealth Secretariat and the Commonwealth Foundation.

Please contact the above email address for information regarding visits and tours. *Area Map p.6, A:2*

Other buildings by Christopher Wren:

- **St Clement Danes,** see 'Strand Walk' p.338
- **The Royal Observatory** see 'Greenwich Walk' p.301
- **The Monument,** see 'Architecture with a View' p.394

NICHOLAS HAWKSMOOR
(1661-1736)

Born in Nottingham Nicholas Hawksmoor was, by the age of 18, employed in London as Sir Christopher Wren's 'domestic clerk'. He assisted Wren in making drawings for St Paul's Cathedral and many of the City churches. He also assisted Vanbrugh on his two most fabulous buildings, Castle Howard in Yorkshire and Blenheim Palace in Oxfordshire. In 1711 Hawksmoor was appointed as one of two surveyors to oversee the Fifty New Churches Act, and at last was recognised as a major architectural force in his own right. Part of the genius of Hawksmoor was his mastery of architectural forms from Classic through Gothic and Renaissance to Italian Baroque, but in a style that remained utterly personal, and almost impossible to categorise.

See 'Walking London's Architecture' for details of Hawksmoor's work in Greenwich (p.300).

Christ Church, Spitalfields

Commercial Street, E1 6LY • Tel 020 7247 7202 • www.christchurchspitalfields.org • Nearest transport Aldgate East LU or Liverpool Street LU & Rail • See website for opening times, services & events

A glorious example of Hawksmoor's genius and considered by many to be his best church, yet it has suffered a chequered history and was nearly demolished during the 1960s. The building was started in 1714, and consecrated in 1729 but became neglected over the ensuing years and had to be closed in 1957 as it was felt to be a dangerous structure. Conservationists fought and won a hard battle and money was raised for the restoration of Christ Church by selling off St John's, Smith Square as a concert hall (see 'Eat and Drink Architecture' p.372).

This church is now used extensively during the Spitalfields Festival and for other concerts during the year. It is a truly fantastic architectural tour de force. Just to look at the giant columns and plaster decorated ceiling is worth the journey alone.

St Anne, Limehouse

Three Colt Street, E14 7HP • Tel 020 7987 1502 • www.stanneslimehouse.org • Nearest transport Westferry DLR • Please telephone for opening times and services

Started in 1714 as one of the first of the 'Fifty Churches' of the 1711 Act, it was not completed until 1724 and then remained unused for six years due to a lack of funds with which to pay the clergy. The huge portico at the west entrance and the tower are characteristically complex. The tower is said to be Hawksmoor's version of a 15th-century lantern tower and is complete with a clock, the second highest in the country after the Big Ben clock face on the Houses of Parliament. The tower and clock were a landmark for generations of sailors, on their way to or returning from every corner of the world; alas the ships pass no more.

The interior is impressive with four huge, full height columns dividing the nave. A superb stained glass window at the east end by Charles Clutterbuck, depicting the Crucifixion of Christ, was installed during a very faithful reconstruction of the interior by Phillip Hardwick, following a serious fire in 1850. St Anne's received further renovation and cleaning between 1983-93 by Julian Harrap.

Left: Christ Church Spitalfields. Hawksmoor's bold and muscular example of Baroque architecture

St George's Bloomsbury

Bloomsbury Way, WC1A 2HR • Tel 020 7242 1979 • www.stgeorgesbloomsbury.org.uk • Nearest transport Holborn LU or Tottenham Court Road LU • See website for opening times, services & events

This is the last of the 12 churches built under the Fifty New Churches Act. At this time Bloomsbury was served by St Giles church, but this arrangement was seen to be unsatisfactory by the new, relatively wealthy residents of the area, who objected to having to enter the unsavoury neighbourhood.

Consecrated in 1731, St George's was the sixth and last of Hawksmoor's London churches, and is considered by many to be one of the finest buildings in the capital. The interior deserves close inspection; the galleried nave is almost a cube, thus complying with the Classical style; the rich mahogany altar and marquetry reredos are a unique feature for a London church.

The exterior is dominated by the large Corinthian portico. It is believed that the inspiration behind the portico was the Roman Temple of Bacchus at Baalbek in the Lebanon. Looking up at the steeple we see a statue of King George I in Roman dress atop the stepped pyramid whose design was based upon Pliny's description of the Mausoleum at Halicarnassus. *Area Map p.2-3, B:1*

St Mary Woolnoth

Lombard Street, EC3V 9AN • Tel 020 7626 9701 www.stml.org uk • Nearest transport Bank LU • Please see website for opening times and services

Aptly described as situated 'on the prow' of Lombard Street and Bank, this church's curious name dates back to a Saxon noble called Woolnoth, or possibly Wulfnoth, who founded a temple on the site. Hawksmoor's church is the only one built in the City under the 'Fifty Churches' Act of 1711. Given a very cramped site, he created a unique exterior, especially when one considers his other churches were built on spacious 'greenfield' sites. The interior feels larger than expected and its design is based on the Egyptian Hall, as described by the Roman writer Vitruvius.

The church has been threatened with demolition many times, especially during the 19th century when City sites were at premium and 18th-century church architecture was of low priority. St Mary Woolnoth is unique in having an underground station below it, during the construction of which The City and Southern London Railway cleared the church vaults, transferring the bodies buried there to a cemetery in Ilford, and sunk lift shafts directly beneath the church. *Area Map p.8, C:2*

West Towers, Westminster Abbey

Dean's Yard, SW1P 3PA • Tel 020 7222 5897 • www.westminster-abbey.org • Nearest transport St James's Park LU or Westminster LU

This project was Hawksmoor's last and he died before it was completed. These towers show his extraordinary ability for imitation and innovation and are one of only two examples of his Gothic work in London, the other being the tower of St Michael Cornhill (see p.80). So well do the towers sit with the rest of the west end of the Abbey, it is hard to persuade the casual onlooker that the towers only date from the 18th century. *Area Map p.6, B:1*

Right: West Towers, Westminster Abbey. One of Hawksmoor's last projects, completed nine years after his death. Inspiration for the design may well have come from the 14th-century west towers of Beverley Minster on which he worked earlier in his career

SIR JOHN VANBRUGH
(1664–1726)

Of Vanbrugh one contemporary said 'Van's genius, without thought or lecture, is hugely turn'd to architecture'. However, Vanbrugh's life was an extraordinary one even if we do not take into consideration his architectural achievements: he was also in his time a wine merchant, soldier, prisoner (in the Bastille of Paris) as well as a successful playwright.

It is not known when Vanbrugh decided to try his hand at architecture but by 1669 he was designing Castle Howard in North Yorkshire for the Earl of Carlisle. By 1702 he was Wren's principal colleague on the Board of His Majesty's Works and the following year was appointed to the Board of Directors of Greenwich Hospital. He was later given the opportunity to create his most memorable building, Blenheim Palace in Oxfordshire, a gift to the Duke of Marlborough as a mark of royal gratitude for his military achievements against the French. A master of the Baroque, Vanbrugh's work was flamboyant, theatrical and exuberant. His massive, muscular style worked best when applied to the large-scale projects he undertook but towards the end of his life Vanbrugh did champion architects of the Palladian movement, such as Burlington.

Vanbrugh Castle

121 Maze Hill, SE10 8XQ • Nearest transport Maze Hill Rail • No public access

In 1718 Vanbrugh bought 12 acres of land at Maze Hill in order to build homes for himself and his family, while he was working on projects at Greenwich nearby. His own, the only building remaining, is now divided into private apartments and so is not open to the public.

Finished in 1726, this turreted, palatial building, resembling a Scottish castle or fortress, still stuns and amuses the unsuspecting. It is thought to be Britain's first sham castle – a sort of Gothic pile without a trace of Gothic detailing!

Royal Arsenal, Woolwich

Woolwich SE18 6ST • Nearest transport Woolwich Arsenal Rail, Riverbus & DLR • www.royalarsenaltours.co.uk

During the building of Blenheim Palace the Duchess of Marlborough had a spectacular falling-out with Vanbrugh, which led to his resigning the commission in 1716. His friendship with the Duke continued and this led to the architect being given the commission to design buildings for the Board of Ordnance. The most important buildings in this group, and still extant in London, can be found at the Royal Arsenal at Woolwich which is just along the River Thames from Greenwich.

It is probable, but by no means beyond doubt, that Vanbrugh was responsible for the building of the Brass Gun Foundry of 1717; the Model Room of 1719 and the Gun Bore Factory of the early 1720s. All the buildings are simply constructed in brick and together make a very interesting group.

The 76-acre site at Woolwich has a long history. In 1512 Henry VIII established a Royal Dockyard here and by 1671 it became the largest complex for the manufacture and storage of armaments and military equipment in Britain. King George III gave the Arsenal a Royal Charter in 1805 in honour of its importance in the Napoleonic Wars. During the First World War some 80,000 were employed here in armament manufacture. Despite this glorious past the site was closed by the Ministry of Defence in the late 1960s.

The London Development Agency took control of the land in 2000, when it was decided to create a new mixed use urban quarter. There will eventually be somewhere in the region of six thousand homes created on the site, from a combination of converted Grade I and II listed buildings and new-build, as well as a health centre, hotel, offices, cafés, shops, outdoor spaces with landscaping and public art and a new cinema, making this a new London neighbourhood with transport links that include the Riverside Thames Bus and the London Crossrail route. Open access to public areas and tours of the site are available, see above.

See also:
- King William Block, Greenwich Hospital, 'Greenwich Walk' (p.298)

THOMAS ARCHER
(1668-1743)

Born to a wealthy Warwickshire family and educated at Oxford, he travelled in Europe for four years. During his time in Italy he studied the work of Bernini and the influence is evident in Archer's designs, which are almost pure Continental Baroque.

St Paul's Deptford

Diamond Way, Deptford, SE8 3DS • Tel 020 8692 7449 • Nearest transport Deptford Bridge DLR • Please telephone for opening times and services

Pevsner described St Paul's as 'one of the most moving 18th-century churches in London: large, sombre and virile'. Built 1713-30 as part of the 1711 'Fifty Churches Act', it is certainly one of the foremost Baroque churches in London, if not the country. The visitor is greeted at the west end by a large semi-circular portico, surmounted by a tall English steeple. The interior has notable features such as a curving Venetian window at the apse on the east end, great solid Corinthian columns and the original pulpit with graceful iron stairs.

Russell House, Covent Garden

43 King Street, Covent Garden, WC2E 8JY • Nearest transport Covent Garden LU • no public access other than ground floor shop when open

If you stand with your back to the porch at the front of St Paul's, Covent Garden and glance to your left you will see Russell House. A lovely stuccoed house built 1716-7 by Archer as a home for Admiral Russell, 1st Earl of Oxford, it has four giant Composite pilasters on street-level rusticated piers, and tall, slim windows with gentle elliptical heads. It was restored to its former glory in 1977 having for many years been used as a fruit store for Covent Garden Market. The ground floor of this handsome building is now a fashion shop. *Area Map p.6, B:3*

See also:
- St John, Smith Square, 'Eat and Drink Architecture', p.372

Left: St Paul's Deptford

JAMES GIBBS
(1682-1754)

Born into a modest Scottish Catholic family, Gibbs was unable to fund a 'Grand Tour' and as a young man stayed with relatives in Holland before enrolling at the Scots College in Rome with a view to taking Holy Orders. Fortunately for us, the young Gibbs decided that his real calling was architecture and he became a pupil of the great Carlo Fontana. Consequently Gibbs had a thorough, professional training in Italian architecture, unlike his contemporaries who were merely observers. On his return to England in 1709, the only obstacle to a glittering career was his religion. Ironically, one of his first major commissions was to design the church of St Mary-le-Strand as one of the 'Fifty New Churches' under the Act intended to promote Protestant worship! Not averse to self-publicity, he published two editions of his drawings and in 1732 published his *'Rules for Drawing the Several Parts of Architecture'*.

St Mary-le-Strand

Strand, WC2R 1ES • Nearest transport Temple LU, Charing Cross LU & Rail • Tel 020 7836 3126 • www.stmarylestrand.org • See website for opening times & services

Marooned in the middle of a busy London thoroughfare and a short walk from the delights of Covent Garden, this small church is worth dodging the traffic to visit. The advantage of it being stranded on an island is that it can be viewed from all sides. Dating from 1714-17, this building, probably more than all his others, reflects his training under Fontana, even though Gibbs had to make modifications to please his masters. The original design for the tower was too 'Roman' for Whiggish taste and so something a little more Palladian was produced instead. The semi-circular entrance porch is exquisite as is the interior with its richly coloured stained glass windows, particularly the work in the apse by Sidney Toy (1947). *Area Map p.6, C:3*

Octagon of Orleans House

Riverside, Twickenham, TW1 3DJ • Tel 020 8831 6000 • www.richmond.gov.uk/arts • Nearest transport St Margaret's Rail or Richmond LU then bus 33, 490, H22, R68, R70, 290 alight at The Crown Pub / Lebanon Park • See website for opening times

Built in the early 1720s as an almost freestanding garden room and place for entertainment, the building is of brick with stone window dressings. The fairly plain exterior is in stark contrast to the richly decorated Baroque interior. This is the work of renowned Swiss stuccatori Giovanni Baguttl and Guiseppe Artari, who also decorated St Peter, Vere Street and St Martin-in-the-Fields for Gibbs.

Set in a peaceful woodland area near the River Thames, the Octagon is part of the Orleans House Gallery and is maintained by the London Borough of Richmond.

St Peter, Vere Street

Vere Street, W1G 0DQ • Nearest transport Bond Street LU

Of brown and orange brick with stone quoins and Tuscan portico and pediment, this church sits on its own little island just off busy Oxford Street and was built for the Earl of Oxford in 1721-24. With very pretty plasterwork by Bagutti and Artari, this church has been cited by some as the 'testing ground' for Gibbs' much larger work – St Martin-in-the-Fields.

The building is now the offices of the London Institute of Contemporary Christianity.
Area Map p.4, C:1

See also:
- St Martin-in-the-Fields, see 'Whitehall Walk' p.347
- St Bartholomew's Hospital, see 'Bartholomew Walk' p.283

LORD BURLINGTON (RICHARD BOYLE, 3RD EARL OF BURLINGTON) (1694-1753)

Having inherited extensive properties in the country and London at the age of ten, wealth enabled Burlington to travel as well as patronise the talented. He championed the music of the young Handel, the paintings of Kent and supported the Italian sculptor Guelfi. He employed the talent of Colen Campbell in his quest to restore the principles of Palladian architecture to the position enjoyed at the time of Inigo Jones before the cultural wilderness that was the Commonwealth intervened. Campbell and Burlington collaborated on the remodelling of the latter's family home in Piccadilly, which was subject to further, more extensive, alterations during the 19th century.

However by the early 1720's Burlington was acting as his own architect, assisted by Henry Flitcroft, who was later to design the church of St Giles-in-the-Field. Their earliest work is the Dormitory at Westminster School (gutted during World War II and much altered since with no public access).

Chiswick House

Burlington Lane, W4 2RP • Tel 020 8995 0508 • Nearest transport Chiswick Rail • www.chgt.org.uk • See website for opening times and admission charges

Described by Sir Kenneth Clark in his book *Civilisation* as a 'masterpiece of domestic architecture', Chiswick House was inspired by Palladio's famous Villa Rotonda – but it is no slavish copy. Built between 1727 and 1729 the house was designed by Burlington to be the setting for his extensive art collection. This was housed on the first floor along with a bedchamber and dressing room for Lady Burlington. The lower floor housed Burlington's library and his private apartments. The domestic offices, such as the kitchen remained in the adjacent Jacobean house.

The plan of Chiswick House is a square with an interior of octagonal halls and a slightly flattened dome, also octagonal, with four small windows. The elegant exterior double staircase leads to the portico, which, even with six solid Corinthian columns, appears to float. Burlington ingeniously used obelisks to contain the chimneys so necessary for the English climate and on either side of the portico are statues of Inigo Jones and Palladio by the leading 18th-century sculptor Rysbrack.

The sumptuous interior is at odds with the monochrome exterior, but is very much in the spirit of the work of Inigo Jones. Indeed most of the chimneypieces in Chiswick House are based on designs by Jones in Burlington's collection and many of the rooms have painted ceilings by William Kent.

The original Jacobean house was demolished in the 1780s in order to add wings to Burlington's villa, but these were taken down shortly afterwards. Chiswick House stayed mostly within the ownership of Burlington's family but by the early 1950s it needed extensive repairs. This was undertaken by the Ministry of Works at the behest of Middlesex Council and since 1984 Chiswick House has been cared for by English Heritage. Connoisseurs of architecture will have fun spotting Burlington's influences in the house and references to the works of classical interpreters Palladio and Scamozzi. For the rest of us it is just a joy to behold – a sparkling gem of a building set within an exquisite public park.

Also of note is the gateway and modern café. The gateway was originally designed by Inigo Jones for a house in Chelsea and erected at Chiswick in 1738. The café was named RIBA London Building of the Year 2011; see 'Eat and Drink Architecture' p.361 for more details.

WILLIAM KENT (1685-1748)

Although from a humble Yorkshire family, as a talented painter Kent enjoyed the patronage of wealthy gentlemen who financed his visits to Italy over a period of ten years. In the winter of 1715 whilst in Rome he met the Earl of Burlington who became a patron, collaborator and friend. On his return to England in 1719 Kent received commissions from the great and wealthy, being called upon to restore Rubens' ceiling at the Banqueting House and in 1739 he became Portrait Painter to the King – a post he never assumed.

Kent became interested in architecture during his stay in Italy and had studied the works not only of Palladio but also buildings in Rome by Guilio Romano and Raphael. The influence of these latter two artists/architects can be seen in Kent's preference for rusticated wall surfaces over the smooth exteriors associated with Palladian architecture.

Among Kent's most prestigious works outside the capital are the garden buildings at Stowe in Buckinghamshire and Holkham Hall in Norfolk, on which he collaborated with Lord Burlington. One of Kent's major London projects, the Courts of Justice, originally stood approximately where the public entrance to the House of Commons is today, but was irreparably damaged by fire in 1834.

44, Berkeley Square, Mayfair

44 Berkeley Square, W1J 5AR • Nearest transport Green Park LU

One of the finest town houses in London, this house was built 1742/44 for Lady Isabella Finch. She was sometime Lady in Waiting to Queen Caroline, who, being a single woman, required a house for entertaining as much as for domestic convenience. The house is of brick construction with stone quoins and detailing at the ground floor, particularly around the front door. The interior has an exquisite staircase which, starting with a single flight, fans out to both sides taking guests up to the important first floor, the piano nobile, and the great salon with its three tall pedimented windows overlooking the square.

The house is now owned by the Clermont Club, a private members' club with no public access. However, the club's website has some superb photographs of the interior.

See also:
- Treasury Building and Horse Guards Parade, see 'Whitehall Walk' p.349
- Chiswick House (interior), see p.108

SIR WILLIAM CHAMBERS
(1723-96)

During the period of the 1770s and 1780s English architecture was dominated by two very talented men. The first, William Chambers, initially made his name by producing work in the Chinese style and later as the leading exponent of Palladianism; the second was Robert Adam who gave his name to a style of his own.

Born in Gothenburg to Scottish parents, William Chambers showed a great interest in architecture but was obliged to work for the family mercantile business. In this capacity he travelled extensively to Africa, India, Ceylon and, most importantly China, where he studied and drew the buildings he saw. It was not until the age of 27 that Chambers began his architectural studies in earnest in Paris, under the tutelage of Blondel at l'Ecole des Arts, and he went on to study for a further five years in Rome.

Within two years of his return to England in 1755 he published his first book, *Designs for Chinese Buildings*, and was appointed 'Tutor of Architecture' to the future King George III. Princess Augusta employed Chambers to lay out the grounds at Kew and furnish it with buildings of an Oriental flavour. His royal patronage continued when he was appointed Treasurer of the newly founded Royal Academy in 1768 and the King's Surveyor-General in 1782.

The King's Observatory, Richmond

04

Old Deer Park, Kew Road, Richmond, TW9 2AZ • www.kingsobservatory.co.uk • Nearest transport Richmond LU & Rail

Set in the centre of the historic Richmond Deer Park, which majestically sweeps down to the Thames, the King's Observatory was designed by William Chambers for George III. Made of Portland stone, the building contains two octagonal rooms surmounted with what appears to be a fashionable cupola, but is in fact a moveable dome, inside which were the main telescopes. The building was completed in time for the King, a keen astronomer, to observe the transit of Venus across the face of the sun on 3rd June 1769.

Currently access to the Observatory interior is under review - please see the website for details.

See also:
• Somerset House, see 'Strand Walk' p.340

ROBERT ADAM (1728-92)

Born the second son of William Adam, a successful Scottish architect and entrepreneur, Robert Adam enjoyed a background of relative privilege. He moved in intellectual circles, had access to his father's excellent library and was sufficiently wealthy to be able to travel extensively in Europe. However, Adam was not a gentleman of leisure and, like his father, was thoroughly versed in the craft of building. One important result of this was his concern with every detail of his architectural projects – very different from the dilettante gentleman architects of this period.

On his return from his travels in early 1758 Adam decided to settle in London and was soon joined by his two younger brothers, James, also an architect and William junior, a banker. In 1761 Robert Adam was given one of two new posts of Architect of the King's Works (the post until then had been 'Surveyor of the King's Works'). The other post went to Sir William Chambers who was Adam's rival rather than his colleague. Indeed Chambers was successful in blocking Adam's membership to the Royal Academy on the grounds that his work was 'too eclectic'. However, Adam proved his scholarship by producing three volumes entitled *Works in Architecture of Robert and James Adam*. Perhaps more importantly, Robert Adam had a whole style of architecture named after him and even for those with little interest in the field, the term 'Adam Style' will bring to mind buildings and interiors in the Classical manner.

Over the next 30 thirty years Robert Adam went on to expand the repertoire of English domestic architecture from strict Palladianism to include a much wider range of classical sources. He became one of the most sought after and busiest architects of his day and his wealthy clients adored this new decorative style all of which was designed by Adam himself, right down to the door fittings. Although public commissions eluded him, at the time of his unexpected death in 1792 at the age of 63, Robert Adam had over 30 commissions from all parts of the country in hand. At his funeral in Westminster Abbey his coffin was borne to its last resting place by a Duke, two Earls, a Viscount and a Baron.

There are very few unaltered, from the foundations to the chimney tops, Adam buildings. Indeed there is little of his work to see in central London – much was swept away by road-widening schemes, 'improvements' and enemy bombing. Despite the sad loss of much of his work, Adam was a master of renovation and interior design, as three of his most important houses Syon, Osterley and Kenwood, all described below, illustrate.

The vast collection of plans and drawings by Robert and James Adam was obtained by Sir John Soane in 1833, and can be viewed at his museum, see p.127.

Syon House

Syon Park, Brentford, TW8 8JF • Tel 020 8560 0882 • www.syonpark.co.uk • Nearest transport Gunnersbury LU & Rail then bus 237 or 267 • See website for more details

Originally the site of a 15th-century abbey and of a noble house since 1547, Syon House has belonged to the Percy family, Earls and Dukes of Northumberland, since 1594 and was extensively reconstructed by the tenth Earl in the 17th century. The title died out with his son and was not recreated until 1750 when Sir Hugh Smithson became Earl of Northumberland. It was for him that Robert Adam refashioned the old house by creating a first floor, or piano nobile, and a complete set of parade rooms, through which the guests and hosts would promenade at the frequent, fashionable parties. These new rooms were created within the old structure. The exterior is very simple, castellated and stuccoed.

Entrance to the house is through the Hall to the Ante-room (see below right), the Great Dining Room and the State Drawing Room to the Gallery. This principal route takes the visitor through a sequence of splendid chambers, each different from the last yet all related by similar uses of classical motifs. Adam's use of colour adds to the drama with the prevailing ivory and black of the Hall giving way in the next room, the Ante-room, to an essay in sumptuous gold. Adam draws on a wide range of sources, mixing ancient Greek and Roman motifs in an idiosyncratic manner and then arranging them in a unified scheme.

Lansdowne House

9 Fitzmaurice Place, Berkeley Square, W1J 5JD • www.lansdowneclub.com • Private members' club, no public access

Now a private members' club, Adam designed this house for Lord Bute between 1762 and 1768 as a town mansion standing in its own, large garden. This is an early example of Adam's town houses. Road improvements in the area during the 1930s meant major alterations to the property were necessary and part of the Adam interior had to be sacrificed when the original stone façade was pushed back 40 feet to make way for the road. The discarded Adam Drawing Room, complete with exquisite decorations executed by Cipriani and Zucchi, was shipped off to America and now resides in the Philadelphia Museum of Art and can be viewed on www.philamuseum.org.

Home House

20 Portman Square, W1H 6LW • www.homehouse.co.uk • Private members' club, no public access

The commission for this house was originally given to the architect James Wyatt, but after a falling out with the Countess of Home a year into the project he was sacked and Robert Adam was engaged to complete the job in 1775. The interior is everything one imagines an Adam house to be – very light, elegant and glamorous. The exquisite staircase, reminiscent of Kent's at 44 Berkeley Square, has a single flight to the first floor and then swings out on both sides, lit by a circular skylight. Miraculously, much of Adam's original interior decoration survives.

Home House remained a private residence until, in 1926, Samuel Courtauld housed his growing art collection here, becoming the basis of the Courtauld Institute of Art; the collection moving to larger premises at Somerset House in 1989 (see p.343). The house was then listed on the 'Buildings at Risk Register' until it received extensive and highly successful renovation by Fielden and Mawson, conservation architects, between 1996 and 1999.

Home House is now a private members' club which has a superb website giving an excellent impression of the interior of the property. *Area Map p.4, B:1*

Osterley Park

Jersey Road, Isleworth, Houndslow, TW7 4RB • Tel 020 8232 5050 • www.nationaltrust.org.uk • Nearest transport Osterley LU then 25min walk• See website for opening times and admission charges

Osterley Park was originally built as the country seat for Thomas Gresham in 1575 and purchased in 1761 by wealthy banker Robert Childs, who, like many of his contemporaries, employed Robert Adam to transform his home. As with Syon, the old-fashioned exterior of the house, with its red brick wings around a courtyard and towers at each corner topped with ogee caps, belies its interior. Adam added a magnificent screen of Ionic columns to form a double portico at the centre of the front elevation, with the house being entered by a flight of stairs. Inside, the decorative scheme is sumptuous, in particular the Etruscan Dressing Room, where Adam draws on ancient Herculaneum and the classicising work of his contemporary Josiah Wedgwood for inspiration.

In the ownership of the National Trust since 1949, the house is considered to be the most perfectly preserved of all Adam's work. The grounds have a magnificent lake complete with anglers, water fowl and a flashing kingfisher. The stable block has interesting Elizabethan brickwork and an early 18th-century cupola and clock. All this is a mere 45 minute tube ride from the centre of London.

Kenwood House

The Iveagh Bequest, Kenwood, Hampstead Lane, NW3 7JR • Tel 020 8348 1286 • www.english-heritage.org.uk • Nearest transport Golders Green LU then bus 210, Gospel Oak & Hampstead Heath Rail • Admission free • See website for opening times

Kenwood House stands on the crest of the ridge between Hampstead and Highgate and looks towards central London. On the site of a much older house, Kenwood was rebuilt in about 1700 and between 1764-79 was remodelled by Robert Adam for its owner William Murray, 1st Earl of Mansfield. To the existing brick house Adam added the porch, library and ante chamber, embellished and decorated the remainder of the interior and encased the whole exterior in white stucco.

On the north façade of the house Adam added the huge portico, with four fluted Ionic columns and Grecian scrolled capitals supporting the massive pediment. As you pass through the portico look up to see the rather striking decoration beneath the pediment. The wings of the house are a post-Adam addition.

The Library, sometimes referred to as 'The Great Room', is regarded as one of the finest 18th-century British interiors, and is of an unusual shape, a double cube with semi-circular apses and a coved ceiling, inspired by ancient Roman baths.

Kenwood houses a renowned art collection, which includes works by Jan Vermeer, Frans Hals and Rembrandt, as well as portraits by Gainsborough, Reynolds and Romney.

This elegant house sits in extensive grounds, landscaped by Repton in 1793, which beautifully incorporate some fine 20th-century sculpture by, among others, Reg Butler, Barbara Hepworth and Henry Moore.

Above: Kenwood House south front
Opposite: The Library

Apsley House

149 Piccadilly, W1J 7NT • Tel 020 7499 5676 • www.english-heritage.co.uk • Nearest transport Hyde Park Corner LU • See website for opening times and admission charges

Built 1771-78 by Robert Adam for Lord Apsley, but extensively remodelled by James Wyatt and his family from 1807 onwards. Further renovations have largely ignored its Adam origins, although a few of the rooms still conform to his ideals – if you look really hard.

Originally the house address was 'No 1 London' because it was the first building past the tollgate into the capital for travellers eastward. Apsley House was once the home of Arthur Wellesley, 1st Duke of Wellington, soldier and politician, and today houses the Wellington Museum and a glittering array of artworks acquired courtesy of the Iron Duke's military successes, among them paintings by Velasquez and Correggio.

The Adelphi

Royal Society of Arts, 8 John Adam Street, WC2N 6EZ • Tel 020 7930 5115 • www.thersa.org • Nearest transport Charing Cross LU & Rail • Usually open to the public first Sunday of the month from 10am-1pm, but please telephone to confirm

This building's name is derived from the Greek 'adelphoi' meaning 'brothers' – in honour of Robert, John and William Adam, who, between 1768 and 1774, built a development of grand terraced houses in this area using a series of arches and subterranean streets to counteract the slope from the Strand to the river. The scheme was a financial disaster and only by resorting to a public lottery for the unsold houses, did the family avoid ruin.

Regrettably, most of the scheme was demolished in 1936. Only a few of the original houses remain – Nos 6-10 and 18 Adam Street, 4-6 John Adam Street, 1-3 and 9 Robert Street. The buildings are now offices without public access.

No. 8 John Adam Street, now home to the Royal Society of Arts, was one of the last buildings to be completed in 1774. Built from stone with a temple front of fluted Ionic columns, it is perhaps the best Adam façade in London. *Area Map p.6, B:3*

Frederick's Place

Off Old Jewry, EC2R 8AB • Nearest transport Bank LU • No public access

A surprising find at the heart of the City, these houses were built during the same period as the Adelphi project and were also constructed as a speculative venture. It has been many years since these buildings served as private residences, most are now offices, and consequently they have been subject to alteration. However, it is fun to look for original Adam traces. See – Numbers 6, 7 and 8 Frederick's Place and Number 35 Old Jewry.
Area Map p.8, B:2

Fitzroy Square

Off Tottenham Court Road, W1T 5DX • Nearest transport Great Portland Street LU • For information about the Georgian Society telephone 087 1750 2936 or consult their website www.georgiangroup.org.uk and www.sixfitzroysquare.com

Some of Robert Adam's last London work can be seen in Fitzroy Square. In early 1790 Charles Fitzroy, Lord Southampton, commissioned the highly fashionable Adam to design a handsome square of houses on his land here. However, at the time of Adam's sudden death in 1792 only the south and east sides had been completed. These buildings are typically Adam – light, elegant, stuccoed with rustication at the ground floor.

'Victorianisation', 'improvement' and bomb-damage during World War II has left this square in rather a sorry state but the efforts of caring residents and organisations such as the Georgian Group ensure a better future for this wonderful group of buildings.

Indeed, the Georgian Group, a national charity for the preservation for our Georgian heritage, occupies one of the best-preserved buildings at number 6. The Group often hosts exhibitions and lectures that are open to the public.
Area Map p.2-3, A:2

See also:
• The Admiralty Screen, 'Whitehall Walk' p.349

JOHN NASH (1725-1835)

Nash was the leading architect of the English Regency period, pursuing a neo-classical vision with the patronage of the Prince Regent. He began his working life as a designer of country houses with the landscape gardener Repton, and by the early 19th century had become a prosperous member of the Whig party and in an ideal position to put his architectural ideas into practice in the capital. The forging of a form of classical architecture with stucco walls, huge porticos and various orders of columns and entablatures defined the Regency style.

Among Nash's key works are the Regent's Park terraces, All Souls Church (1822-24) as well as the layout of Regent Street and Trafalgar Square. For more information about Nash refer to John Nash Walk, p.308.

Right: Cumberland Terrace, Regent's Park. The grandest of the Nash terraces built around the park. Best described as 'Romantic Picturesque', his work is often criticised for its impure style, see p.310

GEORGE DANCE THE YOUNGER (1741-1825) & GEORGE DANCE THE ELDER (1695-1768)

George Dance Senior and Younger are often considered collectively simply because they often worked together in the City. However the father's reputation has been somewhat eclipsed by his son's prodigious talent. The building George Dance Senior is noted for is the Mansion House, built at the heart of the City and described below.

Dance the Younger spent his early years learning the craft of architecture in his father's studio, but only after he had spent many years of travel in Europe and study in Rome accompanied by his brother Nathaniel, an accomplished painter.

His first work was to design the church of All Hallows, London Wall, detailed below. Dance was only 26 when he was given this extraordinary commission in 1765, but this may have been due to his father's position as Clerk of the City Works, an influential and potentially lucrative post that would be passed to the son in due course.

It was in this capacity that both Dance Senior and Younger executed some of their most notable projects, such as the now demolished Newgate Prison, built 1770/8 – and, despite its grim purpose, said to have been the most impressive Classical building in the whole of London. It was pulled down in 1900 to accommodate the present Central Criminal Courts.

George Dance the Younger turned his hand to an array of interesting design projects throughout his career including town planning patterns such as at Finsbury Square (1777); the road pattern of Southwark, radiating from St George's Circus (1785); the highly original façade to the Guildhall (p.40); he was also responsible for adding the Sculpture Gallery (now the Ballroom) to Adam's Lansdowne House (1792); and the design of the building for the Royal College of Surgeons in Lincoln's Inn, now much altered (1806/10), and alterations to the Mansion House, as described below. He is noted for his stormy relationship with his brilliant pupil, the irascible John Soane, who purchased Pitzhanger Manor in Ealing, designed by Dance in 1770, and promptly rebuilt it.

Mansion House

Mansion House Place, EC4N 8BH • Tel 020 7626 2500 • www.cityoflondon.gov.uk • Nearest transport: Bank or Mansion House LU • No public access except tours by a City Guide every Tuesday at 2pm • See website for details

This prestigious commission was won by Dance the Elder in 1734 with a brief to provide living accommodation for the Lord Mayor, who until then lodged at one of the City Halls during his term in office. Dance was forced to squeeze a lot of building into a small, awkward space.

The grander front of the building is no longer used as the main entrance due to its close proximity to the busy road. In 1846 stables at the (west) rear of the building in Walbrook, were demolished and a Doric porch was erected as the new main entrance to the building. As with the exterior, the interior makes a nod toward Palladian architecture, but many find the rather excitable ornamentation difficult to digest.

The Mansion House is still in use today for its original purpose and is the venue for lunches, dinners, banquets and meetings with guests of the Lord Mayor. There are two very large ceremonial rooms in the building, the Ballroom and the Egyptian Hall. The latter has a magnificent tunnel vault roof added by George Dance the Younger in 1795/6, which rests on the giant Corinthian columns of his father's design. *Area Map p.8, B:2*

All Hallows Church

All Hallows on the Wall, 83 London Wall, EC2M 5ND • Tel 020 7588 2638 • www.allhallowsonthewall.org • Nearest transport Moorgate LU and Liverpool Street LU & Rail • Open to the public most Fridays 11am-3pm (please telephone to check)

Built in the 1760s to replace a medieval church that had stood on Roman foundations on the same site, hugging the City wall.

The plain exterior is of yellow and pink brick, Portland stone was used for the dressings and for facing the short Italianate tower placed at the west end, with a pedimented door, clock and a domed cupola. The aisleless interior has engaged Ionic columns supporting an enriched plaster vault. The elegant, simple space was a great inspiration to one of Dance's pupils – John Soane.

The church has been adapted to provide meeting and exhibition space for charitable organisations and other users but the main sanctuary area is in its original state.
Area Map p.8, C:3

Right: All Hallows Church, London Wall. George Dance the Younger designed this church on his return from study in Italy, his first commission when he was a mere 24 years of age

Crescent, City of London

Crescent, off The Minories, EC3 • Nearest transport Tower Hill LU • No public access

A fine row of eleven handsome four-storey houses which date from 1765 to 1770. When originally built the crescent stood in a field between, what were then, London's two largest hospitals for the mentally insane – St Luke's and Bedlam. It was here Dance the Younger introduced London to the concept of residential crescents and circuses, so fashionable and popular in Bath.

The section of Roman and medieval City wall to the rear of the Crescent is the best surviving section of the structure in the City and one of the highest intact sections of medieval work.

Today offices, rather than private residences, occupy the site. The Crescent is certainly worth a visit, although difficult to find amid the towering buildings that now surround it.

See also:
- St Bartholomew the Less, 'Bartholomew Walk' p.281

From Restoration to Georgian London

Sir John Soane
(1753-1837)

'The ruling passion of my life (is) to be distinguished as an architect', so said Sir John Soane, the son of a Reading bricklayer who did indeed become a distinguished architect, was awarded many prestigious surveyorships (Whitehall, Bank of England) and undertook the role of Professor of Architecture at the Royal Academy for many years.

Soane was a pupil of George Dance the Younger and it has been suggested that together they introduced what the latter liked to call 'the poetry of architecture' into the rather austere classical tradition, by which he meant the role that natural light could play in a building. Soane's buildings are characterised by an innovative approach to lighting and fenestration with devices such as top lighting and coloured glass used to particular effect.

Right: Sir John Soane's Museum, see p.127

Bank of England

Bank of England Museum, Bartholomew Lane, EC2R 8AH • Tel 020 7601 5545 • www.bankofengland.co.uk/museum • Nearest transport Bank LU • Admission free • See website for opening times

The Bank of England was formed in 1694, and moved to its current position in Threadneedle Street in 1724. Architect George Sampson (died circa 1759), Surveyor to the Bank designed what is now referred to as 'The Old Bank' between 1732-4. John Soane described the building as being 'in a grand style of Palladian simplicity'. However, as business for the Bank grew, so did the need for larger premises and in 1788 Soane was appointed to the Surveyorship at the commencement of a programme of enlargement. Soane wrapped the building in a secure, windowless wall of portland stone and refined and extended the existing banking halls, treating them to his own brand of genius top lighting.

Soane's work would be altered and, in the case of the much-admired banking halls, swept away by later architects, amongst others, C R Cockerell and Sir Herbert Baker. Thankfully a replica of the very finest of Soane's work at the Bank, the domed Stock Office built in 1792, can be seen at the Bank of England Museum. *Area Map p.8, B:2*

Dulwich Picture Gallery

College Road, SE21 7AD • Tel 020 8693 5254 • www.dulwichpicturegallery.org.uk • Nearest transport West Dulwich Rail • See website for opening times and admission charges

Designed and built between 1811-14 this was Britain's first purpose-built public art gallery and a natural vehicle for Soane's clever use of top lighting. Using brick with stone dressings, Soane produced a wonderful building on a very limited budget. Thanks to a major restoration programme the galleries once again look magnificent and an exciting bronze and glass 'Visitor Wing' by Rick Mather houses a café.

The Gallery contains some outstanding works of art by Poussin, Rembrandt, Murillo, Gainsborough and Watteau, amongst others.

04

From Restoration to Georgian London

Sir John Soane's Museum: Soane left this house, really a gigantic cabinet of curiosities, for 'students and amateurs' to enjoy

Sir John Soane's Museum

13 Lincoln's Inn Fields, WC2A 3BP • Tel 020 7405 2107 • www.soane.org • Nearest transport Holborn LU • Admission free • See website for opening times

Soane moved to this house in 1812 and in 1833 obtained an Act of Parliament which enabled him to leave it to the nation intact, as a museum for the study of 'Architecture and Allied Arts'. The building is packed with the items he collected throughout his long life – architectural drawings, models, casts, pieces of sculpture, stunning items from antiquity, a collection of paintings by Hogarth including all eight stages of The 'Rake's Progress', as well as some very good sculpture by, amongst others, Flaxman and Banks.

The Museum is actually three houses knocked into one and the exterior is more eclectic than its Georgian Mannerist Neo-classical neighbours. Soane added a three storey stone loggia to the façade, topped with statuary. The interior contains a series of architectural delights: the oval staircase which sweeps gracefully up to the yellow drawing room, the clever use of mirrors to create light and space in the main ground floor room, the neo-Gothic 'Monk's Parlour' and the basement rooms whose arrangement is reminiscent of a Roman catacomb which has been crammed with interesting objects. Make an appointment in advance and you will be able to peruse some of the 30,000 architectural drawings Soane collected, including some by Wren and Robert Adam. *Area Map p.2-3, C:1*

Holy Trinity Church, Marylebone

Holy Trinity Church 'One Marylebone Road', NW1 4AQ • Tel 020 7380 1663 • www.one-events.co.uk/marylebone/ • Nearest transport Great Portland Street LU • No public access

Built 1824/28 as a Commissioners' Church, one of a number of churches built during the first half of the 19th century in response to the population shift from rural to urban areas. The term is derived from the Church Building Commission which was established in 1824 to organise the building of these Anglican churches.

Unusually the altar was placed at the north end, rather than the more conventional east. The main entrance is at the south, through Soane's unpedimented portico of four huge Ionic columns. The rather busy two stage tower, complete with clock and weather vane, sits atop the building. Deconsecrated in 1955, the church served as offices for various publishing houses until 2007 when it was sympathetically restored to become a smart social venue. If you are not fortunate enough to receive an invite, do look at their website where you can see some excellent photographs of the interior.
Area Map p.4, B:2

SIR ROBERT SMIRKE
(1781-1867)

At the age of 16 Smirke began working in the office of Sir John Soane, but left within months to work with George Dance the Younger. Smirke enjoyed an immensely successful career, being awarded some very plum commissions. A dedicated Greek Revivalist, it has been suggested that his work consisted of the same couple of Grecian formulae used over and over and that his reputation for reliability and as a good business manager outweighed his architectural flair.

Right: The main frontage, The British Museum, by Sir Robert Smirke and considered to be his finest achievement

British Museum

Great Russell Street, WC1B 3DG • Tel 020 7636 1555 • www.thebritishmuseum.ac.uk • Nearest transport Holborn LU or Russell Square LU • Admission free except for major exhibitions • See website for opening times

Arriving at the corner of Great Russell Street, particularly from Gower Street, it's hard to imagine that such a narrow street could possibly accommodate a museum, let alone this monumental neo-classical building. It was built by Smirke 1823-47 as a massive extension to Montague House, the original, rather modest museum building, and was designed to a courtyard plan. Wings and floors were added piecemeal, when funds allowed. The first phase was built on the east side specifically to house George III's library acquired by the Museum in 1823. The King's Library, as the wing is known, was renovated and re-opened to the public as the Enlightenment Gallery in December 2003, but minus the books (which are housed in the new British Library).

The façade, one of the most memorable and imposing in London, was the last part of Smirke's project to be built in 1847, when Montague House itself was demolished to make way for the great Ionic colonnade and portico.

The architect's brother, Sidney Smirke, designed and built the domed Reading Room, finished in 1857, which filled Robert's courtyard. For a description of the 21st-century alterations and additions see Chapter 7. *Area Map p.2-3, B:1*

Other buildings by Sir Robert Smirke:

- **Canada House**, see 'Whitehall Walk' p.344
- **King's College**, see 'Strand Walk' p.340
- **St James's Palace**, see p.42

OTHER 18TH-CENTURY BUILDINGS OF INTEREST:

Geffrye Museum

Geffrye Museum

Kingsland Road, E2 8EA • Tel 020 7739 9893 • www.geffrye-museum.org.uk • Nearest transport Hoxton Overground Station • Admission free • See website for opening times

This excellent museum takes the form of a series of rooms each one displaying the interior of a period home, from Elizabethan times up to the present. The museum is housed in a row of beautifully built 18th-century almshouses and also features a lovely garden with period garden 'rooms'.

In the early 1990s the Geffrye Museum commissioned Branson Coates Architecture to design a bold modern extension to the existing buildings at a cost of £5.3m. The extension opened in 1998 and has almost doubled the museum's size, adding display areas as well as a café and shop.

The contemporary structure proved a great success because it blended with the existing almshouses and maintained the essentially 18th-century atmosphere of this unique museum.

Increased visitor numbers (over 120.000 a year) have put pressure on the existing buildings and currently the Geffrye Museum is closed for a major redevelopment which is being designed by Wright & Wright Architects. The museum is scheduled to reopen in Spring 2020

Handel House & Hendrix Flat

04

From Restoration to Georgian London

25 Brook Street, W1K 4HB • Tel 020 7495 1685 • www.handelhendrix.org • Nearest transport Bond Street and Oxford Circus LU • See website for opening times and admission charges

The great composer George Frederick Handel was the first occupant of this house built by George Barnes as part of a four-building, speculative development in this genteel area of the town. Since that time the property has had many uses. In 2000 the upper part of number 25, was leased to the Handel House Trust and since November 2001 the house has been open to the public.

This house not only tells the fascinating story of this genius composer but gives us a glimpse into an early Georgian household. The Trust has been meticulous in restoring this house to its 18th-century state, using a neighbouring property, number 27/29 Brook Street, which retains much of the detail of the original Barnes development, as the model. The plain fireplaces now installed in the Handel House came from properties in Covent Garden, demolished in 1996.

The adjoining apartment on the upper floor at 23 Brook Street has also been restored to a time when another famous musician was in residence – Jimi Hendrix. He lived in the flat between July 1968 and March 1969 and referred to it as 'my first real home of my own'.

Dr Johnson's House

17 Gough Square, EC4A 3DE • Tel 020 7353 3745 • www.drjohnsonshouse.org • Nearest transport Chancery Lane LU and Blackfriars LU & Rail • See website for opening times and admission charges

The lexicographer, writer and conversationalist Samuel Johnson (1709-84) lived in this atmospheric house while he wrote his *Dictionary of the English Language*. The house, built in 1700, contains furniture and fittings dating from Dr Johnson's time here. This house is a real gem, an oasis of calm surrounded by a sea of offices.

Keats House

Keats Grove, NW3 2RR • Tel 020 7435 2062 • www.cityoflondon.gov.uk • Nearest transport Belsize Park and Hampstead LU and Hampstead Heath Rail • See website for opening times and admission charges

This was the home of the eminent poet John Keats (1795-1821) who was 23 years old when he moved into the eastern half of this house (it used to be a pair of semis). At this date Hampstead was not really part of London but a fairly secluded village surrounded by fields. Keats wrote some of his finest poetry here, including 'Ode to a Nightingale' while sitting under a plum tree in the garden. Sadly he died of tuberculosis at the age of 25 in Italy, having written some of the most memorable poetry in the English language.

Built in 1815, the interior of Keats House has been sensitively restored thanks to a Heritage Lottery Grant of almost half a million pounds. The refurbishment sought to reflect the original decoration of the property, creating a living space that Keats would have recognised and providing an authentic example of Regency style.

Dennis Severs' House

18 Folgate Street, E1 6BX • Tel 020 7247 4013 • www.dennissevershouse.co.uk • Nearest transport Liverpool Street LU/Rail and Shoreditch High St LU • See website for opening times and admission charges

Not a museum but a 'living image' of how life once may have been within the walls of this house. The house was the brainchild of its late owner, Dennis Severs, an American artist who 'created' the fictional Huguenot Jervis family and placed them in this real 18th-century house and let them fill the space with what might have been. The house is set in the heart of Spitalfields, an area rich in history and constantly under threat from encroachment by City high-rise office blocks but which has much to reward the casual visitor. Spitalfields, as well as Soho in west London, was a place of refuge for the estimated 30,000 Huguenots fleeing from France to escape religious persecution following the repeal of the Edict of Nantes. Many of these refugees were weavers, building their houses with large windows to provide the light with which to work by.

John Wesley's House

49 City Road, EC1Y 1AU • Tel 020 7253 2262 • www.wesleysheritage.org.uk • Nearest transport Old Street & Moorgate LU/Rail • Admission free • See website for details

Although thought to have been designed by George Dance the Younger, as part of a large complex, this attribution is uncertain. Only one house and the adjoining chapel were built in 1778/79 and this is where John Wesley (1703-91), evangelist and founder of Methodism, spent his last eleven winters – in the summer he would tour the country preaching. The four-storey stuccoed building with Coade stone dressings is a good example of a Georgian town house. Since 1898 the house has been a museum and the interior has been, as far as possible, restored to look as it did when Wesley was in residence. The website has an excellent virtual-tour section, illustrating how Wesley and his servants lived.

Perhaps the most touching feature of the house is the small room leading off Wesley's bedroom. This room, simply furnished with a chair, kneeler and a small bureau holding a candle and Bible, is known to Methodists as the 'power house', for it is here that Wesley spent the first hours of each day in prayer. The Chapel is a small, but good example of Georgian design, with a porch that was added later, in 1897. Wesley is buried in the chapel graveyard and there is a splendid bronze statue of him by J Adams Acton dated 1891.

St Pancras Station, see p.156

05

VICTORIAN LONDON

VICTORIAN LONDON

"Oh mine in snows and summer heats. Those good old Tory brick-built streets!" Wilfred Whitten

For much of the 19th century London resembled a giant construction site. Industry, imperialism, philanthropy and 'the coming of the railways' brought massed building projects to the capital and each new institution needed to find an appropriate architectural language. The cottage hospital required a different form of expression to the railway station, music hall or the department store, and on occasion the forms chosen could be controversial.

When the Houses of Parliament burned down in the 1830s the Government decreed, after much debate, that its replacement must be of a Gothic or Elizabethan design. Had the fire happened 30 years earlier we may well be the proud custodians of a purely Classical building, a form of architecture associated with learning and authority, whilst Gothic said religion, Egyptian hinted at something exotic and the characteristics of Palazzo meant pomp. However a surge of nationalism throughout Europe in the 1820s and 1830s saw some British artists, craftsmen and architects looking back to the medieval Gothic, a style regarded as 'English' and thus deemed especially appropriate for the Houses of Parliament.

Most of the major railway stations were built between 1836-76, and within that 40 years much of London was carved up as the railway companies vied with each other to acquire land. The cost was not merely a financial one, for example, 7,000 people were rendered homeless when The Great Eastern Railway inched its tracks towards Liverpool Street station.

The first terminal to be completed to the north of London was Euston station, which took its name from 'Euston Grove', the picturesque nursery garden it was built on. Opened in 1837 the line initially only went as far as Boxmoor, just outside Hemel Hempstead. The following year the line was extended to Birmingham, the 112-mile journey taking just over five hours. In celebration of this feat the railway company commissioned the eminent architect Philip Hardwick (1792-1870) to design a grand entrance to the London terminal. This 'Euston Arch', with four gigantic Doric pillars of stone, 72 feet high, was the tallest freestanding structure in London at the time. Sadly, this potent symbol of the glory days of the railway was swept away in 1963, despite a great outcry.

King's Cross station opened in 1852 and St Pancras station in 1863, disgorging commuters in their thousands on to New Road (now the Euston Road) to find their own way to office and workshop before the coming of underground trains and a bus network. It is estimated that by the late 1850s just over 200,000 workers went to the City every day on foot, many walking from major railway stations.

'Underground' train lines linking major London stations began operation with the opening of the Paddington to Farringdon branch of the Metropolitan Railway in 1863. By 1884 the route encompassed the centre of London and thus the Circle line was born. Deeper excavations were needed for lines such as The City and South London Railway which ran between Stockwell and King William Street in the City, and which forms part of today's Northern line.

Many villages and small towns around London were swelled by mass housing built for commuters, people who once would have 'lived above the shop', or at least nearby. This is especially so south of the river, where places such as Clapham, Peckham, and Southfields grew rapidly. The population of Streatham, for example, in 1811 was 2,729 – by 1900 it was 70,000, due in the main to the opening of Streatham Hill station in 1856. The plain 'two-up, two-down' house with a garden proliferated in the new suburbs.

During the 19th century industrialisation and mass production touched almost every aspect of life and this is true of building too. Brick, in particular, became cheaper and more widely available. Red brick was more usual until about

Above: King's Cross Station

1870 when yellowish-bricks made from London clay, known as London Stock bricks, became more popular.

London's population shift was particularly dramatic in the City and Westminster, 123,000 and 241,000 people respectively in 1841 declining to 27,000 and 183,000 by 1901. Those who stayed in the centre of London were generally at either end of the economic scale. The wealthy still built mansions in town, but in far fewer numbers than the century before. The price of building land soared during the 19th century and the mansion block, with large, spacious flats complete with designated servants quarters became practical and fashionable. Many who could afford it lived in the west of London, where the prevailing wind meant the smoke-filled air, polluted by the myriad of belching industrial and domestic chimneys, was, to a certain extent, blown east.

However, during the unusually long, hot and dry summer of 1858 nearly all Londoners had to endure weeks of such a terrible stench that the period has gone down in history as 'the Great Stink'. The source of the ghastly smell was the Thames, into which newly installed sewers discharged their untreated contents. Indeed the windows of the Houses of Parliament were draped with sheets soaked in chloride of lime in an attempt to fend off illness as it was wrongly believed that outbreaks of cholera were caused by 'miasma' or bad air. The Stink was not only very unpleasant but was seen to be a health hazard.

Engineer Sir Joseph Bazalgette's solution was to construct 83 miles of underground brick sewers to intercept sewage outflows and 1,100 miles of street sewers to regulate the raw sewage which flowed through the streets of London. The outflows were diverted downstream where they were dumped, still untreated, into the Thames. Extensive sewage treatment facilities were built only decades later, see 'Crossness Pumping Station' (p.155).

The very poor existed among the rookeries and slums of Seven Dials, St Giles and the edges of the Fleet Valley, often in close proximity to a festering open sewer. Slum clearance took place when new roads needed to cut through such areas. The notorious St Giles, Hogarth's 'Gin Lane', was pulled apart 1841-47 when a thoroughfare from Oxford Circus to High Holborn became necessary.

The slum problem and continuing outbreaks of cholera led to the publication of the Report on the Sanitary Conditions of the Labouring Classes in 1842, which resulted in various philanthropic organisations taking on the practicalities highlighted by the document. Again, blocks of flats were seen as the solution and from the mid 1840s model dwellings were constructed with various degrees of success. In 1862 American philanthropist George Peabody gave £500,000 of his fortune to a Trust for the provision of 'cheap…healthful dwellings for the poor' and between 1864 and 1890, 5,000 such dwellings had been provided, usually in blocks with five or six floors, fairly close-set and made from red brick, some white brick banding, stucco dressings, and with leaded mansard roofs. As a mark of their enduring quality, there are still currently approximately 12,000 Peabody properties on 70 estates of varying size in inner London (see image opposite).

Philanthropy extended to hospital provision and the improvement of existing facilities. In the 1890s wealthy furniture manufacturer John Blundell Maple made a vast donation to University College, Gower Street for a new hospital to be built at, what was then, the only university in England, other than Oxford

Above: Peabody housing

and Cambridge, to award medical degrees. Architect Alfred Waterhouse designed a spectacularly innovative cruciform-shaped building in red brick and terracotta Gothic style, which was in contrast to the Classical form of the rest of the College's buildings. The hospital's offices and operating theatres were placed at the centre with wards suitably isolated in the four 'wings' of the cross pattern. The building is now used by the University's Medical School with no public admission. However, it is often accessible during the Open House weekend, see p.403 for more information.

During the 19th century there were generally two types of hospital in London – 'voluntary' and 'workhouse'. The former were independent charities established for the benefit of the 'deserving poor', who, according to contemporary values, were respectable working-class people who had fallen on hard times because of sickness. The latter, the 'workhouse hospitals', were for those who were destitute and had no alternative. Many of these people had been reduced to poverty through either sickness or old age and the workhouses opened hospital wards and even purpose-built infirmaries to treat them. Eminent architect, George Gilbert Scott, whose buildings include the Midland Hotel at St Pancras station, and the Albert Memorial, started his career designing workhouses; large, grim buildings.

Local authorities were obliged to at least attempt to provide public libraries funded by ratepayers following the Free Libraries Act of 1850 and public baths were provided to serve a dual purpose, firstly as recreational swimming pools and secondly as baths for those with few or no washing facilities at home. When a new municipal building was erected it was usually built in red brick or terracotta, quite often decorated with the sculpted profiles of inspirational figures, such as Shakespeare and Milton. In Great Smith Street, Westminster Council provided both library and bathing facilities in one building, although both activities were kept quite separate! The building is no longer used for its original purpose and is now a restaurant.

Education was not confined to schools, the notion of 'improvement' being an important Victorian value with large museums built in Kensington, not far from the Albert Hall, see p.148. The railways made travel not only easier but also relatively cheaper and hotels were required to satisfy this demand.

Prison planning and construction was of special interest during the 19th century when the number of prisoners rapidly grew as a consequence of the reduction in the number of offences carrying the death penalty or transportation. Pentonville Prison, built 1840-42 by Sir Joshua Jebb, took Jeremy Bentham's Panopticon plan of 1791, which exposed the confined to 24-hour observation, whilst also drawing on models of American provincial prisons and ideas of solitude and silence. The crank, a hard-labour machine, which produced nothing but 'exhaustion of the body and boredom of the mind', was invented at Pentonville.

The Education Act of 1870 ushered in the compulsory provision of schooling for children and necessitated the building of hundreds of schools all over the capital. Church schools naturally favoured designs in the Gothic vein, whilst Board schools preferred red brick and gables. Adult education was encouraged and within the City three charity funded institutes were founded. The most architecturally interesting of the trio is without doubt the Bishopsgate Institute, see p.165.

London in the 19th century was the booming and self-confident hub of an Empire. In 1851 this confidence manifested itself in the Great Exhibition, inspired and championed by the monarch's husband, Prince Albert. The purpose of the exhibition was to put on a global display of manufactured goods and works of art in order to prove Britain's superiority as a rapidly industrialising country, and by using raw materials from all over the world the Exhibition functioned like a giant shop window.

The event attracted some six million visitors who came to view the wares of 17,000 exhibitors. The event was held at Hyde Park in what became known as the 'Crystal Palace', a structure made from glass and cast-iron, six times the size of St Paul's Cathedral and created not by an architect but by a gardener, Joseph Paxton. He had previously designed and constructed the Palm House at Chatsworth in Derbyshire, but this project was on a much bigger scale – taking nine months to construct, not by conventional builders but by members of the Royal Engineers. The entire 'Crystal Palace' was dismantled and moved to a park in Sydenham, south-east London, but perished in a fire in 1936 and only its name lingers on.

Those who witnessed the array of goods on display at the Great Exhibition wanted to purchase such items for themselves. Purpose-built department stores, such as Harvey Nichols in Knightsbridge (1889-94), sprang up all over London. Market places have been important throughout history, particularly in large towns and cities and during this period Sir Horace Jones, official architect to the City of London, designed some fine buildings specifically for this purpose including Smithfield Market (see 'Bartholomew Walk' p.281) and Leadenhall Market (see 'Shopping and Architecture' p.384).

London in the 19th century saw massive social change, and not all of it was for the better. One only has to read the novels of Charles Dickens to see that Victoria's London was not always a pleasant place to live and that the hand of charity was often a harsh and cold one. The rise of industrialisation was seen as the death-knell to craftsmanship. Indeed William Morris stated that 'you cannot educate, you cannot civilise man, unless you give him a share in art.' Such sentiment expressed itself in the Arts and Crafts movement, whose principles included the ideals of an original architecture closely linked to nature and of a unity in buildings of the arts of architecture, sculpture and painting. Mass production was largely rejected by the movement, and its members set about reviving high standards of individual craftsmanship. This included not only woodwork, metalwork, and other decorative arts, but also such things as brick making.

Many people will happily state a preference for architecture of the Victorian era above any other, and yet it was a period of great diversity.

Smithfield Market

EXAMPLES OF BUILDINGS FROM THIS PERIOD:

Right: The Victoria Tower, Palace of Westminster. Designed to house the historic records of Parliament, at 325 feet (98.5 metres) this is the tallest part of the Palace and gives the building its iconic profile

Palace of Westminster & Houses of Parliament
Charles Barry and A W Pugin, 1835-60

Houses of Parliament, Palace of Westminster, SW1A 0AA • www.parliament.uk/visiting • Nearest transport Westminster LU • Entrance by ticket – please apply to your local MP or your embassy (apply at least six months ahead), alternatively visitors can queue outside the St Stephen's entrance for admission that day (although not guaranteed), paid guided tours are also available during the Summer Opening, see website for more details

The need for a new Palace of Westminster arose from the fire of October 1834, which destroyed the totally inadequate set of buildings that housed Parliament. It was decided to build a new Houses of Parliament on the same site and what we have as a result is one of the most immediately identifiable buildings in the world.

The Palace had been the site of the principal residence of the kings of England from the 11th century until 1512 when it was first destroyed by fire and the remaining buildings were used as the administrative centre for the Crown. Parliament met in St Stephen's Chapel, sitting in the choir, one group facing the other, and this gave the seating configuration to the chamber of the House of Commons as we see it today.

The only buildings surviving from the 1834 fire are Westminster Hall, the crypt of St Stephen's Chapel, the cloisters and the Jewel Tower. The architect Charles Barry, who won the commission in 1835 following an open competition, cleverly incorporated all of these remains into the design of the new Palace of Westminster.

The government had specified to all those submitting designs that the new building must be of a Gothic or Elizabethan style; only a handful of the hopeful contestants chose the latter. Debate was taking place at the time over the merits of 'Gothic' architecture, seen as English and Christian, versus 'Classic', which was seen, by some, as foreign and pagan. Charles Barry had previously celebrated the 'Classic' in his distinctly Italianate Travellers Club in Pall Mall, so he was a rather odd choice for the commission in that respect. However, Barry employed the talent of A W Pugin, a keen 'Gothicist', who had recently published his 'manifesto' wordily entitled *Contrast or a Parallel between the Noble Edifices of the Middle Ages and the Corresponding Buildings of the Present Day, showing the Present Decay of Taste*.

The partnership appears to have developed well. As a middle-aged, respectable, workaholic architect, Charles Barry had to deal with the grinding tedium of endless battles with numerous committees that were involved in such a huge project. His private practice was to suffer financially as his time and energy were spent working on Westminster Palace. Indeed, he died in May 1860, at the age of 65, just weeks before the building was completed.

Pugin, on the other hand, was an intelligent, exacting young man of 23 when he started work with Barry. An immensely gifted draughtsman, he was employed, initially, to draw the many complex plans for the building. Later he was officially employed to work on the Palace interior as 'superintendent of woodcarving', but with a brief to design everything from the stained glass in the windows to the coat hooks. Pugin too died before the project of Westminster Palace was completed. He was just 40, insane, and a patient at the Bethlem Hospital in south London.

Despite his pitifully short life, Pugin was hugely influential on a whole generation of architects who understood his 1836 statement that 'the greatest test of architectural beauty is the fitness of the design to the purpose it is intended'.

Two towers dominate Barry and Pugin's building. Firstly there is the Elizabeth Tower which was completed in 1852; it is 316 feet high, 40 feet square and the top can be reached by climbing 393 steps. The clock it contains is the largest in Britain and has worked perfectly since 1859. The great bell, known as Big Ben, strikes the quarter hour and each hour and was cast at the Whitechapel Bell Foundry in east London.

The Elizabeth Tower and Big Ben is currently undergoing major conservation, which has necessitated the temporary halting of Big Ben's famous 'bongs' for the duration of the works, which are due to be completed in 2012

The most massive tower is the Victoria Tower at 323 feet tall and it is perhaps this, combined with the long stretch of rhythmic façade, which gives the building its familiar shape. The Tower is used for storage and currently holds papers relating to the 1.5 million or so Acts of Parliament passed since 1497.

The Palace of Westminster contains almost 1,000 rooms, including the House of Commons, Commons Lobby, Central Lobby, Peers' Lobby, House of Lords, Prince's Chamber, and the Royal Gallery. There are also 11 courtyards, 8 bars and 6 restaurants (none of which are open to the public). Prince Albert chaired the committee responsible for the interior decorations, helping to choose suitable subjects for the many frescoes as well as the positioning of statues and other details.

The best view of the Palace is probably from a boat on the Thames or, looking down upon it from the London Eye and you can see the fine detailing of the south façade by standing in Victoria Tower Gardens. The interior of the Palace of Westminster, and in particular the two debating chambers, need to be seen 'in the flesh', so to speak. Photography and television pictures do not convey adequately the rich, warm and splendid decoration of this surprisingly small space.
Area Map p.6, B:1

The Roundhouse
Robert Dockray 1846/
John McAslan & Partners, 2004

Chalk Farm Road, NW1 8EH • Tel 0844 482 8008 • www.roundhouse.org.uk • Nearest transport Chalk Farm LU • See website for opening times and details of concerts and courses

An outstanding example of 19th-century industrial architecture, built in 1846 as an engine-turning shed and designed by Robert Dockray innovatively using cast and wrought iron to support the slate roof. Only used for its original purpose for a short period it then became a warehouse for Gilbey's Gin and then in 1964 playwright Arnold Wesker established Centre 42, using the space for arts performances which included Pink Floyd and Jimi Hendrix. Lack of funds closed the project in 1983 and the future of the Roundhouse looked uncertain.

In 2004 the Grade II listed building was subject to a £29.7 million redevelopment by John McAslan and Partners architects. The Roundhouse's circular glazed roof-lights have been re-instated, allowing the public to see interior daylight for the first time in over 100 years. The New Wing built alongside the main building houses the box office, bar and café, foyer, offices and an creative centre for young people aged 11-25 years.

Banco Commerciale Italiana (former)
Sancton Wood, 1850-52

44 Gresham Street, EC2V 7AY • Nearest transport Bank LU • No public access inside the building

Originally built for the Queen's Assurance Company in 1850 by Sancton Wood, a pupil of Smirke, until recently the building was occupied by an Italian bank, somewhat appropriately given the Italianate nature of its architecture. The open arcade on the ground floor has slim Tuscan columns, a fairly recent innovation in the City at the time, but one that was to become popular, and the upper floors have close-set windows, which occupy most of the stone-faced façade. This is a fairly early example of the Italianate style being expressed in office accommodation; until this date the style had been considered acceptable for gentlemen's clubs and little else (for example – Charles Barry's Travellers Club, Pall Mall, 1832).

The top storey, with its very small windows, is a fairly recent addition replacing a pitched roof with large chimneystacks. This was 19th-century office building of the grandest order on a prominent corner site and is a welcome survivor, now Listed Grade II, while so many of its contemporaries have been bulldozed.
Area Map p.8, B:2

Victorian London

All Saints Church, Margaret Street
William Butterfield, 1841-59 / Ninian Comper, 1911

Margaret Street, W1W 8JG • Tel 020 7636 1788 • www.allsaintsmargaretstreet.org.uk • Nearest transport Oxford Circus LU • See website for opening times, services & events

This church was the pioneer building of the High Victorian phase of the Gothic Revival and is perhaps one of the finest examples of eminent architect William Butterfield's work. Just a short step from Oxford Circus, All Saints is the expression of the Ecclesiological Society's movement to restore Catholic privileges (before the 19th century the celebration of the Eucharist every Sunday was not practised within the Anglican tradition).

Completing the project in 1859, Butterfield was able to incorporate the Society's requirements for a church, a choir school and a clergy house on a plot that is a mere 100 feet square. He did this by placing the church at the rear with the school and house at the front, level with the street, and arranged around a small courtyard. The spire is 227 feet high and was influenced by the great spire of St Mary's, Lubeck; with the nave 63 feet in length and 73 feet in height. Controversially, but with great success, Butterfield chose to build in pink brick (at the time more expensive than stone) in a bold chequered pattern; the first major building on such a scale to be built from brick rather than stone.

Walking from the outside into the spectacular interior is an experience not to be missed as one is greeted with a riot of colour and patterning in granite, alabaster, marble and tiles. The Lady Chapel (1911) designed and decorated by the architect and artist Ninian Comper in a richly decorated, late Gothic style is of particular note.

William Butterfield's other surviving major church in the centre of London is St Augustine, Queens Gate, Kensington. *Area Map p.4, C:1*

Right: The Lady Chapel, All Saints Church. Designed and decorated by (Sir John) Ninian Comper. Noted for his superb altar screens, or reredos, Comper's work was always well rooted in both liturgy and history

Albert Memorial
George Gilbert Scott, 1863-72

Kensington Gardens, SW7 (opposite the Albert Hall) • Tel 020 7495 0916 • www.royalparks.gov.uk • Nearest transport Knightsbridge LU • The memorial can be viewed at any time, see website if you would like to book a guided tour

When Queen Victoria's consort died in December 1861 at the age of 42 it was mooted, by the Lord Mayor of London and others, that a national memorial should be erected in Prince Albert's honour. Various plans by some of the country's most eminent architects of the day were submitted and the Queen chose Sir George Gilbert Scott's design. The whole project was to be funded partly by national subscription and a massive £50,000 donation from the Government.

Scott's work stands tall at 175 feet and at its centre is a larger than life bronze statue of the seated Prince holding a copy of the catalogue from the 1851 Great Exhibition; the overseeing of this event was thought to have been his proudest achievement. There are a further 175 life-size statues arranged at different levels and these groups of marble figures represent the four continents of the world; agriculture; manufacturing; commerce; engineering; architects; poets and musicians; painters; sculptors; astronomy; geology; geometry; rhetoric; music; astrology; medicine; physiology; faith; hope; charity; temperance; justice; fortitude and prudence. In addition there is a host of bronze angels. All these figures, which are the work of leading British sculptors of the day, are housed under an iron-framed canopy raised on a flight of stone steps.

The whole project was completed in 1872 and was hailed as 'a fitting memorial to our blameless prince' as well as being dismissed as 'vulgar'! Sir George Gilbert Scott considered it to be his finest piece of work and certainly the whole memorial is a testimony to High Victorian Gothic architectural taste and values.

During World War I the original gilding from the memorial was removed lest enemy Zeppelins were attracted by its shine and was only restored during an £11 million, four-year restoration programme completed in 1998.

Other buildings by George Gilbert Scott:

- **Midland Grand Hotel**, see p.156
- **Foreign and Commonwealth Office**, see p.352
- **St Mary Abbots**, on the corner of High Street Kensington and Church Street, is a good example of Scott's London churches with its Early English Gothic interior and notable, fine spire.

Holborn Viaduct
William Haywood, 1863-69

Holborn Viaduct, EC1 • Nearest transport Farringdon LU/Rail or City Thameslink Rail

Being stuck in London's traffic is nothing new and even before mass car ownership the capital's roads were often at a standstill. The Holborn Viaduct was built in 1863-69 as part of a congestion relief measure and to form a link between the West End and the City. It was designed by William Haywood, the City Surveyor and spans Farringdon Street, which runs part of the course of the Fleet, now trickling down to the Thames in pipes under the road.

The most noticeable element of the Viaduct is the cast iron bridge, being 1400 feet in length and 80 feet wide resting on granite hexagonal piers. The marvellous open ironwork is painted red and gold and looks much better than it sounds. The parapet has four bronze statues representing 'Science' and 'Fine Art' on the north side and 'Commerce' and 'Agriculture' on the south.

The Viaduct is best viewed from Farringdon Street but there are staircases at either end of the bridge to access the upper level.

Linley Sambourne House
Joseph Gordon Davis, 1868-71

18 Stafford Terrace, W8 7BH • Tel 020 7602 3316 • www.rbkc.gov.uk/linleysambournehouse • Nearest transport High Street Kensington LU • See website for opening times and admission charges

This house gives us a marvellous opportunity to see the interior of a late Victorian house which has been preserved rather than 'recreated'. It was the home of Edward Linley Sambourne (1844-1910), chief political cartoonist at *Punch* magazine and is full of his work and collection of photographs. He lived here from 1874 until his death in 1910.

The house was built 1858-60 of brick with good quality stucco enriching the exterior and is part of the grid of streets in the popular Holland Park area of London (Phillimore Gardens and Essex Villas complete this small complex). The interior is a picture of cluttered Victorian domesticity with heavy drapes, some original William Morris wallpaper still in situ and a downstairs lavatory the quality of whose workmanship needs to be seen to be believed.

Arab Hall, Leighton House

Leighton House
George Aitchison, 1866

12 Holland Park Road, W14 8LZ • Tel 020 7602 3316 • www.rbkc.gov.uk/leightonhousemuseum • Nearest transport High Street Kensington LU • See website for opening times and admission charges

From the outside, this unassuming house with its red brick façade gives nothing away about its quite extraordinary interior. Architect George Aitchison (1825-1910) designed the body of the house in 1866, but the interior is a pure reflection of its owner's highly aesthetic taste. Lord Frederic Leighton was a much respected artist, the first professional painter to be raised to the peerage, one-time President of the Royal Academy and counted Queen Victoria as one of his customers.

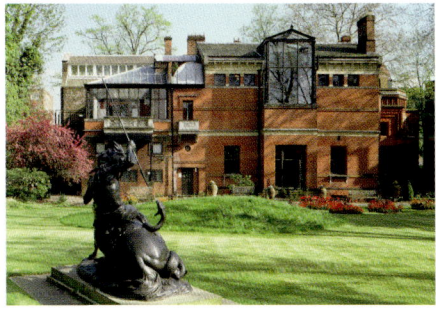

Lord Leighton had travelled extensively abroad since early childhood and his house was a marvellous backdrop to his extensive collection of paintings and memorabilia. At the centre of the house, both physically and spiritually, is the Arab Room, believed to be based on the chamber of the 12th-century Islamic palace of La Zisa at Palermo. The walls and floors are decorated with Leighton's unique collection of Moorish tiles with additions by William de Morgan. In the middle of this room is a pool and fountain. A 'Silk Room' was added in 1895 to house part of Leighton's collection of paintings and to this was added a zenana, originally a place where women could watch proceedings but remain unseen, which overlooks the Arab Hall and adds to the sensuous air of exoticism. It is in the Arab Hall where Lord Leighton held his famous soirées at which he entertained the great and the good. However in order not to encourage the outstaying of any welcome, Leighton had only two bedrooms in this large house.

Visitors to the house can see Lord Leighton's studio and paintings by his contemporaries such as John Millais, Edward Burne-Jones, and of course some of his own pictures.

The House recently underwent a £1.3 million refurbishment which has restored the house to its original spectacular appearance, recreating Leighton's private 'Palace of Art' as it appeared at the time of his death.

Royal Albert Hall
Captain Francis Fowke, 1867-71

Kensington Gore, SW7 2AP • Tel 020 7589 3203 • www.royalalberthall.com • Nearest transport South Kensington & High Street Kensington LU • See website for opening times & events

Prince Albert had suggested that profits from the Great Exhibition of 1851 should be used to build museums, schools and, in particular, a central hall containing a library, concert and exhibition rooms. Following the Prince's death in 1861 it was hoped some of the money raised in 1851 would be used to build such a hall, but funds proved inadequate. However in 1863 the idea was conceived to finance the building by selling 999-year leases on seats in the hall and over 1,300 were sold at 100 pounds each. This allowed the purchasers free entrance to every concert – an arrangement still in existence today, but modified to allow owners access to just 80 concerts a year.

With a capacity of 8,000 people, this huge elliptical hall (not round, as most casual observers believe), was designed by Captain Francis Fowke (1823-65). His design was based on the work of Gottfried Semper, a close friend of Prince Albert and architect of the renowned Dresden Opera House. The foundation stone was laid in 1867 by Queen Victoria, who unexpectedly announced that the building was to be called 'The Royal Albert Hall'; until then it was known as the 'Hall of Arts and Sciences'. The Prince of Wales officially opened the Hall four years later; his mother felt the occasion 'too emotional' to attend.

The brick domed building is decorated in marble and terracotta, the latter being in profusion in the area, such as the neighbouring blocks of flats and Alfred Waterhouse's Natural History Museum nearby. Four double height entrance porches and a balcony encircle the building as does the magnificent frieze entitled 'The Triumph of Art and Letters'.

The splendid interior of the main hall has three tiers of boxes, stalls and a huge gallery, however the acoustics were dreadful and a problem for many years. The eminent conductor Sir Thomas Beecham said that the Hall could be used for a hundred things – but music was not one of them! In the late 1960s a solution was found for the notorious echo by suspending huge fibreglass diffusers from the ceiling, which look like giant fungi - but do the job.

The Hall hosts many varied events but none more famous than the annual festival of music 'The Proms', which runs from July to September.

Crossness Pumping Station
Sir Joseph Bazalgette, 1865

The Old Works, Thames Water S.T.W., Bazalgette Way, Abbey Wood, SE2 9AQ • Tel 020 8311 3711 • www.crossness.org.uk • Nearest transport Abbey Wood Rail, a bus runs from the station to the Crossness site at half hourly intervals • See website for opening times and admission charges • There is a museum and refreshments are available

The Crossness Pumping Station was built by Sir Joseph Bazalgette as part of the London sewage project, opened by the Prince of Wales in 1865.

Of truly outstanding architectural interest is the Beam Engine House, a Grade I Listed Industrial Building constructed in the Romanesque style in gault brick made from a mixture of a heavy clay soil and sand from the south east of London. The interior features some spectacular ornamental Victorian wrought and cast ironwork. It also contains the four original pumping engines, one in each corner of the building, possibly the largest remaining rotative beam engines in the world, with 52 ton flywheels and 47 ton beams. Although modern diesel engines were subsequently introduced, the old beam engines remained in service until work on a new sewage treatment plant commenced in the mid 1950s, and this building was eventually abandoned, and the engine house left to decay. The original spectacular 207 foot chimney has been demolished.

Work commenced on the Pumping Station's restoration by a group of volunteers in 1985 and in 1987 the Crossness Engines Trust was established to replace the original Preservation Group in order to put the enterprise on a sound business and legal basis.

Crossness is a unique part of Britain's industrial heritage and an outstanding example of Victorian engineering and architecture, it is a privilege and a pleasure to be able to visit such an unlikely gem.

The other major pumping stations built as part of Bazalgette's scheme were at Deptford (1864), Abbey Mills (River Lea) (1868), and Chelsea Embankment (1875).

St Pancras Station and The Midland Grand Hotel
W H Barlow, 1865 (St Pancras)
George Gilbert Scott, 1866 (Midland Grand Hotel)

St. Pancras International, Pancras Road, NW1 2QP • Tel 0207 304 3921 (for tours information only) • Nearest transport King's Cross & St Pancras LU & Rail

St Pancras Renaissance London Hotel (formerly The Midland Grand) • Euston Road, NW1 2AR • Tel 020 7841 3540 • www.marriott.com

A frequent response to the question 'What is your favourite building in London?' is often 'St Pancras station'. The station is undoubtedly a wonderful feat of engineering, but what most people think of as St Pancras station is in fact the Midland Hotel, an entirely separate building.

At the beginning of 1866 Sir George Gilbert Scott's design for a hotel to mark the extension of the Midland railway to a London terminus was chosen by the Directors, even though his design was larger and more expensive than other plans submitted.

There is hardly any relationship between Scott's hotel and the terminus, designed by W H Barlow. Barlow's plan for the south end of the train shed was adapted to include a second gable and glazed screen, thus protecting the hotel from the noise and pollution of the station. Barlow's roof over the platforms is 689 feet long with an unprecedented clear roof span of 245 feet 6 inches across the station. The 25 ribs of channel and plate iron lattice ribs rise some 100 feet to meet in a slightly pointed apex. The ironwork was made by the Butterley Company and originally painted sky-blue. The terminus is listed Grade I.

Grade I listing has also been granted to Scott's hotel which was opened in 1876 to great acclaim: '…obliterating its rivals; making Euston appear the old fashioned muddle it was and King's Cross a very ordinary and austere engineer's building'. It is interesting to note that the contemporary view of Scott's Gothic design made the 30 odd year old Classic Euston station 'old fashioned' – such was the rapid and violent change of taste in the 19th century.

The frontage of the hotel, 565 feet in length with a 270 feet tall clock tower and a wider 250 feet tall west tower, is a mass of balconies, windows, gables, dormers, ironwork, columns and carving. The interior is richly decorated throughout with finely carved details on capitals, turrets, stringcourses and friezes, much of which is made from honey-coloured Ancaster stone. Columns are of polished limestone, pink from Devonshire and green from Connemara, and much of the detailing of the principal window surrounds is in Red Mansfield sandstone. The wooden panelling is also finely carved. The flooring is either of geometric ceramic tiles made by Minton and Company or specially commissioned Wilton Axminster carpet.

The hotel had 250 bedrooms, a sumptuous curved dining room and a Grand Staircase, which is one of the finest examples of High Victorian decoration. Also provided was a Ladies' Smoking Room, the first in London, which must have been quite shocking when it opened. The hotel was the most opulent in

London at the time of its opening and at 14 shillings a night, which included breakfast, dinner and a personal attendant, it was considered to be quite expensive.

However, the demand for en-suite facilities and the rising costs of employing an army of staff to run the business smoothly meant that by 1935 the hotel had to close. From that date until the 1960s the building was renamed 'St Pancras Chambers' and used as offices, amid bids for its demolition. It was at this time the building received Grade I listing status.

During the 1980s the building failed its fire certificate requirements making it unusable. During the early 1990s British Rail and English Heritage funded the £10 million structural renovations and exterior cleaning of the building so badly needed. Internally, beneath layers of 'slapped-on' office paint was the original fabulous decoration, just waiting for time and money to be lavished on it once again.

The solution to this problem came when in January 1994 it was announced that St Pancras had become the Government's preferred London terminus for the new route to the Channel Tunnel. St Pancras International, as the station is now known, is also part of a much wider regeneration project that is transforming the King's Cross area. New life was given to the Midland Hotel, when on 5 May 2011, exactly 138 years to the day that the hotel was originally opened, the St Pancras Renaissance hotel welcomed guests once

more. The hotel has everything one would expect from a modern five-star establishment; spa, fitness room, whirlpool, meeting rooms, valet parking, luxurious rooms and suites.

Within the original gloriously decorated entrance hall and coffee room is the 'Gilbert Scott' restaurant and bar, run by Michelin star chef Marcus Wareing, open to hotel patrons and the public alike. Designer David Collins has enhanced the marble pillars and lofty painted ceilings with oxblood red walls and gold leaf flourishes, bringing to the project the glamour and romance that was once synonymous with rail travel. *Area Map p.2-3, B:2*

Previous page left: Statue of Sir John Betjeman, St Pancras Station. Betjeman helped to save St Pancras station from demolition in the 1960s
Previous page right: St Pancras station
This page: former Midland Grand Hotel

London Oratory Church of the Immaculate Heart of Mary
Herbert Gribble, 1876-84

Thurloe Place, Brompton Road, SW7 2RP • Tel 020 7808 0900 • www.bromptonoratory.co.uk • Nearest transport South Kensington LU • Please telephone for opening times, services and events

Pevsner called this church 'the most thoroughgoing 19th-century import of the Italianate style' and indeed one could be forgiven for the feeling of having been transported to Rome when visiting the Brompton Oratory, as it it known.

Completed in 1884, the church was a celebration of the English Catholic revival of the latter-half of the 19th century and was the first Catholic church of substance built in London since the Reformation. It was designed by the young Herbert Gribble, himself a Catholic convert, who was only 29 years old when he was given this huge commission. However it was not until 1896 that the west front and dome, which give the church its familiar face of today, were added.

The interior has a broad nave, some 50 feet in width, giving an impression of spaciousness. Instead of aisles Gribble built side chapels. The whole building is light and richly decorated with some striking altarpieces and statues.

In the nave there are huge marble statues of the Apostles carved by Giuseppe Mazzuoli between 1679-1695 for Siena Cathedral. Also of particular note is Rex Whistler's altarpiece of the English Martyrs in the Chapel of St Wilfred. Completed in 1938, this triptych shows St Thomas More and St John Fisher (both of whom had been canonised in 1935) on the side panels with a depiction of executions at Tyburn at the centre. A fine First World War memorial by L Berra is grouped with an Italian marble pietà.

It is rumoured that during the Cold War era the Brompton Oratory was used by the KGB as a dead letter box – one can only congratulate them on their excellent choice of building!

Natural History Museum
Alfred Waterhouse, 1872-81 / C F Moller Architects, 2009

Cromwell Road, SW7 5BD • Tel 020 7942 5000 • www.nhm.ac.uk • Nearest Transport: South Kensington LU • Admission free • See website for opening times

Following on from the success of the Great Exhibition of 1851, it was felt that a more permanent building was required to show off the British made goods that had been displayed to such an advantage. A plot of land was found in South Kensington and the young Captain Fowke of the Royal Engineers, who was to go on to design the Royal Albert Hall, was engaged as architect. Unfortunately the project did not draw the crowds and the building, described as the ugliest in London, was rapidly demolished. It was decided to replace it with a museum housing the natural 'curiosities' collected by Sir Hans Sloane, the bulk of whose vast collection was held at the British Museum.

A competition was held to design this new Museum of Natural History, with entries submitted anonymously. Captain Fowke won, much to the despair of the judges, many of whom had been critical of the earlier building. However, Fowke died before the work had begun and Alfred Waterhouse was appointed as architect in his place.

Building work began on this huge project in 1872 and the first phase of the museum was opened in 1881. The exterior is completely made from terracotta, with beautiful carvings

of extinct and extant animals and plants to the left and right of the main door respectively. The main façade of the building is huge with two tall, slim towers topped with spires. The rounded arches of the grand entrance were

Hintze Hall, Natural History Museum

Natural History Museum
Alfred Waterhouse, 1872-81 / C F Moller Architects, 2009

Cromwell Road, SW7 5BD • Tel 020 7942 5000 • www.nhm.ac.uk • Nearest Transport: South Kensington LU • Admission free • See website for opening times

Following on from the success of the Great Exhibition of 1851, it was felt that a more permanent building was required to show off the British made goods that had been displayed to such an advantage. A plot of land was found in South Kensington and the young Captain Fowke of the Royal Engineers, who was to go on to design the Royal Albert Hall, was engaged as architect. Unfortunately the project did not draw the crowds and the building, described as the ugliest in London, was rapidly demolished. It was decided to replace it with a museum housing the natural 'curiosities' collected by Sir Hans Sloane, the bulk of whose vast collection was held at the British Museum.

A competition was held to design this new Museum of Natural History, with entries submitted anonymously. Captain Fowke won, much to the despair of the judges, many of whom had been critical of the earlier building. However, Fowke died before the work had begun and Alfred Waterhouse was appointed as architect in his place.

Building work began on this huge project in 1872 and the first phase of the museum was opened in 1881. The exterior is completely made from terracotta, with beautiful carvings

of extinct and extant animals and plants to the left and right of the main door respectively. The main façade of the building is huge with two tall, slim towers topped with spires. The rounded arches of the grand entrance were

Hintze Hall, Natural History Museum

apparently inspired by basalt columns at Fingal's Cave on Staffa in Western Scotland. Waterhouse had earlier travelled to Southern Germany and was evidently inspired by the Romanesque churches he saw there. Indeed the museum has often been likened to a large cathedral, with one enthusiast at the time of its opening declaring it 'the animal's Westminster Abbey'. However, one critic commented that 'a serious mistake has been made in the erection of a building with such elaborate and ornate internal decorations for museum purposes'.

For many years the front of this building was dulled by the grimy, polluted London air but has recently been the subject of a major cleaning project and now looks wonderful.

The internal layout of the museum was heavily influenced by Richard Owen, expert naturalist and superintendent of the Natural History collection during its move from the British Museum to South Kensington. He and Alfred Waterhouse worked together on the best way to harmonise the architectural decoration with the exhibits.

One of the most memorable parts of the building is the grand entrance hall, where the glass of the roof, the exposed iron structure and the grand staircase to the upper floors dominate. As with the exterior of the building, the interior is decorated extensively with sculptured forms depicting nature: animal, vegetable and mineral.

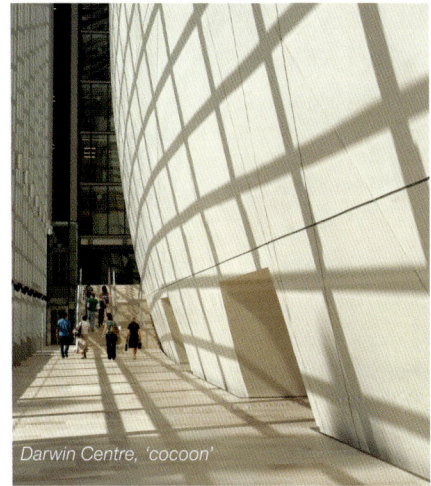
Darwin Centre, 'cocoon'

In 1985, the museum incorporated the nearby building belonging to the Geological Society, in Exhibition Road, designed in 1914 by Sir Richard Allison, and this is now part of the 'Red Zone', where visitors can take the escalator up through the giant Earth sculpture made from iron, zinc and copper.

The latest addition to the museum is the Darwin Centre, opened in late 2009. Designed by the Danish C F Moller Architects, the structure is an 8-storey 'cocoon', the largest sprayed-concrete, curved structure in Europe. Its cool whiteness contrasts brilliantly with the older part of the museum.

St Mary's Church
John Francis Bentley, 1877-82

Cadogan Street, SW3 2QR • Tel 0207 589 5487 • www.stmaryscadoganstreet.co.uk • Nearest transport Sloane Square LU • See website for opening times, services & events

The rather unexciting exterior of this church belies its lovely interior. John Francis Bentley, architect of Westminster Cathedral, designed St Mary's 1877-82 to incorporate the mortuary chapel designed by A W Pugin in 1845 and a chapel of 1860 by Edward, Pugin's eldest son, both of which had been added to an earlier church building.

Holy Trinity Church, Chelsea
J D Sedding, 1888-90

Sloane Street, SW1X 9DF • Tel 020 7730 7270 • www.holytrinitysloanesquare.co.uk • Nearest transport Sloane Square LU • See website for opening times, services & events

Former Poet Laureate Sir John Betjeman referred to Holy Trinity Church as the 'Cathedral of the Arts & Crafts Movement'. This is a fine example of an Arts and Crafts church designed in 1888-90 by J D Sedding, a pupil of Norman Shaw. Sedding believed that the building should be 'wrought and painted over with everything that has life and beauty – in frank and fearless naturalism'.

Sedding was an enthusiastic member of the Art Workers' Guild, a society of artists, craftsmen and designers with a common interest in the interaction, development and distribution of creative skills, based in London. Other members at the same time included architect C F A Voysey, who built the Sanderson Wallpaper Factory, Chiswick, and William Lethaby, architect and academic, who worked in the office of Norman Shaw.

The great east window of 48 small panels, designed by Edward Burne-Jones, was the largest ever made by Morris & Co.

Left: East window by Edward Burne-Jones and William Morris, Holy Trinity Church

Bishopsgate Institute
Charles Harrison Townsend, 1892-94

230 Bishopsgate, EC2M 4QH • Tel 020 7392 9200 • www.bishopsgate.org.uk • Nearest transport Liverpool Street LU/Rail

During the last decades of the 19th century, some Arts and Crafts influenced architects were developing a style of building with its roots firmly in the British vernacular past, but whose expression would be typical of only its own time. One of the most celebrated proponents of this style was Charles Rennie Mackintosh, who worked mainly in Scotland, but it was for Charles Harrison Townsend to give London some of the best examples of this free style of design. Like his contemporary J D Sedding, Townsend was a member of the Art Workers' Guild.

Townsend has, happily, provided us with a trio of good buildings to consider. The terracotta façade of the Grade II listed Bishopsgate Institute is covered with stylised leafy trees and topped by two turrets. The interior has an impressive clerestoried Great Hall, panelled Boardroom and glass-domed Library, much of which has been recently restored as part of a £7.1 million refurbishment programme. The Bishopsgate Institute is entered through a wide, arched door way, quite Romanesque and yet highly original at the same time.

Horniman Museum
Charles Harrison Townsend, 1898-1901

100 London Road, Forest Hill, SE23 3PQ
• 020 8699 1872 • www.horniman.ac.uk
• Nearest transport Forest Hill LU & Rail •
Admission free • See website for opening times & exhibition details

Wealthy tea merchant F J Horniman decided to put his anthropological collection on public display and engaged Charles Harrison Townsend to design a suitable building. As with his other buildings, Townsend gives the wide arched entrance a welcoming feel, but with admittance to the building at almost street level, there is no intimidating grand staircase to climb. The clock tower to one side of the building has a lovely play of squares and circles. This building is one of the best buildings of its age and perhaps the finest example of Art Nouveau architecture in London.

Since its completion in 1891, the museum has been expanded, first with a library and lecture hall added in 1910 by Townsend himself and more recently with further galleries, a shop and a café. There are 16 acres of gardens and a huge Victorian conservatory to explore.

Whitechapel Art Gallery
Charles Harrison Townsend, 1899-1901

77-82 Whitechapel High Street, E1 7QX • Tel 020 7522 7888 • www.whitechapel.org • Nearest transport Aldgate East LU and Liverpool Street LU/Rail • Admission free • See website for details of opening times and exhibitions

The Art Gallery built 1899-1901 was a smaller affair than Townsend had originally designed four years earlier. Financial constraints were also blamed for the exclusion of the planned mosaic by Townsend's fellow Art Workers' Guild artist, Walter Crane, which would have adorned the front of the building. Indeed, the whole project was rather disappointing - just two plain exhibition rooms, one above the other, behind a very plain exterior. Despite its lack of charm, Whitechapel Gallery over the years has hosted acclaimed exhibitions by the likes of Mark Rothko Jackson Pollock, and Gilbert and George.

The recent acquisition of the neighbouring red brick and terracotta Passmore Edwards Library has increased the Gallery's exhibition space considerably. The Library was built at the same time as the Gallery by architects Potts, Son & Hennings, and designed in the free classical style known as Queen Anne, which had strong associations with liberal philanthropy. The programme of restoration, alteration and marrying up the two buildings was undertaken 2003-7 by London architecture studio Witherford Watson Mann in collaboration with Ghent-based Robbrecht en Daem Architects. Much of the original interior furnishings and staircases have been beautifully preserved in both buildings, whilst the overwhelming feel of the place is of quiet, ordered space. The project won a RIBA National Award in 2010.

Fitzrovia Chapel
John Loughborough Pearson, 1890-1891

2 Pearson Square, W1T 3BF • Tel 020 3409 9895 • www.fitzroviachapel.org • Nearest transport Goodge Street LU and Warren Street LU • Admission free see website for details of opening times

This exquisite little Grade II listed chapel is all that remains of the once sprawling group of buildings that was the Middlesex Hospital, which served this area from 1745 until its closure in 2005. The chapel was designed by John Loughborough Pearson, an architect steeped in church construction and renovation since his studentship with Durham-based Ignatius Bonomi. Pearson had undertaken conservation work at Lincoln Cathedral and Westminster Abbey, as well as work on new-build churches such as St Augustine, Kilburn in London and, perhaps his most noted success, Truro Cathedral (1880/7).

The pleasingly plain brick exterior of the chapel belies its sumptuously crafted interior, an essay of colour in marble and mosaics. Despite its diminutive dimensions, the building holds a small organ loft over the entrance, which would have originally adjoined a hospital corridor; a green marble font in the little south transept and a marble altar in the apse. Lancet windows in the apse and tracery windows in the nave bring light into the building. There is also a small window on the north wall which allows patrons sitting at one particular table of the adjoining Percy and Founders Restaurant a perfect view into this building, even when it is closed to the public.

The chapel is currently open on Wednesdays for visiting and quiet contemplation, but primarily earns its keep as a venue for weddings and parties.

Fitzrovia, as this area is known, was, like its neighbours Soho and Bloomsbury, the haunt of artists and writers such as Dylan Thomas. Now one is more likely to find an architect's studio or a public relations company, since in recent years Fitzrovia's little tavernas and public houses have made way for smart offices and apartments. The chapel sits in one such area, nevertheless there are now pleasing public spaces with benches at which to stop, rest and wonder at it all. *Area Map p.4, C:1*

Two Temple Place
John Loughborough Pearson, 1890-1891

Two Temple Place, WC2R 3BD • Tel 020 7836 3715 • www.twotempleplace.org • Nearest transport Temple LU • See website for opening times and information about exhibitions and events

Built as an estate office and London apartment for the Ist Viscount Astor, this was one of the last projects by architect John Loughborough Pearson. Usually associated with church-building and conservation, Pearson produced here a beautiful little two-storey property, with a Portland stone frontage and a sumptuous interior.

On entering the building, you will pass a couple of bronze standard lamps depicting putti playing with telephones and electric light bulbs. A nod, perhaps, to the idea that this was the first property in London to possess a telephone. The interior is all carved mahogany figures, particularly on the staircase, highlighting the client's love of literature. The first-floor Great Hall, with views out towards the Thames, has a mahogany hammerbeam roof and two bay windows with stained glass made by Clayton and Bell, leading exponents in the field and whose work was much favoured by Pearson.

A programme of exhibitions, concerts and talks is held here and regular 'architecture tours' are available. A very interesting building to visit, with a tea room and visitor facilities on the ground floor.

Senate House, see p.197

06

EDWARDIAN LONDON & THE RISE OF MODERNISM

EDWARDIAN LONDON & THE RISE OF MODERNISM

"If you're blue and you don't know where to go to
Why don't you go where fashion sits – Puttin' on the Ritz..."
Irving Berlin

The Edwardian period was short, Edward VII was monarch for a mere nine years, from 1901-10, and yet the very term 'Edwardian' conjures a powerful image of ladies in large hats, boating parties, amusing automobiles and ponies in paddocks. False though this image may have been for the majority, the economic climate around 1900 meant that architects such as the eminent Edwin Lutyens were commissioned by clients whose new-found wealth from retail, coal and textiles afforded them picturesque houses and a small stake in the land. What they really wanted, but couldn't quite afford, was a country house and pedigreed estate, so their desires were satisfied with oversized stairwells and room layouts which gave odd vistas but still felt informal and its sexteriors tended to be vaguely Tudor with hipped gables and tall chimneys.

The style was referred to as the 'Domestic Revival' movement, Lutyens translated some of this emotion to his London buildings and the office blocks he designed were treated to his genius for composition and balance. However, Lutyens soon became unfashionable, being seen as a self-flaunting Victorian who failed, or refused, to 'move with the times'.

The Edwardian period may well have been a short one but it saw the introduction of a plethora of artistic styles and movements; Post-Impressionism, Fauvism, Expressionism, Cubism. These new conceptual themes and philosophies in building were more popular on the Continent at the beginning of the century and it would take time and the catastrophe of a war to bring such radical ideas to Britain to any serious degree. Even then they usually remained as ideas rather than anything material.

Art Nouveau, was at its apogee on the continent at this time but, unlike Paris or Berlin, London was largely immune to its curvaceous charms. The minor exceptions are the monuments to Lord Shaftesbury and Queen Alexandra by Alfred Gilbert, who received much of his artistic education in Paris. The indigenous Arts and Crafts Movement was more influential on this side of the Channel, but the style's pastoral tone found limited expression in the architecture of London save for a few more minor residential developments.

Familiar Gothic Revival forms were still used for church building while large scale public buildings were more often than not of a

'Wrenaissance' form – a sort of grandiose Baroque in the mode of Wren and Vanbrugh. The French form of classical Baroque, as taught by the influential Ecole des Beaux Arts in Paris, was also deemed a suitable form for large scale buildings such as banks. The distinctive Venetian form of Baroque was used for the groundbreaking Methodist Central Hall (see p.184) that at once marked its independence from forms of Anglican church building.

Advances in technology at the dawning of the 20th century affected architecture. The advent of electric lighting, first installed in the City at the now demolished Lloyds Bank in Lombard Street in 1887, meant that by the turn of the century the provision of natural light within buildings became less of an issue. The first passenger lifts were introduced in 1890 and this together with the introduction of concrete and steel framed buildings ten years later, meant that larger, taller buildings were possible.

This was good news for the City in particular, where numbers pouring in each day increased dramatically in the first quarter of the century; 364,000 people in 1911 compared to 437,000 in 1921. The City was the financial capital of the Empire and prospered year on year. Even when industry and manufacturing no longer boomed, as they had in the previous century, the City was still 'doing nicely' and had fully recovered by the early 1920s from the dark days of the 1914-18 war. However, the Great Depression of the early 1930s shook the very foundation of the City.

Westminster was very much aware of its place as the capital of the Empire. Street widening schemes took place as much for aesthetic reasons as for the accommodation of the motor car. Gentlemen's clubs were built and thrived. Shopping occupied happy hours for those who could afford it, and it appeared that more and more could do so. When Nash built his 'Via Triumphalis', he made provision in Regent Street for small shops that gave customers a personal service or sent staff out to their houses, and where haute couture was usual. By the beginning of the century these arrangements were seen to be wholly inadequate by shopkeepers who complained about the lack of space for the stock to satisfy this new army of shoppers.

Mr Gordon Selfridge opened his department store in Oxford Street on 15 March 1909, bringing to London his brand of Chicago consumerism and, in Knightsbridge, Harrods was expanding at a pace that required new premises to be built and in 1905 the first part of its terracotta emporium was opened (see 'Shopping and Architecture').

Hotels and restaurants also thrived. The Ritz Hotel, built on Piccadilly, was of a pioneering design as well as a byword for glamour (see 'Eat and Drink Architecture') whilst, at the other end of the scale, the now defunct Lyons tea-rooms were also doing well and in 1909 the first Lyons Corner House was opened in purpose-built premises in Coventry Street. The novelty of 'brand' architecture, good, value for money fare and waitresses nicknamed 'nippies' because of their speed of service, all proved popular with a broad cross section of society.

Cinema and theatre audiences grew steadily. This was the era of Frank Matcham who built the magnificent Coliseum in 1902-04 (see p.180), the Hackney Empire in 1901, both the subject of recent major renovations, and the London Palladium, in 1910.

Certainly much of the impetus for the Edwardian love of outings to shops or cinemas was the ease of transport within the capital. In 1900 the opening of the Central line took passengers from Bond Street to the Bank of England in what seemed like no time at all.

Car ownership soared during this period. In 1900 there were only 8,000 cars in the whole country, but by 1920 the number of driving licences issued to London addresses alone numbered 100,000 and rose to 261,000 by 1930. The 1920s saw the first traffic-control measures appearing in central London in the form of manually operated traffic lights and white line road markings. Garages and car parks became necessary, a few examples of which are still with us – see former Lex Garage p.192.

However, this cosy vision, false or not, of Edwardian life as expressed in its architecture was to come to an end with what was then called the Great War, the European conflict of 1914-18. The mood of those involved in the world of the arts throughout Europe had been changing, perhaps from the end of the 19th century and certainly from the beginning of the 20th. This change was characterised by a consistent rejection of tradition and a self-conscious effort to explore other possibilities of living. The fact that such philosophies were being considered by a wide swathe of the arts, painting, literature and music as well as architecture, in a Europe-wide forum, is significant. Notwithstanding the above, this was seen by some as the response to the carnage of World War I and the subsequent rise of social equality. Such changes may simply have been the response to photography providing access to images, which previously could only have been seen by the very few privileged enough to travel and which must have had an impact on many levels.

The term 'Modernism' has been given to this shift in thinking and was particularly important in the field of architecture and is most properly identified with the Modern Movement. This was the 20th-century European movement which desired architecture appropriate to modern society and which used all the technical advances at its disposal, such as the reinforced concrete frame.

The first wave of the Modern Movement in architecture was by 1917 already being defined by a small group of Dutch artists, designers and architects, named after their influential magazine, De Stijl. This movement was dedicated to clean, uncomplicated abstract purism and a fondness for straight

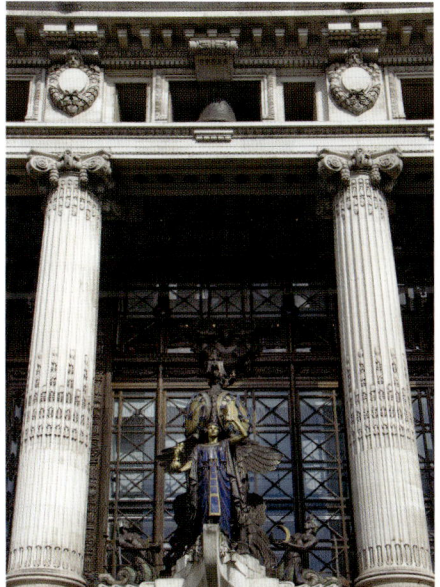

Above: Selfridges, see p.387

lines. The early Modern Movement can also be closely identified with the setting up of the Bauhaus school in Germany in 1919. This groundbreaking unit thrived until repressed by the Nazis in 1933. The first Bauhaus director was Walter Gropius (1883-1969) who taught the ideal of the committed craftsman knowing his place in the arts. However, it was the ideal of functionality in architecture that was the main Bauhaus message whereby practical considerations and not aesthetics determined the form of a building. At its heart was the desire to improve the material conditions of modern society through good, honest design.

Any idea of a supposed resonance with the Arts and Crafts and William Morris can be scotched by the fact that the Modern Movement did not look back to a golden age of medieval craftsmen for its inspiration but instead explored all the possibilities available through modern technology. The breaking-down of social and cultural barriers was also of concern to Modernist architects.

However, those who commissioned building works in London, and Britain as a whole, had been traditionally suspicious of anything foreign, including architecture, unless it had a Roman or Greek pedigree. Nonetheless émigré architects such as Erno Goldfinger succeeded in bringing the Modern Movement to London during the 1930s (see '1-3 Willow Road' p.213).

Britain never did develop its own Bauhaus equivalent, adapting instead an Arts and Crafts aesthetic. Mock Tudor, 'Tudorbethan' and Jacobean-style was the order of the day, particularly in domestic building from the 1920s onwards. Buildings were, typically, half-timbered with a mix of brick and pebble-dash and featured wooden framed windows with iron casements and a generous dose of stained glass, with perhaps an elaborate chimneystack or a slate hung roof.

Despite the economic depression of the 1930s house building continued apace. Speculative builders lined the roads heading out of town with ribbon developments and filled the suburbs with houses, usually in semi-detached pairs and these more often than not were owner-occupied rather than rented. In 1919 there were approximately eight million homes in Britain but by 1939 there were 12 million.

Generally smaller than the houses of the previous generation these 1930s houses are often mocked and derided. The perceived bastardisation of designs such as the afore-mentioned Arts and Crafts resulted in the less-decorated style of the 1930s semi with large bay windows and generous use of chrome. However, given the level of privacy these houses afforded, combined with the luxury of indoor plumbing, they must have seemed like a glimpse of heaven itself to their owners.

One particular style seems to have summed up the mood of post Great War Europe and was called variously 'Moderne', 'Jazz-Moderne' or 'Domestic Cubism', but which we know better as 'Art Deco', a term understood to have been coined by the historian Bevis Hillier in the late 1960s. However, the style was perhaps inspired by the 1925 Paris exhibition known as the 'Exposition internationale des arts décoratifs et industriels modernes'. The dominant style of the twenties and thirties, its exuberance and eclecticism were reactions to the austerity of the war years. In many ways the exhibition consisted of 'modern' versions deriving from earlier periods, e.g. Egyptian or Roman, but given a less ornate, almost geometric style as could be seen in the 20th-century art movements of Cubism and Futurism.

Hillier referred to 'Art Deco' as the last of the total styles and from ocean-going liners to handbags, glamorous cinemas to Bizarre Ware pottery designed by Clarice Cliff there seemed to be something for everyone.

One of the best exponents of Art Deco architecture in London was Charles Holden. He was commissioned by Frank Pick, the head of London Transport during its glory years of the 1920s and 30s, to design more than 50 London Underground stations. Holden was also the architect of the London Transport Headquarters as well as other major projects such as Senate House and Zimbabwe House.

Then came World War II and from the 7th September 1940 the enemy blitzkrieg relentlessly pounded London killing thousands and reducing many of her buildings to rubble. When the war ended and the damage was surveyed what, everyone asked, would lift London's spirits now?

EXAMPLES OF BUILDINGS FROM THIS PERIOD:

Euston Fire Station
W E Riley & LCC Architects Department, 1901-02

172 Euston Road, NW1 2DH • Nearest transport Euston LU/ Rail • No public access to the interior

A lovely example of an Arts and Crafts influenced building in the style adopted by London County Council. There are two similar such buildings in Hampstead but this one must surely be one of the most overlooked gems in this area. Situated to the east of the Euston Station complex, the top floor of the building was designed as the residence for the Chief Fire Officer of the station.

This remarkable fire station is built from red brick and Portland stone. Note the tall, plain chimneypieces and the stylised lettering over the doors facing the Euston Road.
Area Map p.2-3, A:2

Westminster Cathedral
John Francis Bentley, 1903

42 Francis Street, SW1P 1QW • Tel 020 7798 9055 • www.westminstercathedral.org.uk
• Nearest transport Victoria LU/Rail • See website for opening times, services & events

Westminster Cathedral is the principal Roman Catholic church in England. Cardinal Vaughan had been the instigator of the building of a cathedral here and wanted something constructed as quickly as possible, but a shortage of funds was always going to hamper any project that was too ambitious. Nonetheless, John Francis Bentley, a Roman Catholic convert, was appointed architect and his inclination was to design something Gothic in nature. This was thwarted by Cardinal Vaughan who felt an early Christian basilica would compete less with nearby Westminster Abbey.

Bentley was dispatched to do his own 'grand tour' of Italy, and it was a visit to St Vitale in Ravenna that 'really told me all I wanted'. On his return work started almost immediately and by the time Bentley died in 1902 he had witnessed the completion of his cathedral, apart from the tower. Ironically, the first service in the cathedral in 1903 was the funeral of Cardinal Vaughan.

The cathedral nave is made up of three great domed bays each 60 feet in width, with chapels set to either side. At the east end a fourth domed bay serves as the Sanctuary. The cathedral's exterior form is dominated by a spectacular campanile 284 feet high and the whole building is strikingly faced in red brick with bands of Portland stone. Much of the interior is derived from Italian sources, such as the pulpit which is in an appropriately early Christian style by Aristide Leonori, dating from 1899. The 14 Stations of the Cross, carved in low relief by Eric Gill between 1914-18, decorate the piers of the nave and are worth a visit alone. Look out for the inscription at the foot of the Sanctuary steps marking the Mass celebrated here by Pope John Paul II during his visit to London in 1982, the first to be celebrated in England by a reigning Pope.

This is one of the more surprising and memorable buildings in London. On entering the nave, the eye is drawn to the colourful, sparkling myriad of mosaics that adorn the walls of the nave and side-chapels. However, the undecorated domes are like black voids awaiting their decoration, when funds allow, which makes the building all the more interesting to visit. *Area Map p.6, A:1*

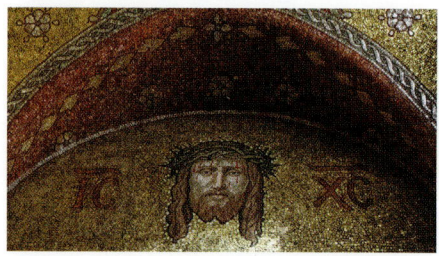

EXAMPLES OF BUILDINGS FROM THIS PERIOD:

Euston Fire Station
W E Riley & LCC Architects Department, 1901-02

172 Euston Road, NW1 2DH • Nearest transport Euston LU/ Rail • No public access to the interior

A lovely example of an Arts and Crafts influenced building in the style adopted by London County Council. There are two similar such buildings in Hampstead but this one must surely be one of the most overlooked gems in this area. Situated to the east of the Euston Station complex, the top floor of the building was designed as the residence for the Chief Fire Officer of the station.

This remarkable fire station is built from red brick and Portland stone. Note the tall, plain chimneypieces and the stylised lettering over the doors facing the Euston Road.
Area Map p.2-3, A:2

Westminster Cathedral
John Francis Bentley, 1903

42 Francis Street, SW1P 1QW • Tel 020 7798 9055 • www.westminstercathedral.org.uk
• Nearest transport Victoria LU/Rail • See website for opening times, services & events

Westminster Cathedral is the principal Roman Catholic church in England. Cardinal Vaughan had been the instigator of the building of a cathedral here and wanted something constructed as quickly as possible, but a shortage of funds was always going to hamper any project that was too ambitious. Nonetheless, John Francis Bentley, a Roman Catholic convert, was appointed architect and his inclination was to design something Gothic in nature. This was thwarted by Cardinal Vaughan who felt an early Christian basilica would compete less with nearby Westminster Abbey.

Bentley was dispatched to do his own 'grand tour' of Italy, and it was a visit to St Vitale in Ravenna that 'really told me all I wanted'. On his return work started almost immediately and by the time Bentley died in 1902 he had witnessed the completion of his cathedral, apart from the tower. Ironically, the first service in the cathedral in 1903 was the funeral of Cardinal Vaughan.

The cathedral nave is made up of three great domed bays each 60 feet in width, with chapels set to either side. At the east end a fourth domed bay serves as the Sanctuary. The cathedral's exterior form is dominated by a spectacular campanile 284 feet high and the whole building is strikingly faced in red brick with bands of Portland stone. Much of the interior is derived from Italian sources, such as the pulpit which is in an appropriately early Christian style by Aristide Leonori, dating from 1899. The 14 Stations of the Cross, carved in low relief by Eric Gill between 1914-18, decorate the piers of the nave and are worth a visit alone. Look out for the inscription at the foot of the Sanctuary steps marking the Mass celebrated here by Pope John Paul II during his visit to London in 1982, the first to be celebrated in England by a reigning Pope.

This is one of the more surprising and memorable buildings in London. On entering the nave, the eye is drawn to the colourful, sparkling myriad of mosaics that adorn the walls of the nave and side-chapels. However, the undecorated domes are like black voids awaiting their decoration, when funds allow, which makes the building all the more interesting to visit. *Area Map p.6, A:1*

Coliseum Theatre
Frank Matcham, 1904

St Martin's Lane, WC2N 4ES• Tel 020 7836 0111 • www.eno.org • Nearest transport Charing Cross LU & Rail • See website for details of tours of the building and access

The Coliseum Theatre was designed by Frank Matcham for the impresario Oswald Stoll as a variety house. Its proscenium stage, a revolving one at that and the first in England, has been graced by the talents of Ellen Terry, Sarah Bernhardt and Diaghilev's Ballet Company. At its opening it had the largest audience capacity (2,358) in London and was pure Edwardian (some at the time said elephantine) Baroque, with touches of Renaissance, Louis XVI and Italianate styles for good measure. It can be safely said that Matcham's designs were 'eclectic'. The architecture may well have been looking to the past for its inspiration, but this was a steel-framed construction with lifts and telephones. The exterior has a terracotta façade with a domed short column on top, supporting a huge globe that once revolved until Westminster City Council made it stop, for reasons that would baffle us ordinary mortals.

Since 1968, the theatre has been the home of the English National Opera and has been a popular and well-patronised venue. However, the interior had always been a little awkward and the facilities for staff and patrons had become outdated by the time a four-year programme of improvements was begun in 2000. A certain amount of restoration to Matcham's original design, which had been re-built over the years, was also included.

The £40 million project was completed almost on time and has been praised by critics and audiences alike. The glass barrel roof to the St Martin's Lane façade has been reinstated and the improvements to the public facilities, including better front of house and foyer arrangements are a joy. All patrons now enter from St Martin's Lane, whereas before, those in the 'gods' had to negotiate the daunting flight of stairs from the door in the adjacent alleyway.

The auditorium is an essay in red and cream 'plush', the seats are comfortable and no longer squeak; the number of ladies' lavatories has been doubled; a silent, air-cooling system has been installed and even the roof top globe, albeit a replica of the original, spins again.

During his long career as an architect, Frank Matcham designed 82 new theatres, including the Hackney Empire and the Victoria Palace and was responsible for the reconstruction of 78 others. *Area Map p.6, B:3*

38 & 39 Cheyne Walk
C R Ashbee, 1904

38 and 39 Cheyne Walk, SW3 •
Nearest transport Sloane Square LU •
Private dwellings – no public access

These properties are important examples of the work of Charles Robert Ashbee (1863-1942), Arts and Crafts architect and designer par excellence. Although he was heavily influenced by William Morris and John Ruskin as well as the principles of Socialism, Ashbee's house building was confined to the upper end of the artisan class. These houses are the only two remaining from a group of eight, one having been demolished as late as 1968 to make way for some frankly rather boring flats.

The detailing on these houses, the ironwork railings for example, was the product of Ashbee's influential School and Guild of Handicraft, a cooperative group of craftsmen.

Country Life Offices (former)
Sir Edwin Lutyens, 1904

Country Life Offices, 2-10 Tavistock Street, WC2 • Nearest transport Covent Garden LU • Private offices – no public access

Lutyens built these offices as a new head office for his friend and client Edward Hudson who had founded the magazine *Country Life* in 1897. This was his first commission in London but was followed by many more.

Wren's work at Hampton Court Palace is clearly echoed here in the flat front, sash windows and carved stone decoration. The quirky window placed within the entrance pediment is a nice touch. The chimneystacks have looked a little insignificant since windows were added to the attic level in the mid 1950s.
Area Map p.6, B:3

06

Edwardian London & the Rise of Modernism

Central Criminal Court (Old Bailey)
E W Mountford, 1907

Old Bailey, EC4M • Tel 020 7248 3277 • www.cityoflondon.gov.uk • Nearest transport St Paul's LU • See website for opening times and details of tours of the building

Designed by E W Mountford (1855-1908) and completed in 1907, the building's most dominant feature is its dome, which was inspired by the one at the Royal Naval Hospital Greenwich and which also echoes the huge dome of nearby St Paul's Cathedral.

Considered to be the finest example of Neo-English Baroque inspired by Wren, Vanbrugh and French classicism, it was built on a solid base of Cornish granite with Portland stone facing on the upper part of the building, the material favoured by this movement.

The original building contained four courts and 90 holding cells but this has been extended to 19 court rooms over the years. The richly decorated marble Grand Hall and Lower Hall have lunettes painted by Gerald Moira with scenes from the Old Testament and English history. The building's most famous feature is the 12 foot high statue of Justice cast in bronze and covered with gold leaf which stands on top of the dome. In her right hand she bears the sword of retribution and in her left hand she holds the scales of justice. Interestingly this Justice is not blindfolded, but all-seeing.

Built on the site of the notorious Newgate Prison and place of public execution since at least the second half of the twelfth century, the Court has tried many famous cases – including William Penn, Daniel Defoe, Oscar Wilde, William 'Lord Haw Haw' Joyce, Dr Crippen, and the Kray brothers. *Area Map p.8, A:2*

Zimbabwe House
Charles Holden, 1907-08

429 Strand, WC2R 0JR • Nearest transport Charing Cross LU & Rail • No public access

These offices were originally built for the British Medical Association and sold to the Southern Rhodesian High Commission in 1930.

Pevsner described this building, an early work by the architect who went on to design Senate House and underground stations for London Transport, as 'virile'. Indeed Holden has here succeeded in making the classic form solid without being overly clumsy and used a variety of classic devices, such as blank arches and columns, to great effect.

However, the building is probably more noted for being the sculptor Jacob Epstein's first large commission. The naked figures he carved into the Portland stone were highly controversial in that their 'manhoods' were deemed to be excessively large. Such was the offence caused, the neighbouring property was obliged to use frosted glass in windows that overlooked Holden's building. Some thought that these figures were mutilated in the 1930s, but frost damage is more likely to have caused the said appendages and heads of the figures to drop off. See Whitehall Walk for more information, p.344. *Area Map p.6, B:3*

Edward VII Galleries – British Museum
Sir John Burnet, 1904-11

British Museum, Great Russell Street, WC1B 3DG• Tel 020 7636 1555 • www.britishmuseum.org • Nearest transport Holborn and Russell Square LU • See website for opening times and details of special exhibitions

We have considered the familiar front façade of the British Museum in a previous chapter - this is the 'back entrance' in Montague Place. A neoclassical approach to this building was made by Burnet using a giant order of three-quarter engaged Ionic columns. This is of course a nod to Smirke's colonnade and yet its composition as a whole owes much to Burnet's education at the Ecole des Beaux-Arts, and gives the composition an edgy flourish. It's worth having a wander through the museum and out of the rear exit to have a look.

This extension to the museum was part of the plan to clear Bloomsbury of many of its residential properties and create an area that would be associated with scholarship. Within a few years Charles Holden was to build Senate House for the University of London opposite Burnet's work. *Area Map p.2-3, B:1*

Methodist Central Hall
Lanchester and Rickards, 1905-11

Storey's Gate, SW1H 9NH• Tel 020 7654 3826 • www.methodist-central-hall.org.uk • Nearest transport St James's Park or Westminster LU • Tours of the building are available by booking in advance – see website for service details, events and opening times

This is one of those buildings which from its exterior is hard to imagine exactly what it is used for as it gives no visual clues as to its purpose. It seems too isolated to be a bank and it certainly doesn't look like a church; the eminent architectural historian Nikolaus Pevsner said it could easily be mistaken for a very substantial casino! It is in fact a Methodist Hall, a multi-purpose building which functions as a Methodist church, a conference and exhibition centre, an art gallery, and an office building.

It was constructed on the site of the Royal Aquarium, which had been built as recently as 1876 as a place of entertainment for London's intelligentsia who, alas, stayed away in their droves. However, sights had to be lowered to attract a different, hopefully paying, clientele but the tone plummeted so much that the Aquarium was obliged to close and sell-up in 1903. The building was demolished to make way for the Methodist Hall.

Funds to build the Hall were raised by a 'one million guineas from one million Methodists' campaign and building begun in 1905 to a design by Henry Lanchester and Edwin Rickards. They chose the Baroque style as a suitable foil to the nearby Gothic Westminster Abbey and Houses of Parliament. However, it was not the 'Wrenaissance' Baroque influenced by the works of Wren and Vanbrugh being practised elsewhere in London, but an even more flamboyant style from Austria.

The building is framed in concrete and steel with brick arches and the huge main meeting hall, which seats 2,353 people, is almost square, as is the impressive dome that tops the construction. The interior has a sumptuous staircase, which sweeps visitors up to a spacious landing with smaller meeting rooms off.

There is very impressive sculpture on the exterior by Henry Poole, who collaborated with Lanchester and Rickards on other projects. One contemporary described the architects' work as 'combining opulence and taste with a touch of refined swagger'.
Area Map p.6, B:1

Cadogan Hall, formerly the First Church of Christ Scientist
R F Chisholm, 1908

5 Sloane Terrace, SW1X 9DQ •Tel 020 7730 4500 • www.cadoganhall.com • Nearest transport Sloane Square LU • See website for opening times & events

The architect, R F Chisholm, had previously worked in India and this could account for the exotic touches to this lovely building. Despite its bell tower, the passer-by may be surprised to learn that this building was once a place of worship. The light ashlar exterior is beautifully maintained; the interior has a barrel vaulted ceiling, a large balcony running around three sides and is free of columns. The furnishings are of a very high quality and include windows of handmade opaque glass.

When the congregation became too small to sustain this building in the mid-1990s, it was acquired by Cadogan Estates. It now serves as a music venue, renamed as the Cadogan Hall and is the home of the Royal Philharmonic Orchestra, who gave their first concert here in November 2004.

Left: Cadogan Hall

County Hall (former)
Ralph Knott, 1909-1933

County Hall, Westminster Bridge Road, SE1 7PB • www.londoncountyhall.com • Nearest transport Waterloo Station LU & Rail • Limited public access, see website for details

Knott was a pupil of the eminent architect Sir Aston Webb and worked in a similar Edwardian Baroque manner. The construction of this building was protracted with delays caused by, among other things, the finding of a Roman boat in 1910 during the excavations for the concrete raft on which County Hall is built. Parts of the timbers were destroyed before their presence was recognized, but what was left of the boat was carefully lifted, treated with preservative and deposited in the Museum of London, where it can still be seen. At the time it was thought to have been a Roman galley, but experts in nautical research have concluded that her timbers were too lightly jointed for a sea-going vessel and that she was probably a ferry boat, plying to and fro across the Thames.

Work on the building stopped again in 1916 owing to the war, but was resumed in 1919, and the building was opened on 17th July, 1922, though the northern section was not completed until 1933. Ralph Knott was only 29 when he won this prestigious commission, but died in 1929, four years before it was finished.

The six-storey County Hall is planned round a number of internal courtyards with the council chamber placed at the heart of the building. The enclosing blocks form an approximate rectangle whose slightly tapering long sides face westwards to the river and eastwards to Belvedere Road. The continuous river façade is relieved by the broad sweep of the colonnaded crescent, while in the middle of the Belvedere Road front an imposing feature is made of the ceremonial entrance.

The building served its purpose as the headquarters of the local authorities in London for just over 60 years before the Thatcher government abolished the Greater London Council in 1986. It now houses two hotels, an aquarium, the London Eye ticket office, food outlets and various other ventures.
Area Map p.6, C:2

Britannic House
Sir Edwin Lutyens, 1921-25

Britannic House, corner of Moorgate and Finsbury Circus, EC2 • Nearest transport Moorgate LU & Rail • No public access

This is one of Lutyens' largest London buildings at seven storeys tall, with a lovely curved frontage to Finsbury Circus. A rusticated ground floor and small, very deep set windows give the building a solid appearance with the top three floors flanked by giant Corinthian columns and rounded windows, echoing the ground floor fenestration. This building was made, with almost no expense spared, for the British-Persian Oil Company, which later became BP.

Rebuilding of the interior took place In 1987-89 by Inskip and Jenkins who tactfully retained the original marble floors and staircase. The building was eventually sold by BP in 2005.

Now deemed too small for a head office function, the building has become 'multi-occupancy'. Gaunt Francis architects saw that the solution was to radically re-plan the centre of this Grade II listed building, introducing a new lift core and enhanced atrium space with a spectacular new atrium roof. Six new glass lift cars are included in a shaftless lift lobby arrangement. The historic Lutyens interiors were carefully restored and the new works carefully integrated into them. The project won the City Heritage Award in 2009.

Finsbury Circus was laid out to a design by Dance the Younger in 1802. For some of Dance's other work see Chapter 4, 'Restoration to Georgian London', page 87. Previously this site was occupied by the Bethlehem Hospital, known as 'Bedlam', but is now a green oasis in the City with a charming bowling green laid in 1909. *Area Map p.8, C:3*

Carreras Cigarette Factory (Greater London House)
M E and O H Collins, 1926-28

180 Hampstead Road, NW1 7AW • Nearest transport Mornington Crescent LU • No public access – but the best of this building is its colourful exterior

This unique factory was built within a few years of Howard Carter's discovery of Tutankhamun's tomb, when anything and everything Egyptian became the height of fashion. It manages to combine this fascination with Egypt with the then prevalent Art Deco ideals of clean lines and large areas of glass, to create a truly remarkable building.

One of the first factories in the country to be constructed from pre stressed concrete, the building no longer serves its original purpose, but since the 1960s has been known as Greater London House and is used as a mixed-tenancy office complex.

However, the main entrance is still guarded by a pair of large black cats, the black cat being the logo of Carreras Cigarettes. The famous feline is also represented in a series of reliefs along the façade of the building – look closely and you will see they have yellow eyes and wire whiskers.

This is, I understand, the only Egyptian temple in North London.

Right: Carreras Cigarette Factory

Freemasons' Hall (United Grand Lodge of England)
Ashley and Newman, 1927-33

60 Great Queen Street, WC2B 5AZ •
Tel 020 7831 9811 • www.ugle.org.uk •
Nearest transport Covent Garden LU •
The building, Masonic Museum & Library
are all open to the public (see website)

This is the third Masonic Hall on this spot. The first dated from 1776 and was by Thomas Sandby (1721-98), whose Great Hall was much admired and preserved through subsequent rebuilding until irrevocably damaged by fire in 1883. A few remaining sections are held at the British Museum.

This late 1920s building by Ashley and Newman, neither of whom are credited with any other London buildings, bears an uncanny resemblance to the Port of London Authority building. Built from Portland stone, the Hall copes well with its awkward corner plot and exudes an air of gravitas, like the head office of a bank.

The overtly Art Deco interior is certainly worth a visit with a grand marble staircase, vaulted corridors and exquisite, massive bronze doors that lead to the 62 feet high Grand Hall, with seating for 1,700 people. The building is now Grade II listed. *Area Map p.2-3, B:1*

London Transport Headquarters

London Transport Headquarters (former)
Charles Holden, 1927-29

55 Broadway, SW1H 0BD • Nearest transport St James's Park LU • No public access

For this building, described by one admirer as 'a sophisticated essay in massing', Holden used a clever cruciform grouping to gain optimum natural light. To appreciate this building one must think back to what sort of impact it made at the time of its construction, when its 'step back' form was seen as pure New York.

The HQ was built at a time when small, privately owned transport companies were being consolidated into a London Passenger Transport Board and it is possible to read the confident, American style architecture of 55 Broadway as propaganda, persuading often reluctant transport companies of the merits of merger.

This great ziggurat of a building of Portland stone boasts fabulous carved statues by Eric Gill, depicting the Four Winds among others, and the shockingly explicit male and female figures denoting 'Day and Night' by Jacob Epstein. The 175 feet tall central tower of the building housed utilities such as stairs, lifts and lavatories.

The building, which cleverly incorporates St James's underground station at its basement level, is no longer deemed suitable for

the administrative needs of Transport for London and from 2018, 55 Broadway will be transformed from office to residential use. TateHindle architects are redesigning the interior space to incorporate a mix of 'affordable' and private housing as well as retail and office space. *Area Map p.6, A:1*

Rudolf Steiner House
Montague Wheeler, 1926-37

35 Park Road, NW1 6XT • Tel 020 7723 4400 • www.rsh.anth.org.uk • Nearest transport Baker Street LU • See website for opening times and details of exhibitions and courses

Expressionism in architecture found a voice in Germany and the Netherlands circa 1905-30 and was the antithesis of Modernism. Expressionism was concerned that buildings should not be merely functional but creative, free and powerful sculptural forms in themselves. Probably the most notable building of this type is the Goetheanum in Dornach, Switzerland built by Rudolf Steiner in 1928.

Rudolf Steiner House near Baker Street is the only example of Expressionist architecture in London, and is a pretty tame one at that. The stone-faced building is perhaps rather inconspicuous but, nonetheless, it is a well used building with a theatre, bookshop and a particularly good library with a host of archive material relating to the construction of the building. Of particular note is the very fine curved staircase. *Area Map p.4, B:2*

Lex Garage
J J Joass, 1929

NCP, (formerly the Lex Car Park) • 32 Brewer Street, W1F 0ST • Tel 0870 606 7050 • www.ncp.co.uk • Nearest transport Piccadilly Circus LU

The Lex Garage was one of the first ramped multi-storey car parks in the country. It was under the threat of demolition for several years, but was recognised as an important feature in Britain's early motoring history and awarded a Grade II listing by English Heritage in 2002.

It was designed by John James Joass, an advocate of Edwardian Baroque, and also responsible for several London buildings including Whiteley's store in Bayswater. Originally the car park offered waiting rooms for chauffeurs and changing rooms for ladies, but sadly these facilities are no longer available.

Recently refurbished, the car park is administered by NCP. The site was entered for the British Parking Association awards in 2009 and awarded a Special Commendation in the Best Refurbishment Category.
Area Map p.6, A:3

Phoenix Theatre
Giles Gilbert Scott, Bertie Crewe and Cyril Masey, 1930

Charing Cross Road, WC2H 0JP • Tel 0844 871 7627 • www.phoenix-theatre.co.uk • Access to the interior for patrons only • See website for details of productions and ticket prices

Built on a rather awkward plot at the junction of the busy Charing Cross Road and Flitcroft Street, where the main entrance has been placed. The corner position lends itself to the circular entrance lobby, above which is a shallow rotunda with four columns and the attic level has small square windows. The interior was the work of Theodore Komisarjevsky, émigré Russian theatre director and designer, who furnished the Phoenix in gilt and red plush with ornate ceilings and shapely doors. He commissioned fellow countryman Vladimir Polunin to paint panels placed above the theatre boxes in the style of Tintoretto, Titian and Giorgione. Polunin went on to produce artwork for London Transport posters during the 1930s.

The senior architect of this project, Giles Gilbert Scott, was the grandson of George Gilbert Scott and was responsible for some iconic structures such as the Battersea Power Station and the one time ubiquitous K3-6 red telephone boxes. Bertie Crewe was a pupil of Frank Matcham and had enjoyed a long career designing theatres and later cinemas. *Area Map p 6., B:3*

Arnos Grove Underground Station
Charles Holden, 1930

Bowes Road, N14 • www.tfl.gov.uk • Open normal London Transport hours

When the Piccadilly line was extended in 1930, Frank Pick, the legendary head of London Underground, gave Charles Holden the task of designing the new stations. Pick believed that nothing was too good for the travelling public and he felt aesthetics were as important as the trains and buses running on time. Pick commissioned a calligrapher to give London Transport its own typeface, artists to devise posters and a designer to provide a logo – still in use today. 'The best' also ran to architecture and Holden's stations are classics. His Piccadilly line extension stations are all unique and yet are variations on a theme – built from exposed brickwork and concrete, using simple forms such as cylinders and rectangles with ceramic tiles to add colour. Holden designed everything – lighting, kiosks, ticket machines, platform seating and even the clock faces and litterbins.

Holden and Pick had travelled to northern Europe for inspiration – the Arnos Grove building is reminiscent of the much-admired Stockholm City Library of 1928. Arnos Grove has a drum-shaped ticket hall, whose large windows let light flood in during the day; at night electric light shines out. Southgate station is another example of a Holden station.

Unilever House
J Lomax Simpson, with Burnet, Tate and Lorne, 1931

100 Victoria Embankment, EC4Y 0DH • Nearest transport Blackfriars LU & Rail • No public access

This building is on the site of the once renowned De Keyser's Hotel, a very successful enterprise started by Sir Polydore de Keyser, a waiter from Belgium, who eventually opened his 400 room hotel in 1874. De Keyser became Lord Mayor of London in 1887, the first Catholic since the Reformation to do so. The hotel closed at the end of World War I and the land sold to Unilever in 1921.

Sited on a busy corner where traffic roars along Victoria Embankment and over Blackfriars Bridge, this impressive stone building is windowless on the ground floor, presumably to help eliminate some of the noise from the road. From the fourth floor of this lovely curved building is a parapet from which a row of giant Ionic columns stretch upwards. The roots of the design of this building are undoubtedly classical but with more than a hint of Art Deco.

It is a worthwhile building to contemplate for its form alone, despite the traffic. However the real treat is its display of sculpture with huge figures taming sinuous horses, representing 'Controlled Energy', by William Reid Dick and other figures by Gilbert Ledward and Nicholas Munro. During the evening the façade of the building is particularly well lit.

In a six-year programme of refurbishment that ended in 1983, Unilever House was renovated and expanded by the addition of an eight-storey wing. The new wing had to be low enough so that it did not violate the long-standing edict of London planning authorities that no building should be high enough to block the view of St Paul's Cathedral from Waterloo Bridge.

Such efforts did not suffice for the expanding and changing requirements of a multinational corporation such as Unilever and by 2004 a further and more drastic redevelopment was undertaken. The architects Kohn Pedersen Fox Associates were employed to renovate and restore the exterior, while the interior was entirely restructured with extensions of the crescent and watergate wings, a vast new central atrium letting light into the building's interior and the introduction of a contemporary roof garden. Some of the original building's finest features including Eric Gill's pewter lift panels and the fine parquet flooring have been retained but the overall feel of the interior is of a 21st-century building, complete with much improved energy efficiency.

Area Map p.8, A:2

Daimler Car Hire Garage (former)
Wallis Gilbert & Partners, 1931

McCann Erickson, 7-11 Herbrand Street, WC1N 1EX • Private with no public access

Designed by the architectural practice that produced grand projects such as the Hoover Factory and Victoria Coach Station, this building was one of their smallest projects. It first served as a Daimler garage, then as a taxi garage before starting its new life in 2000 as the London office of the highly successful advertising agency McCann Erickson.

The pristine white building has a rectangular office block and a tall central tower housing the stairwell. The long vertical windows of the stairwell now provide light to a central atrium which originally housed a curved car ramp for the building's sleek, four-wheeled, former occupants. As with nearly all the designs from Wallis Gilbert & Partners, this building is in an Art Deco style. This former garage is now Grade II listed. *Area Map p.2-3, B:2*

Right: Daimler Car Hire Garage. One of Wallis Gilbert & Partners' smaller projects – they also designed many large industrial buildings such as the iconic Hoover Factory in west London

St Olaf House
H S Goodhart-Rendel, 1932

27 Tooley Street, SE1 2PR • Nearest transport London Bridge LU & Rail • Private office, no public access

Built as the head office for the nearby Hay's Wharf in 1931-32, see 'South Bank Walk', St Olaf House, which almost abuts London Bridge, is an Art Deco gem faced in Portland stone. The building has curved sides and a lively use of windows, with those on the central four floors having bronze frames. The huge lettering over the entrances on both sides of the building is in a stylised, triangulated Art Deco form.

The staircase is a notable example of the Art Deco style, with a zigzag balustrade – worth pressing your nose against the entrance door to have a peep. *Area Map p.8, C:1*

Senate House
Charles Holden, 1937

The University of London, Malet Street, WC1E 7HU • Tel 020 7862 8000 • Nearest transport Goodge Street LU • No public access, however Senate House usually participates in the London Open House scheme (see p.403)

The plan for this fabulous building was conceived in 1927 with the purchase of a ten and a half acre site from the Bedford Estate to provide buildings for the University of London, which having been formed in 1836 was in need of more space. The proposal was to provide administrative offices, a library, ceremonial hall, students' union, five institutions and two schools; a massive undertaking.

Architect Charles Holden was selected on the strength of his London Underground stations and 55 Broadway, which had recently opened. His masterplan was duly approved and the start of work on the Senate House and Library was completed by 1937. However lack of funding and the intervention of World War II saw the rest of Holden's plans thwarted.

Holden designed this building with the overall massing based on a pyramidal form for stability, thereby giving Senate House its slight Aztec temple flavour. Holden made limited use of the fairly new technology of steel-framing, using it in the floor construction and within the tower to support the many book stacks, but eschewing its application to the building's main structure.

Standing at 210 ft high, London's first true skyscraper is faced in Cornish granite on the ground floor with Portland stone used on the 18 upper floors. It is thought that the exterior was intended to receive carved figures and ornamentation, but these were never realised and, perhaps, the building is better for it.

Great care has been lavished on the interior. The Ceremonial Hall, where graduates of the University receive their degrees, is double-height and lined with travertine marble. The same material is used on the staircase, which has a notable wrought iron balustrade. *Area Map p.2-3, B:1*

Canary Wharf Station (foreground), Norman Foster (see p.305)

07

1945 TO THE 21ST CENTURY

1945 TO THE 21ST CENTURY

"Architecture should speak of its time and place, but yearn for timelessness." Frank Gehry

In 1951 Britain set aside post-war austerity for an all too brief moment of celebration and fun. One hundred years after the Great Exhibition, the Labour government, which had ousted Churchill in the general election of 1945, threw economic caution to the wind and decided to allow frivolity and a modicum of excess to replace the rationing and monotonous drabness which had followed in the wake of peace.

The means the government chose was an exhibition which they called a festival, to distinguish it from the instructive exhibitions held during the war and which had been deadly serious by necessity.

The primary medium the enlightened socialists chose for their festival was architecture. Every major city in the United Kingdom had been ravaged by the Blitz so the idea of reconstruction and redevelopment was in itself a tonic to the nation.

A parcel of land on the south bank of the River Thames between the Waterloo and Hungerford bridges, just north of Waterloo Station, was set aside as the London site of the festival and a young architect, Hugh Casson, was appointed Festival Director.

The Festival of Britain ran for five months, attracted almost ten million visitors and was the nursery for all British post-war modern architects. It was here that Casson and team coined an exceedingly British version of Modernism, that could be said to have been 'contemporary', rather than 'Modern'. Influences were drawn from Scandinavia as well as from French and German sources. Indeed, many of the architects employed were European émigrés who had arrived in London in the late 1930s with ideas formed by Gropius and Corbusier. Even some of the humble exhibition kiosks were designed by Erno Goldfinger and the landscape enhanced with works by Epstein, Hepworth and Moore.

The nation loved the whole thing with its bright colours, strange shapes and challenging new ideas about how the British home should be decorated.

Sadly, however, when Winston Churchill regained power in the general election of 1951, he decided in a fit of pique to clear the whole thing away, with the exception of the Royal Festival Hall. The Dome of Discovery, the Skylon, the Homes and Gardens Pavilion were all unnecessarily demolished and Britain returned to the realities of austerity.

The architects that had so proved their worth during the Festival now set about the business of rebuilding the country. They designed housing, hospitals, schools and shopping centres, rebuilt derelict churches and repaired bombed-out houses. Their buildings in the brave new British Modernist style became symbols of the recently established Welfare State. In time the Festival mood returned as new towns and new housing created new homes that were as different from the pre-war norm as was Dior's 'New Look' from the uniform-like fashions of the 1940s.

Reinforced concrete replaced brickwork in the same way that steel had replaced timber at the beginning of the century - Britain was building, and building fast. But, on a fateful morning in May 1968 this architectural euphoria came to an end, shattered like the pre-cast concrete panels that so dramatically crashed to the ground when part of the 23 storey block of flats that was Ronan Point in Newham, East London collapsed, killing three people. Trust was badly shaken in the architectural and engineering vision which housed families in the high-rise apartment buildings that had become symbolic of Britain's post-war renaissance. Critics began to argue that Modernism was a flawed architectural philosophy and that Britain's architecture should return to its vernacular roots for safety and sanity's sake. Britain, their reasoning went, was historically a country of brick and stone, not concrete and steel, its buildings in the main were low-rise and had pitched roofs.

Above: Lloyd's of London, Richard Rogers, see p.235

Meanwhile, across the English Channel young architects Richard Rogers and Renzo Piano had completed the mind-bogglingly audacious high-tech Pompidou Centre in Paris in 1976, which was immediately voted the 'Most Popular Building in France'. The aspirations of British architecture would not bow down in the face of popular yearning for an unnecessary romanticism. Then in 1978 against all the odds Rogers was appointed by the insurance organisation Lloyd's of London, one of the most conservative institutions in the notoriously stuffy City of London, to design its headquarters. This building is considered, to this day, to be one of the most daring and futuristic in the world.

The American architect Robert Venturi had published his seminal book *Complexity and Contradiction in Architecture* in the 1960s when his views suddenly became fashionable. In his so-called Postmodern world, the deep roots of the psyche could only be satisfied by a complex, non-rational environment which carried with it subconscious references to architectural languages of the past. Office buildings built of brick needed to have references to Classical architecture to satisfy the hunger in the human mind for reassurance from the past. The Postmodern architectural movement came with a rich, some say fraudulent, philosophical system which appealed to a large number of architects. The American Modernist Philip Johnson changed his spots overnight and designed the AT&T building in Manhattan with a Chippendale style split pediment where it reached the sky. James Stirling designed the over-complex No1 Poultry and in 1983 Terry Farrell gave a popular twist to Postmodernism with his building in Camden for TV AM with its jokey coloured boiled eggs on the canal elevation and a steel work keystone classical arch over the car park entrance.

Terry Farrell went on to complete three further grand projects in the Postmodern manner - the MI6 building at Vauxhall, Embankment Place over Charing Cross Station and Alban Gate which spans London Wall in the City.

In 1984 Prince Charles, the Prince of Wales, was guest of honour at a dinner hosted

Above: No1 Poultry, James Stirling

by the Royal Institute of British Architects at Hampton Court Palace to celebrate the Institute's 150th anniversary. The Prince was there to represent the Queen, the Institute's patron, and to present the Royal Gold Medal. He used the opportunity afforded by his speech to attack British architecture and specifically the proposals for an extension to the National Gallery designed by Ahrens, Burton and Koralek (ABK), touching a popular nerve and was praised by tabloid and broadsheet alike for taking a brave stand against an arrogant and out of touch profession. The ABK scheme for the National Gallery was dropped and was eventually replaced with a Postmodern concoction by the ringmaster of the philosophy Robert Venturi, with Denise Scott Brown.

Architects at this time became dab handed at new computer aided design technology, so out went the drawing boards and in came electronic hardware. However, architectural computers did more than replace the T square, set square and Rotring pen. They afforded a new freedom to the architectural imagination, liberating it from the previous constraints which were in effect linear geometry. Whereas plans drawn by hand using the T square and set square had tended, over the course of architectural history, to result in rectilinear and right-angular buildings, those drawn on a computer could turn the strangest lines, shapes and forms into concrete reality. For structural engineers the computer meant more finely honed calculations resulting in new structural systems. Colour photocopying meant that the architect's palette needed no longer to be monochrome – if Mondrian could paint it, architects could now draw it, reproduce it and specify it. The new language was shape and colour.

On Saturday 19 November 1994 the British people experienced their first National Lottery draw – 25% of the profits from the Lottery are set aside for 'good causes'; to date (2018) this has amounted to over a staggering £59 billion. The 'good causes' include those which require building.

As British architecture entered the new millennium fuelled by public enthusiasm and the continuing generosity of the Lottery, Norman Foster emerged as the most successful architect of his generation. The Great Court at the British Museum and the pedestrian Millennium Bridge, linking St Paul's Cathedral to Tate Modern, were both funded by the Lottery.

However, not all Lottery funded projects were quite so well received; the Millennium Dome, a wonderful piece of architecture by Richard Rogers (see Greenwich Walk, p.306), was much derided for several reasons, but mainly on grounds of cost – £700 million overall, £400 million of which was courtesy of the Lottery.

One Lottery funded project, the conversion of a grubby old power station on the south bank of the Thames into Tate Modern by architects Herzog and de Meuron, couldn't be more popular, with over five million visitors a year. Indeed, some of the most exciting public architecture has not necessarily been new-build, but the opening up of areas once redundant or forbidding.

One early example of this approach, the offices of 'Imagination', 25 Store Street, WC1E 7BL (www.imagination.com), set the bar high. Originally this six-storey Edwardian building was two schools, with girls occupying the building to the front, whilst boys were taught in an almost identical one at the rear, with a narrow passage open to the elements,

Imagination, Ron Herron

dividing the two. Various uses were made of the building after the schools closed but it was left in a state of dilapidation until 1988 when the premises were acquired by Imagination, the global communications agency.

This refurbishment project was handed to their in-house architect Ron Herron, who had worked on the conception of the South Bank Centre in the early 1960s and who had been part of the ground-breaking Archigram group of designers responsible for some interesting but unrealised projects. Their vision of disposable, flexible and thus easily extended buildings was influential from the mid 1960s to mid 1970s. Some of their philosophy can be traced in the Imagination building.

Viewed from the street it's impossible to envisage what lies behind the red brick and hanging green ivy of the façade. The original building space has been given a high-specification and smart appearance, but it is the treatment of the 23 foot wide space between the original buildings that is the most astonishing feature. This once dead-end alley, the walls of which have had their bricks painted white, rises six storeys with white steel and aluminium bridges linking the two buildings and criss-crossing the space between, while the whole is roofed by a network of suspension rods that push-up gigantic umbrellas of Teflon-coated PVC fabric.

The refurbishment of the building has won many awards including the 1990 Royal

Institute of British Architects 'National Award for Architecture'. In the same year at the BBC Design Awards, Sir Norman Foster said of the building 'I was so full of enthusiasm, I couldn't stop talking about it. I was stopping people, I was phoning people, I thought it was really wonderful'.

Unfortunately there is no public access to this building, but it sits next to 'New London Architecture' at the Building Centre, Store Street, WC1E 7BL (www.newlondonarchitecture.org: nearest transport Tottenham Court Road LU; see website for opening times). The Centre hosts exhibitions and talks on the topic of contemporary architecture and houses a 1:2000 scale interactive model of central London.

Public venues, such as theatres and concert halls, took advantage of this idea of reinvention to provide their patrons with better facilities. An early example of this can be seen at Sadler's Wells Theatre, Rosebery Avenue, EC1R 4TN (www.sadlers-wells.com), by Arts Team @ RHWL with Nicholas Hare Architects, 1998. This is the sixth theatre on the site. The last was built in 1931 and was fondly remembered but not easy to use with cramped facilities. However, with a Grade II listing most people assumed that little could be done, but when pressed English Heritage confirmed that Sadler's Wells was listed for its historical significance rather than its architectural merit and therefore what we have now is an almost brand new theatre.

Technical and operational facilities were given a badly needed update and an 85 foot fly-tower was built and stands proud – in both senses of the word – above the rest of the theatre. The bar, ticketing and cloakroom facilities are all excellent, as is the provision for wheelchair access. The auditorium has one of the best dance stages anywhere and one only has to note the number of world-class companies who include Sadler's Wells on their performance itineraries since refurbishment for evidence of its success. Importantly the whole foyer area, now feeling like one single space from the ground floor almost to the roof, with its exciting use of light and sheer glass front wall, makes the theatre feel accessible to those who might otherwise find a visit to such a temple of culture rather daunting.

Museums too have benefitted from the new mood for the opening-up of 'dark corners'. Of note is Danish architectural practice C F Moller's outstanding solution to the vexed question of the extent admired landmark buildings of an earlier age can be sympathetically developed for the 21st century.

The Darwin Centre, named after the evolutionary theorist Charles Darwin, is the most significant addition to the Natural History Museum since it opened in South Kensington in 1881. The £78 million extension to Waterhouse's highly decorative Victorian building (see p.163 for details) takes the form of a 65 metre (210 feet) tall, curved shell of dazzling white reinforced concrete, resembling a cocoon and sitting within a massive glass and steel atrium.

However, this cocoon is no architectural gimmick with the exposed thermal mass of the 30cm thick, continuous reinforced concrete shell able to maintain a stable internal environment, minimising energy loading. This regulates the temperature and humidity thereby reducing the risk of pest infestations and ensuring that the collection of 17 million insect and 3 million plant specimens are protected and preserved. Take the lift up eight floors to the top of the cocoon and then follow the sloping spiral path down, past the exhibits and the workspaces for the museum's scientific staff.

The built environment of twenty-first century London has much to offer the even moderately interested resident and visitor. The new 'Crossrail' Elizabeth Line, due to open fully in December 2019 has given some leading architects opportunities to show how good an underground station can be. Norman Foster's Canary Wharf Crossrail station is a feat of engineering. The complex forms an artificial island in the North Dock, with the usual mix of shops, restaurants and cafés, but topped with an impressive public park, where visitors are protected from the elements by a 300 metre timber and glass lattice roof. The interior space, with walkways and seating, is beautifully planted with species which first entered Britain though the nearby docks and feels very different to the nearby Canary Wharf

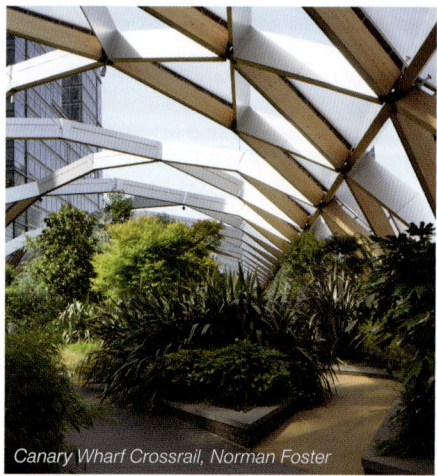
Canary Wharf Crossrail, Norman Foster

Docklands Light Railway station, also by Foster, which is all steel and glass.

Most of the London railway termini stations have been subject to rigorous upgrading during the last decade, King's Cross being the latest. In the not so distant past King's Cross, and neighbouring St Pancras Station, were dirty, rundown post-industrial sites, but their sixty-seven acres have been transformed into a vibrant place to live, work and visit.

A previous redevelopment scheme for the site aimed to sweep away historic landmarks, held to be important by locals and heritage enthusiasts alike, and swathe the area in high-density office buildings. Thankfully the plan was abandoned during the recession of the early 1990s. The present scheme, due to be completed by 2020, includes 2,000 new homes, a new primary school, 10 public squares, three parks, a lido, 500,000 sq ft of restaurant and retail space, and 3.4million sq ft of office space. This prestigious project currently includes a new UK headquarters for both Facebook and Google (by Heatherwick Studio), making King's Cross a new 'knowledge hub'.

However, it's not all new-build at King's Cross, with some splendid buildings of good architectural merit having been re-imagined. Notable are the Coal Drops, mid 19th-century brick and, surprisingly ornate, ironwork buildings, where coal, brought to the site by train, was dropped into huge hoppers awaiting onward transportation by horse-drawn cart and which architects, Heatherwick Studio, have transformed into a high-end retail area (see www.heatherwick.com for full details and some fascinating 'before' pictures).

Likewise, the Granary Building, which was originally designed as part of the Goods Yard complex by Lewis Cubitt, architect of the station itself, for the storage of wheat grown in Lincolnshire and destined for bakeries throughout London. Converted by architects Stanton Williams, winning many awards as a result, this former granary store is now the University of the Arts London Campus for Central Saint Martin's, where five thousand

Coal Drops, Heatherwick Studio

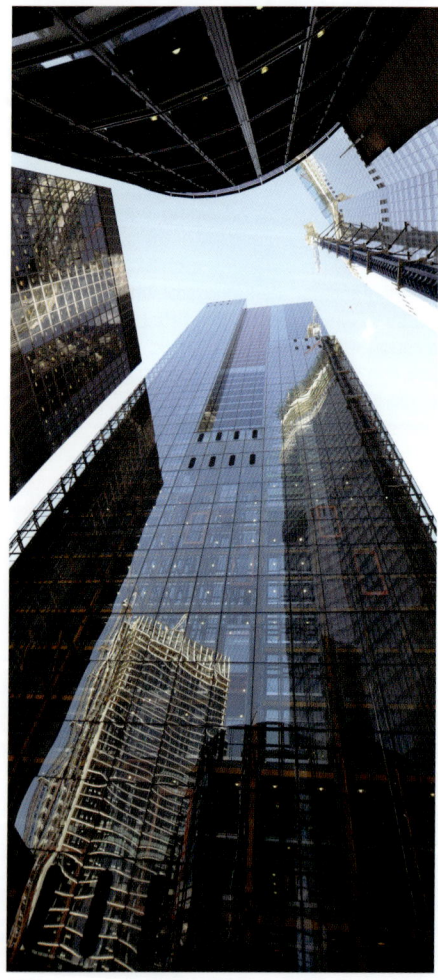

students, plus staff, add to the 'mix' of the area. Stanton Williams were also responsible for the design of the nearby Lighterman, a canal-side restaurant (www.thelighterman.co.uk), with an upper floor seating area and balcony to take in the views.

London has had something of a love-hate relationship with high-rise buildings. We love them, so long as we do not have to live in them. The June 2017 fire which devastated the 24-storey residential block of flats known as Grenfell Tower in North Kensington, taking the lives of seventy-two residents, probably confirmed such concerns. However, tall commercial buildings do not seem to engender the same emotions and, indeed, the plethora of contemporary sky-scraping office buildings excite the imagination, with the bestowing of nicknames such as 'the Cheesegrater' on Richard Rogers Leadenhall Building, 'the Walkie-Talkie' on Rafael Vinoly's 20 Fenchurch Street and 'the Gherkin', as well as many, less polite, tags on Foster's St Mary Axe building.

But are Londoners getting concerned by the sheer number of high-rise, (that is 20 floors or more), developments in the capital? Over four hundred are in the planning stage in 2018. Eric Parry Architects' 73-floor, / 951 feet, No1 Undershaft, in the City, will be the second in height to The Shard (see p.255), with The Pinnacle, Bishopsgate, designed by PLP Architecture and The Diamond, Leadenhall Street, by Skidmore, Owings & Merrill, at a mere 913 feet and 864 feet respectively, not far behind.

Protest groups, such as 'Sky Line Campaign', question this enthusiasm for tower construction – and its effect on ordinary Londoners' lives. There is also worry that the precious 'protected view' of St Paul's Cathedral will, one day, be swept away in the clamour to build high. A 'protected view' is the legal requirement within urban planning to preserve the view of a specific place or historic building from another location by limiting the height of new buildings within or adjacent to the sightline between the two places thus preserving the ability to see the landmark as a focus of the view. Seven out of London's thirteen 'protected views' protect sightlines to St Paul's, for example the new from Parliament Hill in the north of London and from Greenwich Park in the South.

But the question of sightlines is not the only issue, for London property, both residential and commercial, has become very expensive. In part this has arisen out of central government housing policy since the 1980s, but also in consequence of a move to a service economy over the same period. In that time, London has developed into a world leading international financial services centre, which, together with ancillary support services, has not only created considerable wealth, but attracted highly remunerated professional staff and an influx of wealthy overseas investors. The impact has been not only the construction of incredible individualistic commercial skyscrapers, some being purely speculative, but an ever continuing rise in residential property values as a consequence of the wealth generated and a focus by residential developers on high end 'executive' dwellings. Affordable housing for lower paid service providers essential to the operation of a metropolis is in short supply and the gulf between rich and poor has become a chasm. It is ironic that some 75 years after the destruction of 70,000 buildings, with another 1.7 million damaged, during the 1939/45 war, ordinary Londoners are once again finding themselves in housing difficulties. But how long this enthusiasm for building remains, or until the bubble bursts, only time will tell, but Britain's departure from the European Union could well be a test to come.

At present, British architecture, particularly in London, remains as vibrant, if not more so, than it was during the triumph of the Festival of Britain. Architects, themselves, are finding they have become readily recognizable household names; Norman Foster and Renzo Piano being prime examples. For this reason, the following chapter highlights key architectural practitioners, together with examples of their work, which, as set out in a rough chronological order by date of birth, hopefully enables the underlying thinking and development of building design and construction over this period to be discerned.

Berthold Lubetkin
(1901-1990)

Lubetkin was one of the many talented architects and designers who arrived in London as refugees escaping Nazism in the late 1920s and early 1930s. Born in the South Caucasus in Russia, he trained as an architect in Moscow and at the Ecole des Beaux Arts in Paris, before working for Auguste Perret (1874-1954), a pioneer in the architectural use of reinforced concrete.

In accordance with the ideals of the Bauhaus, Lubetkin formed a design group, Tecton, on his arrival in London in 1930. There then followed a period of intense work that would introduce to the public the International Modern movement. Highpoint One (1935) and Highpoint Two (1938) blocks of flats both in North Hill, Highgate; the Gorilla House (1934) and the Penguin Pool (1935) at Regent's Park Zoo; and the Finsbury Health Centre in Pine Street (1939) showed what could be done with excellent design and concrete.

This latter project displays Lubetkin's belief that 'nothing was too good for ordinary people', an ethos that intensified in his post-war work.

Spa Green Estate (1950)

Rosebery Avenue, St John St, Clerkenwell, EC1V 4PP • Nearest transport Angel LU • No public access

Commissioned and designed before the outbreak of World War Two, the Spa Green Estate was built between 1948-50. Using engineer Ove Arup's innovative concrete box-frame or 'egg-crate' construction provided each flat with clear views and interiors uncluttered by beams, columns or pipes. Many of the noted internal features at Spa Green borrowed from Lubetkin's acclaimed Highpoint flats, including lifts, central heating, balconies, daylight and ventilation from multiple directions, large entry spaces, and a roof terrace providing a communal area for drying clothes, social gathering and enjoying the views. Well-designed fitted kitchens included slide-away breakfast counters and ironing boards, electrical and gas appliances, and a central waste-disposal system in stainless steel. The three blocks of flats, 126 units in total, were awarded a Grade II listing in 1998, by which time the whole estate needed refreshing. A £5 million refurbishment, completed in 2008, has brought Spa Green back to its former glory.

Lubetkin also worked on the Dorset Estate and Sivill House, completed 1957 and 1962 respectively, both in Bethnal Green. Eventually, however, he became dissatisfied with post-war politics and society in Britain and retired to Bristol. *Area Map p.2-3, C:2*

ERNO GOLDFINGER
(1902-87)

Budapest born Goldfinger worked in Paris, where he mixed with avant-garde artists and architects before he settled in London in 1934, becoming an immensely influential architect. His London works include the French Government Tourist Offices at 66 Haymarket (designed in 1958) and at 177 Piccadilly (built 1963); Alexander Fleming House, now named Metro Cental Heights, at Elephant and Castle and Grade II listed (1966); Haggerston Girls School (1967), and Balfron Tower (1967).

Perhaps his most noted building, Trellick Tower, is described below, but his most accessible is the house he built for himself in the late 1930s and thus strictly belongs to the previous chapter, but perhaps we can justify its inclusion here by saying the property was 'ahead of its time'. At the time, however, Goldfinger encountered immense hostility from local conservation groups who saw his proposal for the terrace of four dwellings, as originally planned, as being out of step with the rest of the neighbourhood. One disgruntled local, writer Ian Fleming, took so against the architect, he named one of his most notorious villains after him!

1-3 Willow Road (1939)

Hampstead, NW3 1TH • Tel 020 7435 6166 • www.nationaltrust.org.uk • Nearest transport Hampstead or Hampstead Heath LU • See website for opening times & admission charges

This small housing project by the Hungarian-born architect Erno Goldfinger is one of the most important examples of the Modern Movement in London. Goldfingers' original proposal was opposed by local conversation groups but after a great deal of alteration to the original design, planning permission was eventually granted, and the building of the three-house terrace went ahead.

Each of the houses within the terrace has a slightly different internal plan and Goldfinger took the centre house, the largest, as a home for his young family. Mindful of a family's needs, a large amount of interior flexibility was incorporated – with moveable walls so one large nursery could become two bedrooms in the future.

The terrace is three floors high at the front and four at the rear; each house has an integral garage, and is constructed from reinforced concrete with brick-faced walls. Concrete was also used for the framing of the first floor windows and for the ground floor columns. Such unifying motifs make this terrace appear to be one large house and thus it fits well with its Georgian neighbours.

Goldfinger's own house has been in the care of the National Trust since 1994 and is open to the public. The house is filled with furniture designed by Goldfinger and his art collection is displayed, including works by Bridget Riley, Max Ernst and Henry Moore. There are also some family photographs on show, one particular favourite being a picture of Goldfinger with his aged mother when she came to live in Willow Road – along with her incredibly heavy-looking, solid Hungarian furniture, that looks remarkably at home in such a Modernist setting. There is also an opportunity to see a short film on Erno Goldfinger and his work, which is most worthwhile.

Trellick Tower (1972)
5 Golborne Road, W10 • Nearest transport Westbourne Park LU • No public access

Much of Goldfinger's working life was taken up with two massive public housing projects, both for the London County Council. The first was the Balfron Tower (1963-68) in Rowlett Street, Poplar, east London, which, at 27 floors high, was one of the tallest dwellings in Europe at the time.

On completion, Goldfinger and his wife moved in to flat number 130 on the 26th floor for eight weeks, assessing the experience and listing the points raised by their fellow tenants. The problems, such as two lifts not being enough, were taken into consideration in his next major housing project – Trellick Tower.

This was under construction when Ronan Point partially collapsed and public opinion turned strongly against high-rise living. Goldfinger argued that Ronan Point had been constructed using a prefabricated concrete system, which he felt was flawed, whereas he employed a poured concrete method.

Trellick Tower consists of 217 dwellings in a mix of nine different types of flats and maisonettes, all of which are 'through' apartments with windows on both sides, with the block facing south/north. The slab is 31 storeys high with a separate lift/stair tower and bridges to the main block at every three floors. Goldfinger paid meticulous attention to detail, for example, windows pivoted for cleaning, had soundproof double glazing and the entrance hall was marble-lined. The views across London from the upper floors are stunning.

Despite the architect's best efforts, this was not a place where people wanted to live. Goldfinger had employed Le Corbusier's philosophy as set out in his unrealised 'Radiant City' urban masterplan of 1935. However, the *Radiant City* was based on the abandonment of class based stratification, a philosophy not readily attainable in the contemporary city. The block was repeatedly and seriously vandalised and its tenants were hardly comforted by the 1974 blockbuster film *The Towering Inferno* or J G Ballard's 1975 novel *High Rise*, in which he describes tower blocks as 'architecture built for war'.

However, Trellick Tower is still there, Grade II listed no less, and is now a desirable address. Thatcher's 'Right to Buy' policy enabled some tenants to purchase their apartment and over time the social mix of the tower has changed, although many apartments are still allocated to those with social-housing needs. A door entry intercom system and the employment of a concierge were initiated in the mid-1980s. An active residents' association has campaigned for a number of changes to the building and housing policy over the years.

Although Trellick Tower has no public access, it is often included as part of the Open House scheme, see p.403 for details.

Sir Leslie Martin
(1908-2000)

Manchester born and educated, Leslie Martin gave London a vision of a 'modern world'. As Deputy Architect to the London County Council (LCC) in 1948 he led the team charged with producing the Royal Festival Hall. In 1953 he took on the role of Chief Architect to the LCC. Martin believed that society, art, and architecture were all aspects of the same conversation and that a better world could exist where social problems could be solved through intelligent design. He was much influenced by the work of Norwegian architect Alvar Aalto and counted Ben Nicholson, Barbara Hepworth and Naum Gabo among his friends and collaborators.

Leslie Martin was acknowledged as a leading light in the Modern Movement and designed some major additions to various Oxford and Cambridge colleges, as well as the celebrated Royal Concert Hall in Glasgow and the Centre for Modern Art at the Gulbenkian Foundation in Lisbon. In addition to being a practising architect he was an academic, enjoying the role of Professor of Architecture at Cambridge University for over forty years and was knighted in 1957.

Royal Festival Hall (1951)

Southbank Centre, Belvedere Road, SE1 8XX • Tel 020 7960 4200 • www.rfh.org.uk • Nearest transport Waterloo LU & Rail • See website for opening times and details of events, tickets and wheelchair access

Designed in 1948 by a team led by Sir Leslie Martin and which included Sir Robert Matthew (1906-75) the Royal Festival Hall was finished in time for the 1951 Festival of Britain, for which it was a showpiece. It was intended as a taste of what modern architecture could be – solid, functional and accessible. With a budget of £2 million and a lead time of just two years, the project was delivered within budget and on schedule.

The exterior is a display of glass and Portland stone, the river elevation having been extended forward during major renovation work in the early 1960s. The interior is a series of intersecting levels with a pleasing use of wood, marble, lighting and textiles throughout. Leslie Martin stipulated from the start that 'the egg of the concert hall should be surrounded by a box of structure', thus eliminating noise from the nearby Hungerford railway bridge and leaving the whole ground floor as free space for social gathering, refreshment and exhibition areas. The auditorium, designed by Leslie Martin and Peter Moro, accommodates 2,600 in one large stalls area, a substantial balcony, and four tiers of boxes. At the hall's opening one critic carped that the boxes looked like 'drawers pulled out in a hurried burglary raid' and Corbusier thought they were a joke 'but a very good joke'. Now they are more widely appreciated and have been copied many times since. Leslie Martin's wife, Sadie Speight, an architect and designer, was responsible for the striking red wall hangings at the rear of the boxes, which were made by the Edinburgh Weavers.

The Hall, being the first new concert venue to open in post-war Europe, was a focus for musicians, but needed to adapt over time to new demands from performers and audiences. Since 1992 the Hall has been the subject of ongoing refurbishment by the architectural partnership of Allies and Morrison, no mean feat given its Grade I listing. With a budget of £110 million, the Hall has been restored to its original elegance and vitality. By moving all the administrative offices into a new office building between the hall and the railway, many of the internal spaces previously used as offices are now available as public areas. On the river façade, a dingy service road has been transformed into an elegant parade of restaurants and shops.

Close by, and part of the 'South Bank Centre' along with the Festival Hall, are the Queen Elizabeth Hall, opened in 1967, and the Purcell Room, and Hayward Gallery, both opened in

Hayward Gallery, South Bank Centre

the following year, built for the London County Council, with Norman Engleback (1927-2015) as lead architect. This group of buildings is a marvellous example of New Brutalism, with its admiration of the work of Le Corbusier and its use of huge blank walls of rough concrete. These buildings have been much criticised, not least for their interconnecting walkways which are difficult for the able-bodied to negotiate and totally impossible for people with any form of mobility restriction and, worst of all, appear to be unnecessary. On paper the design for this group must have seemed bold and exciting, but given its location next to a grey Thames and under an often dull London sky some observers comment that the buildings seem out of place.

This trio of buildings has been the subject of a three year, multi-million pound renovation, in time for their fiftieth birthday celebrations in 2018. The concrete has been cleaned by applying a coating of latex, which, when pulled off takes away the dirt and grime; the wooden surfaces have been polished, cramped corners have been opened-up and the electrics have been updated. The Queen Elizabeth Hall stage has been widened, thereby enabling this 1,000 seat venue to host dance and orchestral events. The shared Queen Elizabeth Hall and Purcell Room foyer space has also been spruced up and is now a welcoming late-night social venue.

The Hayward Gallery has emerged from this latest make-over as arguably the best gallery in London for the display of contemporary art. The hapless, leaky roof has been replaced with a 'state of the art' solid glass roof, sixty-six open roof pyramids and an electric roller-blind system. The gallery is now flooded with natural light, which, of course, changes pleasingly throughout the day. This once 'ugly duckling' of a building is now truly a swan.

Skateboarders cherish the terraces and undercrofts of the buildings on the South Bank as their playground, although such activity was once seen as evidence of failed architecture. However, a recent successful campaign to save the South Bank skatepark has acknowledged it as one of the great public spaces of London.
Area Map p.6, C:2

Sir Robert Matthew
(1906-1975)

Edinburgh born and educated, Robert Matthew left his post as Chief Architect and Planning Officer in the Department of Health for Scotland in 1946, moving to London to take up the same job-title, but at the London County Council. In this challenging role he oversaw the re-building of much of London's war damaged housing, schools and infrastructure, including the Royal Festival Hall in conjunction with Leslie Martin - see above.

In the early 1950s he formed a partnership with fellow architect Stirrat Johnson-Marshall, establishing the firm of RMJM, with projects in London and throughout Scotland, at the same time accepting the chair of architecture at Edinburgh University. Matthew was vice-president of RIBA in 1962 and knighted in 1971.

Former Commonwealth Institute (1958-1962), now The Design Museum (John Pawson 2010-2016)

205 Kensington High Street, W8 6AG • Tel 020 3862 5937 • www.designmuseum.org • Nearest transport High Street Kensington LU • See website for opening times and programme of talks and workshops • Museum, shop, restaurant and café are free to enter, tickets for special exhibitions can be purchased online or in person

Set back from the western end of Kensington High Street, on the edge of Holland Park, the building has a distinct tent-like copper hyperbolic-paraboloid roof. Designed during the period of post-war optimism, very much in the spirit of the 'Festival of Britain', the Commonwealth Institute was completed in 1962. Its primary function as an exhibition space for British foreign interests was redundant within twenty years and the building had been threatened with demolition, despite its Grade II listing.

The buildings' saviour came in the shape of Sir Terence Conran who, with a need to enlarge his Design Museum and with his very deep pockets, engaged the 'king of minimalism' John Pawson to realise the transformation, which opened to the public to much acclaim in 2016.

New Zealand House
Sir Robert Matthew, 1957-1962

80 Haymarket, SW1Y 4TE • Nearest transport Leicester Square LU • No public access

This was the first tall building to grace post war London, 225 feet in height and fifteen storeys. The first four floors are a sort of podium that the rest of the tower rests upon.

The building, designed to serve as the official face of New Zealand in Britain, functioned as the offices of the New Zealand High Commissioner. Much attention was paid to the interior, with features such as New Zealand timber ceilings. The views from every window are excellent, especially from the bar and terrace at the very top of the building - so I am told.

New Zealand House still looks a little out of place, sitting, as it does, so close to the gentlemen's clubs in Pall Mall and Nash's nearby Regent Street. New Zealand House is Grade II listed. *Area Map p.6, A:2*

Eric Bedford
(1909-2001)

Yorkshireman Eric Bedford was chief architect for the Ministry of Public Building and Works from 1951 until 1970, and as such was responsible for all government buildings of that period. Included within this list, and arguably on of London's most iconic landmarks, is the Post Office Tower, now renamed as BT Tower, but many of his London works have since been demolished.
His role at the Ministry required him to design the backdrop for the 1953 Coronation of Queen Elizabeth. The project included four graceful 65 feet high tubular steel arches over the Mall, spanning 70 feet surmounted by gold an silver lions, white unicorns and a coronet He also designed the striped kiosks in Hyde Park and a temporary annexe at Westminster Abbey. He was appointed CVO (Commander of the Victorian Order for his efforts.

BT Tower
1961-1965

60 Cleveland Street, W1T 4JZ • Nearest Transport Goodge Street and Warren Street LU • No public access

The Tower, which can be seen from all over the capital, combines an office block with the function of a telecommunications tower. The structure is immediately unsettling to the eye, being thinner in the middle than at the top and bottom. This wasp waist effect has always had style and may look futuristic in some ways, but at the time it was built it was an astonishing architectural statement.

The Tower was the first purpose-built tower to transmit high frequency radio waves. Until the construction of the NatWest Tower in the City in the early 1980s, this 620 foot (189 metres) tower of concrete, steel and glass was the tallest building in London. Its cylindrical form reduces wind resistance and improves stability.

For over 20 years after its opening the public were allowed to ride one of the two high-speed lifts, travelling at some 6 metres a second taking 30 seconds to reach any of the three observation floors or up to the 34th floor restaurant which was built on a 3 metre wide (9 feet 10 inch) revolving segment, spinning through 360 degrees every 22 minutes. The restaurant closed in 1980 amid security worries and the tower is now inaccessible to the public.
Area Map p3, A:1

RICHARD SEIFERT
(1910-2001)

Born in Zurich, but educated at the Bartlett School of Architecture in London, Seifert was something of a 'developers' architect', skilled at exploiting loopholes in planning laws to maximise a site's potential. Indeed, one of his most famous buildings, Tower 42, formerly known as the NatWest Tower, was twenty years in the planning and construction and accordingly looked somewhat old-fashioned on completion (see 'Eat and Drink Architecture' on p.377)

Centre Point
1967

101 New Oxford Street, WC1A 1DD • Nearest transport Tottenham Court Road LU • No public access

Located at St Giles Circus, the most congested area in post-war London, the construction of this building aroused strong hostility both for the design and the London County Council's granting of planning permission for a private, speculative office project rather than for much needed housing.

This argument was strengthened by the 10 years Centre Point remained unoccupied – the charity 'Centrepoint' was borne from the plight of the many homeless people who congregated at the foot of this building. Ironically, the building is currently being refitted by Rick Mather Architects into residential use, with retail outlets and coffee shops in the public plaza area at street level.

Notwithstanding the controversy in which it was built, Centre Point is an extraordinary construction. Exceedingly slim, when viewed from the south and north, its glass set within a frame of pre-cast concrete sections gives it a unique surface texture. The structure's size, at 398 feet high and with 34 storeys, was initially seen as being out of scale with its surroundings. This design style was to be employed in several Richard Seifert London buildings – most notably Space House (formerly Aerial House) in Kingsway. *Area Map p.3, B:1*

Sir Denys Lasdun
(1914-2001)

As a schoolboy Denys Lasdun read *Towards a New Architecture* by Le Corbusier (1923), later travelling to Paris to meet the author and both events remained a strong influence throughout his life. London born Lasdun trained at the Architectural Association before taking a job in 1935 with Wells Coates, who had just completed his celebrated Isokon Building, Lawn Road, Hampstead. In 1937 Lasdun joined the Tecton team, led by Berthold Lubetkin, until the firm was dissolved in 1948 when he then worked independently.

Lasdun has been called the greatest English architect working in the early Modern period, not only for his iconic buildings such as the National Theatre, but also for his thoughtful approach to the post-war public housing delivered within government defined budgets in the 1950's. His name is often linked to the 'cluster block' method of design he perfected, for example at Keeling House in Claredale Street, Bethnal Green, completed in 1958. Essentially, a cluster block could be fitted into a small site without disturbing the existing street pattern or character. The design for Keeling House provides three towers of maisonettes, sixteen storeys high, set at different angles to each other and connected by a bridge to a central tower of lifts and staircases. Lasdun sought to provide independent houses in the sky - each maisonette having its own front door, a kitchen balcony at the rear and the noisy service functions sited at the side away from the neighbouring flat - allowing occupants to flush the toilet and run a bath in privacy.

Denys Lasdun was a much sought after, world-class architect, with significant commissions on the continent and in Britain, with many in London. His design for 26 St James's Place, a block of flats overlooking Green Park (1958-60) a finely articulated piece of Modern architecture which remains respectful to its older neighbours. He was also responsible for a large redevelopment project for the University of London in Bloomsbury comprising the School of Oriental and African Studies (1972-74) and the Institutes of Education and of Law (1973-76). He was knighted in 1976 and received the RIBA Gold Medal the following year.

The National Theatre
1967-1976

Upper Ground, SE1 9PX • Tel 020 7452 3000 • www.nationaltheatre.org.uk • Nearest transport Waterloo, Southwark & Embankment LU • Open 9.30am until late, Monday to Saturday but check the website for details.

One of London's best known Brutalist buildings, a layered concrete landscape, the National Theatre stands on the South Bank of the Thames almost abutting Waterloo Bridge. The building is formed of two fly towers rising from the horizontal terraces that surround the core of the construction. The building contains three theatres within: the Olivier, seating 1,600 in its fan-shaped auditorium; the Lyttleton, has a more conventional arrangement of 890 seats, but the space is pillarless and therefore has excellent sightlines, and the smallest theatre, the Dorfman, formerly named the Cottesloe, is a flexible space seating up to 450 people. The cafés, restaurants and bars are open during the day to all, and there is often live music in the foyer space, which Lasdun referred to as 'the fourth theatre'.

The National Theatre building still courts controversy forty-odd years after its opening because of Lasdun's use of raw concrete left rough and 'unfinished' both inside and outside; a method of construction sometimes called *breton brut*. Here the rough-cast concrete surface shows the imprint of the sawn wooden planks used in the casting process. In 1988 Prince Charles described the building as 'a clever way of building a nuclear power station in the middle of London without anyone objecting', but nevertheless it is Grade II listed and is beloved, at least, by the thousands of theatregoers who patronise the place. *Area Map p.6, C:2*

The Royal College of Physicians
1960-1964

St Andrew's Place, Outer Circle, NW1 4LE •
www.rcplondon.ac.uk • Tel 020 3075 1543 •
Nearest transport Regent's Park and Great
Portland Street LU • Building, museum and
garden are open to the public, free of charge,
Monday to Friday, check website

Having acquired the bomb damaged property
Someries House in 1958, the Royal College
of Physicians sought an architect to fulfill the
brief of delivering a complex set of needs of
a particularly sensitive site - the new building
needing to 'harmonise' with the remaining
Nash properties nearby. The young Denys
Lasdun gave them a Modern masterpiece,
a spectacular feat of engineering and one of
the first post-war buildings in London to be
awarded Grade I listing.

It is difficult to choose architectural highlights
of the College, there are so many. However,
the Censors' Room is particularly interesting -
from the exterior the cube-shaped room seems
to float above the ground floor, its interior
walls are covered with the same Spanish oak
panelling dating from 1674 and used in three
previous homes.

This is a building that should be visited to be
truly appreciated and the College generously
opens their doors to share their wonderful
building with the public. *Area Map p.4, C:2*

GEOFFREY POWELL
(1920-1999)
PETER CHAMBERLIN
(1919-1978)
CHRISTOPH BON
(1921-1999)

Powell formed the partnership with two fellow teachers at Kingston Polytechnic having recently won the competition to build the Golden Lane Estate (1952-63), consisting of flats and maisonettes for single people and couples, on the very edge of the City (now Islington, following boundary changes). The commission to build the much larger Barbican Estate on adjacent land was subsequently awarded to the practice. Although the firm's name is synonymous with these two housing estates, the main body of their work can be found at universities throughout the UK. The practice was never particularly affiliated to one philosophy of design, but were obviously influenced by Le Corbusier and his 'house as a machine' ethos as well as Brutalism and Modernism.

The Barbican Estate
1963-1973, with some work ongoing until 1981

City of London, EC2Y 8DS • Nearest transport Barbican or St Paul's LU • www.barbican.org.uk for details of events at the Barbican Centre and tours of the estate

In an attempt to repopulate the post-war City, a thirty-five acre site of extensive bomb damage was cleared for high density housing, a cultural centre, school and a music college, collectively to be known as the Barbican Estate, so named because of its proximity to the Roman and later fortifications along London Wall.

The scheme had to incorporate the idea of a City-wide 'walkway' or 'ped-way', much of which has been achieved, but, until recently, only within the Barbican Estate, see the entry for 'Ken Shuttleworth' later in this chapter. The small church of St Giles Cripplegate (mid-16th century, with heavy 19th-century and post-war restoration) had to be considered, as did the livery halls of the Barber-Surgeons and the Ironmongers. They all sit happily, cheek-by-jowl with their new neighbours.

In the Barbican, Chamberlin, Powell and Bon gave London, arguably, one of the best housing schemes of the twentieth century. Three tower blocks, which for some considerable time were the tallest residential buildings in Europe, and a number of long terraces of flats accommodate up to 6,500 people in a largely car-free environment. Dark grey Welsh Pen Lee granite-faced concrete and deep red engineering brick are the materials that predominate, with the architects giving their full attention to detailing for the one hundred or so differing types of flat, from door handles to waste disposal units. The scheme was conceived as rented housing for City workers of all salary levels, although the consequences of the 'Right to Buy' in the 1980s has left the Barbican Estate well out of reach for all but the very wealthy.

Much attention was also given to the landscaping, with many of the 'cultural' buildings - the 2,000 seater Barbican Hall, the excellent Barbican Theatre, City of London School for Girls and the Guildhall School of Music and Drama, art galleries, as well as the bars, cafés and restaurants - accessible from a pleasant area with a lake and outdoor seating.

Detractors hate the intense use of concrete and the (deliberately) rough finish, although residents and users, generally, love the Estate. A good place to visit and wander, but even better is to take the 'Architecture Tour' offered - see the Barbican Centre website for details. *Area Map p.8, B:3*

ALISON (1928-1993) & PETER SMITHSON (1923-2003)

Often referred to as 'the architects' architects', Alison and Peter Smithson are untypical of their profession in that the buildings they are most noted for were undertaken at the beginning of their working lives. They met at Newcastle School of Architecture, moving to London in 1949 to work with the LCC until the following year when they won a competition to design a secondary school in Hunstanton, Norfolk, to critical acclaim. Two major London projects soon followed, firstly in 1964 The Economist Building, described below, in swanky St James's and the ill-fated Robin Hood Gardens in the Isle of Dogs (1967-72). This unfortunate foray into local authority housing divided opinion – residents hated the inconvenient, dank, leaky flats, whereas non-resident theorists loved them. Demolition of the Robin Hood Garden scheme is currently underway.

The Economist Building
1964

The Economist Building, 25 St James's Street, SW1A 1HG • Nearest transport Green Park LU (Victoria, Piccadilly, and Jubilee lines) • No public access

An office block of 1960s vintage which still looks fresh and relevant. The building consists of three towers of differing heights arranged around a shallow pedestrian plaza. The four-storey smallest tower directly faces St James's Street and was originally designed as bank premises. The tallest tower of 15 storeys was the home of The Economist magazine, the commissioning client of the project, and the third block is an eight-storey residential tower. The towers are made from concrete with Portland stone spandrels and pilasters with aluminium window frames. The minimal structural design of the buildings evokes a high Modernist aesthetic, providing excellent natural light due to their 'centre core' construction. In 1988 Skidmore, Owings & Merrill renovated the building, infilling some of the colonnades around the plaza and reconfiguring the interiors.

The whole building sits well with its neighbours such as Boodles Club (1765) without a hint of imitation or mockery. This was the first 1960s building to be Grade II listed, nevertheless its prime location makes it a sitting target for future development. *Area Map p.6, A:2*

RICHARD ROGERS,
LORD ROGERS OF RIVERSIDE (b1933)

Born to cultivated, anglophile Italian parents, Rogers and his family fled Florence on the eve of war to settle in London. He is the cousin of Ernesto Rogers, Modernist architect of the one hundred metre tall Torre Velasca, built in the 1950s in the centre of Milan, and the young Richard spent time working in his office.

Richard Rogers studied architecture at the Architectural Association, winning a scholarship to Yale where he met fellow British student Norman Foster with whom he formed Team 4, together with their then wives Su Brumwell and Wendy Cheeseman. By 1970 Team 4 was no more. Rogers had met Renzo Piano and the two young architects were rather surprised to find they were the winners of an international competition to design a new arts complex in the historic heart of Paris, the Pompidou Centre, also known as Beaubourg. They gave Paris a building of such futuristic design that it not only turned the world of architecture upside down, but inside out too. The Centre presented to an unsuspecting public the concept of High Tech, a marrying of architecture and engineering expressed in the use of steel and glass, exposed services and flexible interiors. Completed in 1976, it was immediately voted 'Most Popular Building in France'.

Since that time Richard Rogers has been almost a household name, having built some of London's instantly recognisable buildings within various partnerships - The Millennium Dome, now known as the O2 Arena, see 'Greenwich Walk'; the Channel 4 Headquarters at 124 Horseferry Road; 88 Wood Street, in the City, the building with the colourful ventilation funnels; the 225 metre tall so-called 'Cheesegrater' at 122 Leadenhall Street and 'One Hyde Park', a complex of mixed luxury residences and retail units in Knightsbridge.

Richard Rogers was knighted in 1991, awarded the RIBA Gold Medal in 1985 and the prestigious Pritzker Prize in 2007.

Lloyd's of London
1978-1986

One Lime Street, EC3M 7HA• Tel 020 7327 1000 • Nearest transport Monument LU • www.lloyds.com/lloyds/about-us/the-lloyds-building/virtual-tour • Public visiting very limited (pre-booked group tours only)

Not everyone loved Rogers' introduction to the future of architecture in the guise of the Pompidou Centre, Paris, which makes it all the more extraordinary that the very epitome of City conservatism, Lloyd's of London, should ask Richard Rogers to create a new building for them. On this project Rogers worked in collaboration with fellow architect Mike Davies and engineer Peter Roman Rice of Ove Arup and Partners.

Lloyd's of London began providing marine insurance from Edward Lloyd's coffee house over three hundred years ago and has since expanded into many aspects of insurance. Lloyd's is not a company in the conventional sense, but a market where members join together to form syndicates to insure risks, which have included anything from sporting events to actresses' legs. During its long history, Lloyd's business has outgrown various premises around the City and only commissioned its first custom-designed headquarters during the 1920s. That building was the work of Sir Edwin Cooper, but was outgrown and another move was made in the 1950s, which again subsequently proved inadequate.

This is when the notion of High Tech design, with its emphasis on the flexible use of space, became attractive. Many of the features of Richard Rogers' Lloyd's building can be traced back to design elements employed at the Pompidou Centre. Most notable is that all the vertical structures and services, such as stairwells and cloakroom pods, are placed in the rounded stainless steel ribs on the outside of the building, along with essential pipe work, ducts and an array of glass passenger lifts. The pushing of these services to the outer flanks of the structure allows for an uninterrupted floor space within. The construction took eight years to finish and used almost 34,000 cubic metres of concrete, 30,000 square metres of stainless steel cladding and 12,000 square metres of glass in the process.

At the heart of the building is the 'Room', a huge glazed atrium where the underwriters and brokers work, an area that can be expanded, or indeed contracted, should the need arise, and is served by a bank of criss-crossing escalators. The great arched shape of the glass exterior is something of a nod to Sir Horace Jones' Victorian Leadenhall Market next door. The Room contains the famous Lutine Bell, salvaged from a ship wreck of 1859, which has been hung in a succession of Lloyd's Underwriting Rooms and is still rung to herald announcements - one stroke for good news, two for bad. The Bell, weighing some 106 pounds, hangs under carved wooden tempietto, designed by Cooper for his 1920s building.

On the ninth floor of this iconic glass and steel building, sitting within a free-standing stone box, is the Board Room; an elegant 18-th-century space designed by eminent architect Robert Adam. Originally built for the 1st Earl of Shelburne as an addition to Bowood House in Wiltshire, the whole room was rescued from becoming rubble when the rest of the house, in a neglected and sorry state, was demolished in the 1950s. The Adam room had been incorporated into the 1950's Lloyd's headquarters and was again moved, this time to heights unimagined by its original architect, to Rogers' building. Sir Edwin Cooper's galleried, wood-panelled library from the 1920s building has also been preserved and incorporated within the basement area. His 1922 Lloyd's War Memorial portico, made of Portland stone, now forms the Leadenhall Street entrance screen.

This striking, bold building, which was awarded Grade I listing in 2011, made Richard Rogers' reputation as one of Britain's outstanding architects. Public visiting is limited to pre-booked groups, but Lloyd's have participated in the Open House scheme (see p.403) for many years, when staff generously share their love of the place. If you are unable to be in London for Open House, an evening stroll around the City will reveal the building aglow with coloured lights, designed by the ingenious 'Imagination' team.
Area Map p.9, C:2

Maggie's Centre
Rogers Stirk Harbour & Partners, 2008

Charing Cross Hospital, Fulham Palace Road, W6 8RF • Tel 020 7386 1750 • www.maggiescentres.org • Nearest transport Baron's Court LU

Built at the front of Charing Cross Hospital, it is an oasis of calm where people with cancer, their family and friends can access the support they need free of charge.

The Centre is named for the founder of the movement, Maggie Keswick Jencks, a writer and designer who collaborated with her husband, architect Charles Jencks, on a number of projects. When Maggie was diagnosed with cancer in 1993 she decided to spend her time creating a place where people would be helped not just to cope with the disease but to fight it – as she did. The first Centre was opened in Edinburgh in 1996, with two more built in Scotland, designed by internationally renowned architects, Frank Gehry and Zaha Hadid, and many others are in the planning stage around the country.

Very much in the spirit of their founder, the organisation strives to create spaces that are non-institutional and domestic in scale, but which are also unique. Architects are asked to design buildings where people feel safe and valued, and also to create an atmosphere that stimulates their imagination. Richard Rogers has risen to the challenge of an awkward plot facing a busy road and has designed an uplifting building consisting of a double-height kitchen, three sitting rooms, as well as other smaller spaces for more private conversations, and a courtyard garden. Light floods into this cheerful-looking little orange-red building from the glazed walls at the first floor level and roof lights.

This building won Richard Rogers and his team the ultimate accolade of being awarded the prestigious RIBA Stirling Prize for 2009.

NORMAN FOSTER,
BARON FOSTER OF THAMES BANK (b 1935)

'Iconic architecture' is a somewhat overused term, but much of Norman Foster's work is just that. One only needs to think of the simple grace of the Millau Viaduct in France (2004), the ingenious marrying-up of the old with the new at the Reichstag in Berlin and the one-mile perfect circle that is the Apple Inc headquarters in California (2017).

Foster studied architecture at the University of Manchester from the age of twenty-one, winning a scholarship to Yale where he met fellow Brit, Richard Rogers, with whom he went into partnership, together with their wives Su Brummell and Wendy Cheeseman, on their return to Britain, as Team 4. The practice disbanded in the late 1960s, but different and varied partnerships followed, with Foster winning some interesting commissions, mostly abroad or at least outside of London. Stanstead Airport, not in the capital - but nearly - completed in 1991, showed the high-tech elegance for which he would become rightly famous.

Following the success of Foster's Stanstead Airport, London came calling with plum projects that would seal his reputation as one of the world's leading architects. He was knighted in 1990, was appointed to the Order of Merit in 1997 and was raised to the peerage as Baron Foster of Thames Bank in 1999. He was awarded the RIBA Gold Medal for Architecture in 1983, the Pritzker Prize in 1999 and on 24 April 2017 Lord Foster was given the Freedom of the City of London

See also The South Bank Walk in 'Walking London's Architecture' on p.322.

Sackler Galleries
1991

The Royal Academy of Arts, Burlington House, Piccadilly, W1J 0BD • Tel 020 7300 8000 • www.royalacademy.org.uk • Nearest transport Piccadilly Circus or Green Park LU • Admission free – except for special exhibitions) • See website for opening times

Climb the sweep of glass stairs to the Sackler Galleries, passing what used to be the exterior of the old building and take in the sheer beauty of the former façade that could well have gone unnoticed until given this opportunity to be seen on its own level. This tends to happen with Foster's buildings in that, wonderful as they are in themselves, they also open up the surroundings, whether it be a view, another part of the building or simply the sky.

You may prefer to take the glass-walled lift to the Galleries, but whether by lift or stairs, when you arrive you will be greeted by the bright space and clean lines of the top-lit ante room which beautifully displays some of the Academy's best sculpture, including Michaelangelo's Virgin and Child with the Infant St John.

Much of the new gallery space has been gleaned from the isolated and seldom visited Diploma Galleries. Norman Foster's fusion of the old and the new here has been universally acclaimed as nothing short of a masterpiece, sitting very well within Burlington House, one of the few surviving 18th-century mansions in this part of London. The Royal Academy moved to these premises, so much larger than its cramped quarters in the old Somerset House, in 1868, the 100th anniversary of its foundation. (See also the section on David Chipperfield in this chapter, p.271).

Great Court, British Museum

The Great Court, The British Museum
Robert Smirke, 1823-47 / Foster and Partners, 2000

British Museum, Great Russell Street, WC1B 3DG • Tel 020 7636 1555 • www.british-museum.org • Nearest transport Holborn, Russell Square or Tottenham Court Road LU • See website for opening times and details of special exhibitions

When the British Library moved to its new premises in St Pancras in 1998, the round Reading Room and its surrounding space was taken into use by the British Museum. Before the construction of the Reading Room by Sidney Smirke in 1855, the area had been an open courtyard, albeit not one that had been held in affection, having been called a 'miserable-looking space'. Norman Foster and his team have given the courtyard back to the public in spectacular fashion.

The Reading Room forms the core of the space, retaining its original function but now serving as a public reference library and exhibition space, whilst a staircase wraps around its exterior giving access to the restaurant (some of whose tables have fabulous views into Smirke's Reading Room) and to the upper galleries via a short walkway.

The whole Great Court area, the largest enclosed public space in Europe, is covered by a lightweight roof with 3312 glass panels – each one a different size. The roof structure rests on the perimeter walls and slender columns hidden by the skin of the Reading Room. The area feels somehow lighter than out of doors, with the only slight irritation being the noise level. However, even that cannot spoil the overall effect, especially when one can look up and see clouds scudding across the London sky or when the sun shines through the glass and casts shadows on the creamy marble beneath.

Judging by the crowds of people who now use this piazza this is one of the most successful and universally popular architectural and engineering feats of the modern age.

The Great Court has a bookshop, a gift shop, lecture theatres, education room and WCs as well as two cafés and access to galleries on the ground floor. *Area Map p.2-3, B:2*

City Hall
1998-2002

The Queen's Walk, SE1 2AA • Tel 020 7983 4000 • www.london.gov.uk/gla • Nearest transport London Bridge LU & Rail • City Hall is open to the public • See the website for opening times, events and exhibitions

This building is part of the 67 acre development in the area to the west of Tower Bridge on the south bank of the Thames, known as More London. The City Hall provides four acres of space on ten levels, housing the offices of the Mayor of London, five hundred staff members and the assembly chamber for the twenty five elected members of the London Assembly.

The curiously shaped glass building is entered either at the ground level or, better still, through a large, slightly sunken amphitheatre, paved with rather nice blue limestone and the focus of outdoor events. The amphitheatre entrance leads the visitor into a public café and on to an elliptical exhibition space where a dramatic, yet gently rising, ramp takes visitors up through the building affording fantastic views of London through the windows, or should we say walls? Visitors can see into the assembly chamber, which is also open to the public, and which provides two hundred and fifty seats for visitors and members of the press.

Beyond the assembly chamber level, the ramp curls on past the Mayor's Office to the public space at the top of the building. This area is known as 'London's Living Room' and has an external terrace encircling the whole of City Hall.

The form of the building is derived from a geometrically modified sphere, which provides the greatest volume with the least surface area, thereby minimising heat loss and thus saving energy. The building leans back towards the south where the floor plates step inwards to provide natural shading for the offices beneath. Energy saving schemes are employed throughout the building. Typical is the cooling system which uses cold ground water pumped from the water table and passed through beams in the ceilings, reducing, by approximately one quarter, the annual energy consumption. City Hall was the first building completed in the 'More London' complex – see 'South Bank Walk'. *Area Map p.8, C:1*

City Hall

30 St Mary Axe (Swiss Re Headquarters)
1997-2004

St Mary Axe, EC3A 8BF • Nearest transport Liverpool Street LU & Rail • Private offices, no public access

When the architecturally noted Baltic Exchange in the heart of the City was damaged beyond repair by an IRA bomb in 1992, those with an interest in such matters waited with bated breath to see what would replace it. What Norman Foster and his team have produced exceeds expectation for amid the rectangular and pointed City skyline emerged this rounded bullet-shaped building.

The 41 storey, 40,000 square metre construction has been described as 'London's first ecological tall building' and is inspired by Buckminster Fuller's theory of the 'Climatroffice'. Part of the low-energy environmental strategy is the provision of air conditioning whereby stale air is drawn into green garden spaces integrated into the workplace and re-oxygenated by the dense planting. Mechanical air conditioning is only used in a 'back-up' role as, joy of joys, the windows can be opened! The building's services, lifts and stairs are concentrated in a central core leaving the rest of the floor space free. The top two levels accommodate bars and restaurants, with the rest of the building being used for offices.

Opinion is mixed on this building's appearance – it is called the 'gherkin' by some, even worse names by others. However, in an age of computer aided design, architecture does not have to conform to what went before. More importantly, there are sound ecological reasons for curves (see City Hall, above). Such thought has been put into this structure, including the painstaking aerodynamic modelling of the tower to avoid down draughts, thereby ensuring those using the piazza outside are not buffeted by the wind. Tapering at the top into the crown reduces wind resistance further.

The building has 24,000 square metres of glass cladding, but interestingly, for a rounded construction, there is only one curved piece of glass and that is at the very top.

This building was the winner of the 2005 RIBA Stirling Prize. *Area Map p.8, C:2*

Wembley Stadium
Foster and Partners with HOK S+V+E, 2007

Wembley National Stadium, Wembley, HA9 0WS • Tel 0844 980 8001 • www.wembleystadium.com • Nearest Ttransport Wembley Park LU • See website for tours and events

Built on the site of the original 1923 stadium, constructed for the British Empire Exhibition of the following year with the purpose to 'stimulate trade, strengthen bonds that bind mother country to her sister states and daughters', and which became synonymous with football and sell-out rock concerts. Closed in 2000, this stadium was demolished three years later, when work began on its much-needed modern replacement.

The new stadium covers almost twice the area of the old, is nearly four times its height and has increased spectator capacity to 90,000 seated in one 'bowl' rather than four separate stands. A new feature is the partly retractable roof which keeps the spectator dry in the event of rain or snow, but does not cover the pitch. The 11-acre roof, weighing some 6,000 tonnes, is mostly supported by a giant arch, thereby eliminating the need for pillars inside the stadium, thus ensuring all spectators have a clear view of events.

The 133 metre tall arch is as much an iconic feature as the twin towers of the old building, perhaps more so as the new landmark can be seen from all over the capital, especially at night when it is illuminated. Constructed from British-made steel, it is 315 metres in length and of the longest single roof structure in the world. Facts and figures abound regarding this structure, such as the London Eye could fit between the top of the arch and the pitch, but perhaps it suffices to say that it is a truly amazing construction.

Regular tours of the Stadium are available, which include the opportunity to hold aloft the FA Cup, albeit only a replica.

Bloomberg European Headquarters
2017

3 Victoria Street, EC4N 4TQ • Nearest transport Mansion House or Cannon Street LU • Public access only to SPACE art gallery and London Mithraeum, see p.18 for details

Sited between St Paul's Cathedral and the Bank of England, Bloomberg's European Headquarters is the latest design by Foster in the City. The 3.2 acre site comprises two triangular office buildings united by bridges spanning a pedestrian thoroughfare providing access to shops, restaurants and SPACE, a contemporary art gallery which also houses the Roman Temple of Mithras, (see p.18).

Both the client, Michael Bllomberg, and the architect wanted the building to 'fit in' with the City – but this is no ubiquitous high-rise, with the top two floors of the twelve storeys set back so as to give the Illusion of a low-rise complex. In keeping with its neighbours, St Paul's and St Stephen Walbrook, it is enveloped in stone, and features 3,000 cubic square metres of English sandstone. The stone was cut to make three hundred beams and columns, with all selecting and matching done by eye. However, the complex design required curved stone pieces for the façade and these were worked in Tuscany, Italy, cut by hi-tech machinery, but finished by hand.

Skilled hands also worked the bronze fins which were finished in Japan using a unique, secret, colouring and finishing process known as Ryuka Ibushi. The fins change colour throughout the day, depending on the light, and will age gracefully, as well as play a vital role in the cooling of the building in hot weather. The fins have vents which can be opened or closed according to the weather with air pulled into the office spaces, through the atrium and up through the roof.

The building has pushed the boundaries of sustainable design and is the 'greenest' office in the world to date. This was confirmed by BREEAM, (Building Research Establishment Environmental Assessment Method), who gave it the highest score for sustainability. For example, the building uses 35% less energy and 73% less water than a typical office block of the same size.

The project cost a cool £1 billion, but brings's 4,000 London employees together, rather than scattering them across four different locations. The world's most sustainable office and certainly the largest stone building in the City of London since St Paul's Cathedral, Bloomberg European Headquaters won the coveted 2018 RIBA Stirling Prize for the UK's best new building. *Area Map p.8, B:2*

SIR MICHAEL HOPKINS (b1935) & LADY PATTY HOPKINS (b1942)

The name 'Hopkins' probably does not come to mind as easily as 'Foster' or 'Rogers', yet the practice of Hopkins Architects is often spoken of in the same context as those 'superstar' architects, with a portfolio of work that is technically brilliant, edgy and accessible.

Michael and Patty Hopkins, both Architectural Association trained, met whilst working in the studio of architect Frederick Gibberd. From 1969-1976 Michael was in partnership with Norman Foster, whilst Patty had her own practice, but in 1976 they joined forces to set up Hopkins Architects. One of their first projects was to build a home and office for themselves in Hampstead; a lightweight steel and plate glass structure entered via a small bridge and now Grade II listed.

The practice has produced an array of outstanding buildings around the world, as well as in Britain. In 1994, following the success of their work on the new Glyndebourne Opera House, they were jointly given the RIBA Gold Medal, the first British married couple to win the award. The Gold Medal citation describes the Hopkins' work as 'not only a matter of exploiting technology to build beautifully, nor simply of accommodating difficult and changing tasks in the most elegant way, but above all of capturing in stone and transmitting in bronze the finest aspirations of our age'.

Hopkins Architects appear to be busier than ever with master planning, refurbishing, and new buildings. Listed below are a few examples of their work. See also Portcullis House in 'Whitehall Walk' (see p.353), Haberdashers Hall in 'Bartholomew Walk' (see p.285), St James' Café in 'Eat and Drink Architecture' (see p.372) and the Buckingham Palace Ticket Office in 'John Nash Walk' (see p.320).

Evelina London Children's Hospital
2005

St Thomas' Hospital, Westminster Bridge Road, SE1 7EH • www.evelinalondon.nhs.uk • No public access

The practice has completed some outstanding healthcare facilities - the UCH Macmillan Cancer Centre and the Institute of Immunity and Transplantation at the Royal Free Hospital being two recent examples. The construction of the Evelina Children's Hospital, on the site of a former nurses' home at St Thomas's Hospital, won many accolades for Hopkins, not least the RIBA Regional and National Award, the Stirling Prize People's Choice, and the Building Better Healthcare Awards, Best NHS Hospital Design.

This building places the young patient at the centre of everything - no long, forbidding corridors here. Open plan, where possible, the upper floors are reached by two bright red lift towers and the predominant use of glass makes the whole place light and airy, with some areas having views over Lambeth Palace Gardens. *Area Map p.6, C:1*

Wellcome Trust Gibbs Building (2004)

215 Euston Road, NW1 2BE • Tel 020 7611 8888 • www.wellcome.ac.uk • Nearest transport Euston, Euston Square, Warren Street LU • No public access, but weekly tours of the Heatherwick sculpture can be booked - see website

Two major projects, side by side on one of London's busiest roads, undertaken for the Wellcome Foundation, one of the world's largest medical research charities.

The first, known as the Gibbs Building, brings together over 500 staff members of the Wellcome Trust, who had previously been housed in two separate buildings nearby. The ten-storey, 28,000 square metre construction, is open plan with a glazed atrium and a 90 metre 'street' running the length of the building. At the west end of the atrium hangs the Thomas Heatherwick sculpture 'Bleigiessen', made of 150,000 coloured glass spheres suspended on one million metres of stainless steel wire and rising the height of six storeys.

Its neighbour, at 183 Euston Road, was originally built in the 1930s by Septimus Warwick, architect of Lambeth Town Hall, who was commissioned by Sir Henry Wellcome to house research laboratories, a large sculpture court and exhibition spaces. This neoclassical building has been remodelled to

Wellcome Collection (1932)

183 Euston Road, NW1 2BE • Tel 020 7611 2222 • www. wellcomecollection.org • Nearest transport Euston, Euston Square, Warren Street LU • The building is generally open seven days a week (check website for details) • Entrance is free

create the Wellcome Collection. The layout of the building has been simplified and the ground floor windows on to the Euston Road have been enlarged. It is now an inviting, exciting place to visit with permanent and temporary exhibitions, a huge reference library, a bookshop, restaurant and an excellent café.
Area Map p.4, C:2

London 2012 Velodrome
2009-2011

Queen Elizabeth Olympic Park, Abercrombie Road, E20 3AB • www.visitleevalley.org.uk/en/content/cms/london2012/velo-park • Nearest transport Stratford, Stratford International LU

One of the four permanent structures built for the London 2012 Olympics, the others being the London Stadium (Populous Architects), London Aquatics Centre (Zaha Hadid) and the Copper Box Arena (Make Architects).

Perhaps one of the most instantly recognisable buildings in London that is not a skyscraper. The distinctive shape of the roof has been likened to a certain brand of potato crisp, hence its nickname 'the Pringle', but it is a lovely building, simple and elegant. 'Cycling inspired the concept for the Velodrome, the bicycle is an ingenious ergonomic object that is honed to unrivalled efficiency' say the architects. Indeed, it was the most energy efficient building on the Olympic site and has been called the most sustainable stadium ever.

Now part of the Lee Valley Velopark - see the website for details.

RENZO PIANO
(b 1937)

Renzo Piano was born in Genoa into a family of builders and trained at Milan Polytechnic and the offices of Louis Khan in the USA. His passion for construction and 'doing things' is reflected in his architectural practice's name 'Renzo Piano Building Workshop', and its ethos 'We do not only design things here, but we also make things, and test them'.

His first brush with fame came early in his career, when he and Richard Rogers built the Pompidou Centre, Paris, in the mid-1970s. Since that time Renzo Piano's architecture has graced many places in the world - from airports to museums and galleries, from master planning to housing developments and from office blocks to a pilgrim church. He was awarded the RIBA Gold Medal in 1989 and the Pritzker Prize in 1998.

His first building in London, Central St Giles, completed in 2010, is a mixed-use development, consisting of one fifteen-storey residential block and one eleven-storey office block. London seemed underwhelmed with some critics calling it 'tacky', whilst others praised 'a colourful addition to what was a drab part of town'. Likewise, his next London project, The Shard, also divides opinion.

The Shard
2009-2012

32 London Bridge Street, London SE1 9SG • www.the-shard.com • See website for details of visiting the building • Nearest transport London Bridge LU

Renzo Piano apparently took inspiration from the spires of London's churches for his design of The Shard, a building that can been seen from most points in London and some beyond.

The slender pyramidal form contains a mixed-use development with direct access to and from the busy transport hub of London Bridge station at ground level. Immediately above are three floors of restaurants and bars with offices, making use of the large floor plates, occupying levels four to twenty-eight. The Shangri-La Hotel occupies the central section of the building, with residences above, where the building is slender enough for apartments to have views on all sides. The final floors accommodate the highest public viewing galleries in the country - 240 metres above street level.

A spectacular glass and steel spire atop the 95 storeys forms its summit. Eight sloping glass facades, the 'shards', define the shape and visual quality of the tower, fragmenting the scale of the building and reflecting the light in unpredictable ways. The weather, light and colour of the sky change how we see it. Lightness and transparency are key to this piece of architecture - its elegance contrasting with the bulky high-rise blocks elsewhere. Questions have been raised as to the wisdom of using so much glass, but a ventilated double skin façade reduces the heat gain and improves comfort. Excess heat from the offices is used to heat the hotel and apartments and any additional heat Is dissipated naturally through a sixteen storey radiator at the top of the tower. Winter gardens with operable windows are located on each floor, allowing the occupants to connect with the outside world.

The building is designed to maintain its stability under the most onerous conditions. Its early conceptual designs were among the first in the UK to be realised following the publication of the US National Institute of Standards and Technology report into the World Trade Centre collapse, which has resulted in the global re-evaluation of the design of tall structures.
Area Map p.8, C:1

TERRY FARRELL
(b 1938)

Terry Farrell is regarded as one the "big five" of late 20th-century British architecture, along with Norman Foster, Richard Rogers, Michael Hopkins and Nicholas Grimshaw. Farrell and Grimshaw worked together in partnership for fifteen years, but in 1980 they split up, moving in different architectural directions.

While Grimshaw continued working in the High-Tech style (see the Cutty Sark entry in the 'Greenwich' section of 'Walking London's Architecture'), Farrell became one of the few architects who did not shy away from being labelled a Postmodernist and responsible for some of London's first important examples of that style.

Manchester-born Farrell studied architecture at Newcastle University and furthered his studies at the University of Pennsylvania, under Louis Khan and doyens of Postmodernism, Denise Scott Brown and Robert Venturi.

Two examples of Farrell's work are listed below. See also Alban Gate in 'Eat and Drink Architecture'.

Embankment Place
1985-1990

Charing Cross, WC2N • Nearest transport Embankment LU or Charing Cross LU & Rail • Public access along walkways to Hungerford Bridge and Charing Cross Station but no public access to Embankment Place

Embankment Place was built to take advantage of 'air rights' over Charing Cross Station, rising nine storeys over the railway tracks to provide office and retail space, the latter at various points around the complex. Constructed from red brick and polished black stone with a huge curved roof and stone clad towers, Embankment Place is arguably one of London's finest examples of Postmodernist architecture – witty, neo-eclectic and in absolute contrast to the bland concrete blocks of previous decades. *Area Map p.6, B:2*

Vauxhall Cross
1982-1992

85 Albert Embankment, SE1 7TP • Nearest transport Vauxhall LU/Rail • No public access

Seen at its best from the opposite bank of the Thames with one's back to Tate Britain, Vauxhall Cross was designed and built as a general office complex and was only announced as the headquarters of the British Intelligence Service, otherwise known as 'MI6', after the design was commissioned. Until then the Secret Service had been housed in nameless Government blocks, but there is nothing anonymous about this ostentatious building. Indeed, the exterior has featured in many films, notably in two James Bond productions, 'The World is Not Enough', and 'Skyfall', where in the latter the building is 'blown up' – much to the delight of critics of Farrell's Postmodern design. The building incorporates a public riverside walkway, but small windows ensure none of its interior workings can be seen.

Its stepped construction, not unlike a ziggurat – hence its nickname of 'Babylon on Thames' – is emphasised by the use of contrasting materials - pale concrete cladding and dark wall glazing. Unsurprisingly, Vauxhall Cross, for all its 'openness', is very much a modern-day fortress with banks of security cameras, inside and out, with walls, doors and windows that repel electronic eavesdropping and jamming, as well as being bullet and bomb proof.

DANIEL LIBESKIND
(b 1946)

Daniel Libeskind was born in Lodz in Poland before moving to Israel at the age of eleven and then to the United States two years later. He studied at New York's Cooper Union architecture school, then spent two years at the University of Essex where he received a post graduate degree in the history and theory of architecture in 1972.

Following more than a decade of teaching and writing, Libeskind won the commission to build the Jewish Museum in Berlin, and produced a building of such theoretic, physical and emotional dynamism that in 1999 over a quarter of a million people visited the finished site, before any of the exhibits were installed.

Libeskind was now the 'go to' architect for projects where emotions needed architectural interpretation. His Imperial War Museum North, in Salford (1997-2001), takes the form of interlocking shards of a shattered world, and has been much praised. However, his portfolio is a varied one, albeit not always fulfilled. His design for an extension to the Victoria and Albert Museum, the 'Spiral', which one commentator described as 'the Guggenheim in Bilbao turned on its side and then beaten senseless with a hammer', was rather too much for the powers-that-be and the project was sadly shelved in 2005.

Graduate Centre, London Metropolitan University
2004

London Metropolitan University, 166-220 Holloway Road, N7 8DB • Nearest transport Holloway Road LU • No public access to the interior, group visits can be booked by contacting the University's Marketing Department on Tel: 020 7423 0000

How does one go about designing a building that can sing?' Daniel Libeskind posed this question in his book 'Breaking Ground' written during the construction of his Graduate Centre for the London Metropolitan University. The project is the only Libeskind building in London and was completed within a modest budget of three million pounds and on the architecturally unremarkable Holloway Road.

The three dramatically intersecting blocks clad in embossed coloured stainless steel form a shining, ever-changing surface, pierced with windows and doors at irregular angles. Nothing seems to stand still and yet the building sits perfectly poised in its urban setting – not shouting but singing.

The project attracted a string of prestigious awards, notably a RIBA Prize in 2004, a special prize in the Royal Fine Art Commission Trust's 'Building of the Year Awards' and the Jeu d'Esprit 'Future Project Award' made by the Architectural Review.

Graduate Centre, London Metropolitan University

WILL ALSOP
(1947-2018)

Although Alsop's architectural output was not huge, it was certainly original. Born in Northampton, he studied at the Architectural Association School of Architecture and worked in the offices of Modernists Maxwell Fry and Jane Drew as well as Cedric Price. Arguably some of his best work was done abroad, for example the good people of Marseilles have for their local government offices 'Le Grand Bleu', (1990-4), his first great success. A whale on stilts the locals call it, nonetheless, as with most of his designs, it attracted attention and awards. Sadly, Will Alsop died in May 2018.

Palestra
2009

197 Blackfriars Road, SE1 8AA • Transport for London Customer Service Office • No public access

'If you built it, they will come'. In 2000 Will Alsop's Peckham Library not only won the RIBA Stirling Prize, it also made a neglected part of the Borough of Southwark rather funky. There is little doubt that Palestra is doing the same for this part of the Borough – this is the sort of building that stops you in your tracks to say 'wow'!

Reminiscent of a Minorcan prehistoric taula on stilts, the tilted lower part of Palestra is clad in a structurally bonded double glazed curtain walling system, with each panel having a colour printed full height across one-third the width of the glazing, giving a patchwork effect. This highly original piece of architecture was commissioned as speculative office space and is currently the home of the Transport for London Customer Service Office.

Alsop's North Greenwich tube station, next to the 02 Arena, was also much praised and nominated for the Stirling Prize in 1999.
Area Map p.8, A:1

Right: Palestra, winner of 2007 RIBA National Award

JACQUES HERZOG (b 1950)
PIERRE DE MEURON (b 1950)

Both Herzog and de Meuron were born in Basel, within a month or so of each other and both studied at Zurich Polytechnic. In 1978 they opened their architectural practice in their home town, which has now grown to a team of five partners, forty associates and over four hundred projects worldwide.

The architects often cite Joseph Beuys as an enduring artistic inspiration and collaborate with different artists on each architectural project. In 2012 they worked with Ai Weiwei on the Serpentine's annual pavillion commission to much critical acclaim.

In 2001 Herzog and de Meuron were awarded the Pritzker Prize and won the 2003 Stirling Prize for the simply beautiful Leban Dance Centre at Deptford Creek (Trinity Laban Conservatoire of Music and Dance, Laban Building, Creekside, SE8 3DZ). In 2007 they were awarded the RIBA Gold Medal.

Tate Modern
Giles Gilbert Scott, 1947-1963
Herzog and de Meuron, 2000

Bankside, SE1 9TG • Tel 020 7887 8888 • www.tate.org.uk • Nearest transport Southwark LU • Admission free (apart from major exhibitions) • See website for opening times, exhibitions, events and wheelchair access

As the world's most visited contemporary art gallery, the Tate Modern building itself is perhaps as much a draw as the exhibits it contains. This magnificent landmark on the south side of the Thames started life as the Bankside Power Station when post-war London required more energy than it was then producing.

Architect Giles Gilbert Scott, grandson of George, won the commission in 1947 amid great controversy. Londoners were appalled at the thought of something as utilitarian as a power station being constructed directly across the river to the iconic St Paul's Cathedral. Indeed Lord Llewellin made an impassioned plea in the House of Lords against the project stating 'However good the architect,...it will be rather like introducing an alligator into the water-lily pond in one's garden.'

Nonetheless building went ahead but the oil-fired power station was not completed until 1963. The construction is of brick-cladding over a steel frame with a centrally placed chimney, which was limited to a height of 325 feet (99 metres), just shorter than the dome of St Paul's, thus complying with the architectural etiquette of London.

The rapidly rising cost of oil rendered Bankside uneconomical and it was closed in 1981, with its future under threat until 1994 when Nicholas Serota, the far-sighted director of the Tate Gallery, chose this building to display its collection of international modern art. The competition to oversee the £134 million scheme, (much of the funding came from the National Lottery), was won by Jacques Herzog and Pierre de Meuron, who, whilst leaving the visible exterior, including the chimney, almost untouched, fashioned the interior into galleries. The turbine hall, measuring 550 feet long, 75 feet wide and 115 feet high and entered by a huge ramp, provides a perfect space for hosting large-scale temporary exhibitions. This first stage of the Tate was opened in May 2000 and during its two decades an estimated 45 million visitors have been awed by this fabulous building.

So successful was the re imagining of the Turbine Hall and galleries, it was decided to take the project further and in 2005 Herzog and de Meuron were commissioned to conjure further space for the gallery. The result was unveiled in 2016 to great excitement. The 'extension' has yielded over 22,000 square metres of space for exhibition displays, workshops, educational sessions, offices, catering and retail. Three original, subterranean oil tanks have been transformed - two of which provide spaces for live performance art and the third is used as an auxiliary space. Above the tanks, rising ten floors, is the Switch House, also known as the Blavatnik Building, named for a major donor of the project. The pyramidal form of the tower has been constructed from a perforated brick screen. through which light filters in during the day and flows out at night.

A trip to level ten of the Switch House brings the visitor to a 360 degree viewing gallery, providing panoramic views over London. Even if you take the lift to the top of the building, do have a look at the staircases - they have, quite rightly, been likened to a piece of sculpture.
Area Map p.8, A:1

ZAHA HADID
(1950-2016)

It is something of a sad fact that, despite Iraqi-born Zaha Hadid making London her home and work-base, there is little of her architecture to be seen in the capital. There were many plans, but little came to fruition. The London Olympics Aquatics Pool (see below) and the small Serpentine Sackler Gallery (2013), see 'Eat and Drink Architecture' on p.362, are her only public buildings in the capital, but both are fine examples of her work.

A mathematics graduate from Baghdad, Zaha Hadid studied at the Architectural Association, tutored by Rem Koolhaas, for whom she worked in Rotterdam until she returned to London in 1980 and set up her own practice. Her first commission of note was for a fire station in Weil am Rhine in Germany (1993) then a ski jump in Innsbruck, Austria (2002) and as the projects got larger, so the architecture became more extravagant, but always elegant. Hadid was not known as the 'queen of the curve' for nothing. See her practice website www.zaha-hadid.com for her full portfolio.

At the time of her sudden death in 2016, Zaha Hadid had projects, built, in progress or still 'on the drawing board', all around the globe. Her practice, which still bears her name, is now run by her long-time business collaborator Patrik Schumacher.

Zaha Hadid was the first female recipient of the Pritzker Prize in 2004 and her numerous awards included being made Dame Commander of the Order of the British Empire in 2012. She won the RIBA European Award several times and scooped the 2011 RIBA Stirling Prize for The Evelyn Grace Academy in London (no public access). In 2016, a few months before she died, she was awarded the RIBA Gold Medal, again, the first female to receive this accolade. She had held teaching posts at the Architectural Association and the Universities of Harvard, Chicago, Columbia and Cambridge.

Aquatics Centre, Queen Elizabeth Olympic Park

2012

Aquatics Centre, Queen Elizabeth Olympic Park, E20 2ZQ • Tel 020 3201 2000 • www.londonaquaticscentre.org • Nearest transport Stratford and Hackney Wick LU

Of all the buildings that made up the 2012 Olympic Park, Zaha Hadid's Aquatic Centre was hailed as the 'Gateway to the Games'. The roof of this iconic building is wave shaped, the frame of which was made from steel trusses fabricated in Newport from plate rolled in Gateshead, Motherwell and Scunthorpe and rests on just three concrete supports. The construction of this 160 metre long, 2,800 tonne spectacular aluminium-covered roof is thought to be one of most complex projects undertaken in the Olympic Park. The ceiling is made of timber cladding that sweeps outside to cover the northern roof supports.

The interior is a pleasing sweep of curves and glass, the Centre originally comprised a competition pool, a water polo pool and a diving pool, with a total seating capacity of 17,500. The facility is now open to the public, a permanent fixture in the community with facilities that were previously unavailable in London. It is worth visiting to look at the six concrete diving boards alone – they protrude like tongues over the water.

London Wall Place

KEN SHUTTLEWORTH
(b 1952)

Not a name that is widely known, Ken Shuttleworth was a key contributor on many of the projects that came from Norman Foster's studio where he was a partner for many years. Such buildings as City Hall, Wembley Stadium and 30 St Mary Axe (nicknamed the Gherkin), originated from Shuttleworth's hand.

After completing his architectural studies in Leicester, where he was affectionately known as 'Ken the Pen', as he could draw much quicker than anyone else, he joined Foster's practice in the 1970s, eventually becoming a partner. In 2004 he left to form 'Make', an employee-owned architectural practice with 150 people working in three offices - London, Hong Kong and Sydney. Their London work includes residential and educational establishments as well as the inevitable office design.

Of particular note is London Wall Place, consisting of two large office blocks constructed on a site which had to incorporate a sizeable section of Roman Wall and Saxon remains. High-level walkways or pedways have been introduced as have green and pleasant gardens reminiscent of the site's neighbour, the Barbican Estate, making this part of the City very people-friendly.

City of London Information Centre
2007

St Paul's Churchyard, EC4M 8BX • www.visitthecity.co.uk • Nearest transport St Paul's and Mansion House LU • Open daily

Reminiscent of a paper-aeroplane, this dynamic, contemporary little building is situated to the south-west of the South Transept of St Paul's Cathedral and only a few steps from the Millennium Bridge, which is the pedestrian link from the City to Tate Modern.

The folded metallic envelope is constructed as a steel frame braced by a structural ply skin and clad in 220 pre-finished stainless steel panels, the subtly reflected surfaces of which contrast superbly with the pale stone of St Paul's. The interior, lined with a tessellation of 174 vivid yellow panels formed from 'Trespa', a recycled timber product, is bathed in natural light from the full-height glazed frontage and the triangular rooflights.

Constructed off-site in two sections, this building was craned into place during the night and finished off within a couple of days. The rainwater that falls on the roof is collected to irrigate nearby planting and to flush the building's toilets.
Area Map p.8, A:2

DAVID CHIPPERFIELD
(b 1953)

It is somewhat of an irony that for London born and trained David Chipperfield, major projects for the capital have, until recently, eluded him, despite his brilliant work in other parts of the world.

After graduating from the Architectural Association in 1977, Chipperfield worked in the offices of both Norman Foster and Richard Rogers, before setting up his own practice in 1985. He now heads four offices – London, Berlin, Shanghai and Milan-reflecting his global portfolio.

Major international works include public buildings in Anchorage, Des Moines and St Louis in the USA; the City of Justice in Barcelona, the America's Cup Building in Valencia and the Museum of Modern Literature, Marbach, Germany, for which he was awarded the RIBA Stirling Prize in 2007.

In 1997, his practice was chosen to rebuild the Neues Museum on Berlin's Museum Island, a hugely important undertaking not only for German cultural life, but for the architect too. Enemy bomb damage during World War II and subsequent neglect, made for a sorry state of affairs for this beautiful Friedrich August Stuler masterpiece, finished in 1859. Chipperfield coaxed a modest yet triumphant elegance from this building and it is universally admired.

The success of the Neues Museum must have gone some way to the securing of the Royal Academy expansion in London.

Chipperfield's work in Britain, outside of London, has included the Turner Contemporary, on the beachfront at Margate in Kent and The Hepworth Wakefield on the bank of the River Calder, both opened in 2011 to great acclaim. Chipperfield has one new build on the new King's Cross development: 1 Pancras Square, an eight-floor speculative office and one of a cluster in the area. The use of short, cast iron columns make the building stand apart from its neighbours. In the 1980s Chipperfield was commissioned by Anthony Gormley to design a studio for him on a plot north of King's Cross Station, amid warehouses and small factories. The serene, silent space has delighted the client ever since.

The Royal Academy of Arts – Refurbishment
2018

Burlington House, Piccadilly W1J 0BE • www.royalacademy.org.uk • Nearest transport Green Park and Piccadilly LU • See website for opening times and information regarding events and exhibitions

Burlington House was one of a number of aristocratic houses built during the mid-17th century on the quiet country road that later became Piccadilly. Various architects have been associated with the house but it was Richard Boyle, Third Earl of Burlington, inheritor of the property, who was to create its now familiar Palladian style.

In 1867 the building was leased to the Royal Academy and additional buildings constructed around the courtyard. The architects responsible for this 19th-century extension were Robert Richardson Banks (1812-72) and Charles Barry (1823-1900), son of Sir Charles Barry.

Almost twenty years ago, the Royal Academy acquired the property directly to the rear of Burlington House, number 6 Burlington Gardens, which was originally built in 1870 for the University of London by Sir James Pennethorne (1801-1871). The redevelopment of this site by the Royal Academy has been slow, with at least two schemes considered previously before being rejected.

In 2008 David Chipperfield was awarded the commission to undertake the refurbishment and the linking of the two buildings. As with his work at the Neues Museum in Berlin, Chipperfield has unlocked not only a great deal of 'usable' space, but also beauty, which was well hidden until now. Opened in May 2018, coinciding with the Academy's 250th anniversary, the refurbishment has secured considerable additional space for new galleries, a café-bar, a 250-seat lecture theatre and more space for the Art School. Architecture gets its own gallery, where, we are promised, 'major exhibitions' will be housed. The two buildings are now linked by a white concrete enclosed bridge, which, as with the rest of the refurbishment, manages to look like it's always been there. A truly exciting place to visit.

See also separate entry for Norman Foster's Sackler Gallery extension on p.239.
Area Map p.6, A:2

AMANDA LEVETE
(b 1955)

British born Amanda Levete worked in the offices of Will Alsop and Richard Rogers on graduation from the Architectural Association. In 1989 she joined Jan Kaplicky's 'Future Systems' as partner and the pair went on to marry. Their best-known projects are the Media Centre at Lord's Cricket Ground, the pale green 'water boatmen' foot bridge at West India Quay, Canary Wharf and the Selfridge's Birmingham building, the huge, shiny object which landed next to the Bullring in 2003, to great delight.

In 2009 Amanda Levete formed her own practice, with one of her first buildings being the News International headquarters in Wapping (2009). In the same year she transformed the front of a small office block, located in a narrow street just off the busy Oxford Street, by creating a new aluminium façade with 'eyelid' shaped windows which funnel light down into the work space (10 Hills Place, W1F 7SD).

Amanda Levete has a truly international portfolio, notably The Museum of Art, Architecture and Technology built on the banks of the River Tagus in the Belem district of Lisbon, Portugal. The undulating form of the building is covered with 15,000 white, three-dimensional ceramic tiles, winning much acclaim.

Her latest building in London, an extension to the Victoria and Albert Museum, described below, is perhaps her most admired work to date.

Amanda Levete was appointed Commander of the Order of the British Empire for services to architecture in the 2017 Queen's Birthday Honours and in 2018 was awarded the Jane Drew Prize by *The Architects' Journal and The Architectural Review.*

Media Centre, Lord's Cricket Ground
1995-1998

St John's Wood Road, NW8 8QN • Tel 020 7432 1000 • www.lords.org • Nearest transport St John's Wood LU • See website for details of tours of the grounds

Amanda Levete was in partnership with Jan Kaplicky, working under the name of Future Systems, when they designed this truly unique building – a single-shell aluminium monocoque structure which was made, prefabricated in 26 sections, off-site in a Cornish boatbuilder's yard and assembled at Lord's. As futuristic as it first appears, the Media Centre fits well with the other structures at the Ground and, indeed, is the same height, 49 feet or 15 metres, as the Nursery Pavilion (David Morley, 1999) directly opposite, across the square. The Media Centre has space for 100 journalists plus television and radio commentators – this is where 'Tuffers' and 'Aggers' and other stalwarts of the BBC's 'Test Match Special' team broadcast from. The Media Centre was awarded the prestigious RIBA Stirling Prize in 1999.

Media Centre, Lord's Cricket Ground

Exhibition Road Quarter

Exhibition Road Quarter
2017

Victoria and Albert Museum, Cromwell Road, SW7 2RL • Tel 020 7942 2000
• www.vam.ac.uk • Nearest transport South Kensington and Knightsbridge LU •
See website for opening times and information regarding exhibitions and lectures

The Victoria and Albert Museum, affectionately known as 'Britain's attic', is the world's largest decorative arts museum. The collection's foundation goes back to the Great Exhibition of 1851, but the building dates from 1891 to a design by Aston Webb (1849-1930), who was also responsible for Admiralty Arch and the principal façade of Buckingham Palace. The building itself is glorious, witness the refreshment rooms with decorations by William Morris and others.

In 2001, the museum launched 'Futureplan', an ambitious programme of development and transformation to awaken this sleeping beauty. Projects included the cleaning of Webb's Cromwell Road façade, the establishment of the Clothworkers' Centre at Blythe House in Olympia and the refurbishment of various galleries. Of special note is the work of Stanton Williams whose series of elegant, unified and accessible Ceramics Galleries includes a working studio and demonstration area, completed in 2009.

The latest phase of the Futureplan to be completed is the 'Exhibition Road Quarter'. Architect Amanda Levete has most definitely drawn our attention to a part of the museum most visitors have walked by for years. Aston Webb's stone screen, originally built in 1909 to hide the museum's unsightly boiler house, has been slimmed down and transformed into a major new entrance to the museum.

There is a white porcelain tile covered courtyard and a subterranean exhibition area, providing 6,400 square metres of new display space. Even on the dullest day the handmade tiles dazzle – 11,000 were used to pave the new area alone, with a further 4,300 used to cover the roof of the new café and shop.

Go inside and you will find two staircases with lacquered tulipwood balustrades leading to the sunken Sainsbury Gallery exhibition space. Even on a busy day, this new extension oozes calm. But this project was not an easy one, given its proximity to the original, Grade I listed, museum. The exhibition space, some 18 metres below the courtyard, required 22,500 cubic metres of earth to be excavated.

It is envisaged that the courtyard will be used to display large sculptures and will be a welcome addition to what has become one of London's newest and brightest rendezvous spots.

STEVEN HOLL
(b 1947)

Despite an intriguingly eclectic portfolio and global recognition – *Time* magazine's 'America's Best Architect' and the first US winner of Finland's prestigious Alvar Aalto Medal are just two of his many accolades – Steven Holl has only just made his mark on London, but it was worth the wait.

Holl trained in Washington and Rome as well as spending time at the Architectural Association in London, a contemporary of Rem Koolhaas and Zaha Hadid, before going into practice in California and, later, New York. His body of work includes a library in Lilongwe, Malawi (2019); almost 200 houses, shops and other buildings as part of the new town of Makuhari in Japan, sited on reclaimed land on the rim of Tokyo Bay (1996); Danish Natural History Museum in Copenhagen (2012); Reid Building extension to Charles Rennie Mackintosh's 1909 Glasgow School of Art (2014), as well as many and varied projects in the United States.

Maggie's Barts

Maggie's Barts
Steven Holl, 2018

Maggie's Barts, St Bartholomew's Hospital, EC1A 7BE, West Smithfield • Nearest transport Barbican and St Paul's LU

Steven Holl's first project in London, Maggie's Cancer Care Centre at St Bartholomew's Hospital at Smithfield, brings together much of his architectural philosophy – such as his belief that the site is the metaphysical beginning of any piece of architecture. This particular site, within the grounds of the oldest hospital in London, founded in the 12th century, with buildings dating from the mid 18th century by James Gibbs (see the Bartholomew Walk p.281), gave Holl the opportunity to demonstrate his approach to placing a modern construction next to an historic building. He has created, in his words, 'an authentically new piece' that doesn't overwhelm its older neighbour, but instead presents a 'complementary contrast'; to try to mimic the craftsmanship of Gibbs' original stonework work would, in Holl's thinking, be an 'unauthentic' act. Indeed, Holl's building has replaced just such an unsatisfactory piece of architecture, a 1960's extension to the hospital's North Wing.

The exterior of Holl's three-storey 'urban townhouse' is made from double layers of matte white glass, with seemingly random colour fields inserted between the inner and outer glazing. Holl took the neume notation from medieval books of music used by the monks at the nearby church of St Bartholomew the Great.

Holl describes the building as 'a vessel within a vessel within a vessel': three floors, each with its own distinct function, linked by a shallow-tread staircase, and decorated by perforated bamboo giving a cocooning, basket-like quality of calm and gentleness. The building is topped by a roof garden used for yoga sessions and other activities.

Steven Holl's marvellous building has a meditative quality and is one of 21 'Maggie's Centres' dotted around the country, each designed by an eminent architect for use by anyone affected by cancer. The centres are named for Maggie Keswick Jencks (1941-1995) the artist, garden designer and writer who, through her own illness, saw a need for a new approach to cancer care. For further details see: www.maggiescentres.org. *Area Map p.8, A:3*

Trafalgar Square, see p.345

08

WALKING LONDON'S ARCHITECTURE

Walking London's Architecure

Bartholomew Walk..281-289
Fleet Street and Beyond Walk.................................290-297
Greenwich Walk...298-307
John Nash Walk...308-321
South Bank Walk...322-335
Strand Walk..336-343
Whitehall Walk...344-354

Bartholomew Walk

1. **Charterhouse Square**
2. **Florin Court**
3. **No 41 Cloth Fair**
4. **St Bartholomew the Great**
5. **St Bartholomew's Hospital**
6. **Gatehouse of St Bartholomew's Hospital**
7. **St Bartholomew the Less**
8. **St Bartholomew's Hospital Museum**
9. **Great Hall (St Bartholomew's Hospital)**
10. **Maggie's Centre**
11. **Haberdashers' Hall**
12. **Smithfield Market**

A fairly short walk, in terms of distance, but one which takes in the variety London has always offered. Choose any area in the capital and the curious will find all sorts of half-hidden nuggets of history and architectural gems. There are many places to take refreshment in this area, particularly around Smithfield, as well as '14 on The Green', a coffee house in a Georgian house at the gates of The Charterhouse.

We start this walk in ❶ **Charterhouse Square** by the entrance gates to The Charterhouse, where there is much to see in the Chapel Court, only recently opened to visitors. The gates bear the legend 'virtue is the only nobility' in Old French, and were designed by Eric Parry Architects, as was the metal baldacchino-esque canopy which marks the entrance to the Chapel Court. Of note here is the grave of Walter Manny, founder of the monastery that once thrived here, and a bronze model of the building complex. Eric Parry Architects undertook the renewal work on this site in 2013 as part of the 'Revealing the Charterhouse' project, completed in 2017. See p.56 for further details of this fascinating set of buildings.

Walk along the east side of Charterhouse Square, and at numbers 6-9 you will find a block of flats named ❷ **Florin Court**. This lovely, curved building, recessed at the centre, opened in 1936 and was designed by Guy Morgan. The residents of this handsome ten-storey block enjoy a roof garden with wonderful views and there is a swimming pool in the basement. The architectural historian Nikolaus Pevsner described Florin Court as being 'poised between modernism and Art Deco'. Fans of Agatha Christie's 'Poirot' television series, starring David Suchet, will recognise this building as being the home of the dandified detective.

Moving on, cross Charterhouse Street, bear right and take the narrow Hayne Street, cross Long Lane, and take the narrow alleyway next to the 'Red Cow' public house. This brings us to Cloth Fair.

Building first took place on this land when it passed from nearby Bartholomew's Priory to Lord Rich at the dissolution of the monasteries.

Although the Priory was not completely closed, much of its property was confiscated. Until the mid 20th century, houses were packed on both sides of this fairly narrow street, giving a flavour of how much of London looked at the time of the Great Fire. Take a look at the red brick, four storey ❸ **No 41**, which is a private residence, an almost unique example of a 17th-century City merchant's house. The house is hard to date precisely and it could be as early as 1614 when the first land lease was released, although the building conforms to post Great Fire regulations. Nos 39-40 date from about 1830.

The curious name of the street is derived from the cloth merchants who settled here and because of the area's association with the Bartholomew Fair, an annual three day event which always started on the feast day of St Bartholomew, 24th August. Begun in 1133 this fair was an important source of income for the Priory of St Bartholomew, whose canny founder Rahere had instigated the Fair as a way of making money for his hospital. A Royal Charter authorising the Fair had been granted by Henry I to Rahere, who, it is believed, was at one time minstrel to the King.

The Fair soon became a cloth specialists' market, where merchants from all over England and the Continent would flock to sell and buy their wares. During the 17th century wrangling arose over who was to receive the largest portion of the Fair's revenue and the Fair was threatened with closure. Nonetheless, diversions – fire-eaters, magicians, tight-rope walkers – abounded here for a good many years more until 1855 when public disorder, probably related to the vast quantity of drink consumed, was blamed for its eventual closure. Ben Jonson's play 'Bartholomew Fair' is an apparently accurate vignette. This street was also the birthplace of the architect Inigo Jones, his father being a cloth merchant.

After exiting Cloth Fair at West Smithfield bear left where you will shortly arrive at the Tudor gatehouse of the church of ❹ **St Bartholomew the Great** (see p.34 for more details).

On leaving St Bartholomew the Great, walk through the gatehouse again and along West Smithfield, past the entrance to Little Britain and along the perimeter wall of ❺ **St Bartholomew's Hospital**. Often as not there are bunches of flowers left on the ground under the plaque on the wall commemorating the 300 or so Protestants burned at the stake near this spot between 1553 and 1558 during the reign of Queen Mary, a deed which earned her the nickname of 'Bloody Mary'.

The name 'Smithfield' is probably a corruption of 'smooth field', meaning flat land. Jousting tournaments took place here as did public executions until about 1400 when they were moved to Tyburn.

Now we move onto the ❻ **Gatehouse of St Bartholomew's Hospital**. This nice little building dates from about 1700

⑤ *St Bartholomew the Great*

and has a bust of Henry VIII in a niche at the centre of the pediment. The carved figures representing Lameness and Disease are contemporary with the building.

Walking past the gatehouse into the Hospital grounds on your left is the church of ❼ **St Bartholomew the Less**. Some of the church dates from the 15th century, namely the south tower and the vestry, but the rest dates from 1823-25 and is by Thomas Hardwick to a plan by George Dance the Younger. This is a lovely little octagonal, brick-built church with small windows placed high up to give a dramatic light effect. Although the church is now parochial, rather than exclusively for the Hospital, the link can be seen in its early 20th-century stained glass window, depicting a nurse and which was the gift of the Worshipful Company of Glaziers.

This building suffered severe bomb damage during World War II but was sympathetically restored by Lord Mottistone of Seely and Paget, who was responsible for much of the post-war restoration work in the City. The church is open every day from 7am to approximately 8pm.

When you have finished at the church make your way to the 'North Block' where sign posts will direct you to ❽ **St Bartholomew's Hospital Museum**. This small museum has a collection of surgical instruments and illustrates the fascinating history of the Hospital and the changing roles of the staff. Make your way through the museum to the door that leads to the ❾ **Great Hall**.

This building was designed by James Gibbs (1682-1754), also responsible for St Martin-in-the-Fields and St Mary-le-Strand, in about 1730. Gibbs gave his services to the Hospital for free. Security will not let you go very far into the Hall, but far enough to allow a look at the wonderful murals painted on the walls of the staircase by William Hogarth in 1735-37. The paintings represent Christ at the Pool of Bethesda and The Good Samaritan. The figures are larger than life size and the artist is said to have used hospital patients as his models. Hogarth did this work without charge, perhaps as an act of pure charity for he had been born nearby and his sister and mother still lived there. He may also have seen tho gesture as an opportunity to show that British artists could paint as well as the Italians whose work was being brought home as souvenirs by the wealthy from their Grand Tours. Indeed it is rumoured that an Italian artist had been offered the commission at the Hospital, for which a large fee would have been paid, when Hogarth stepped in. To get a better look at the whole work join one of the Friday tours (2pm at Henry VIII Gate).

Many historic events are associated with the hospital, which is not surprising given its location. One of the most famous was in 1381 when Wat Tyler, leader of the Peasants' Revolt, was brought to St Bartholomew's Hospital having been stabbed in the back by the Lord Mayor of London, William Walworth, as Tyler went to speak peaceably to the King. However, before Tyler could be treated he was dragged outside and beheaded by the King's men. After visiting the museum, you may like to walk through to the Court, also designed by James Gibbs as are the buildings to the left and right. The impetus to build separate ward blocks was justified by Gibbs as a precaution against fire, but the elimination of the risk of cross-infection may have been a factor.

As you walk into the Court note the modern building at the far end of the block to your left. This luminous white glass construction is the latest addition to the Bart's complex, having been completed at the end of 2017. The building houses a **❿ Maggie's Centre**, a place for anyone affected by cancer, designed by Steven Holl, see p.277.

Go out of the Hospital grounds and to your left follow West Smithfield, crossing Giltspur Street and Hosier Lane. Still in West Smithfield, at number 18 is **⓫ Haberdashers' Hall**.

The Worshipful Company of Haberdashers is one of the 108 City Livery Companies. These City Companies are in many ways like clubs. Their members are called freemen or liverymen and officers are elected to a committee or court chaired by the Master, usually for one year. Livery companies date back to the middle ages, when they were founded to promote and protect the trades which their members practiced. The livery companies probably had their origins in this country before the Norman Conquest of 1066 and are similar to the fraternities and guilds (or mysteries) that flourished throughout Europe for many centuries. The term 'mystery' is still in use and derives from the Latin 'misterium' meaning 'professional skill'.

Livery was the term used for the clothing, food and drink provided for the officers and retainers of great households, such as those of bishops, barons, colleges or guilds. The term then became restricted to mean just the distinctive clothing and badges which were the symbols of privilege and protection. Since the members of each guild were distinguished from one another in this way, the guilds gradually became known as livery companies. It is still their custom to wear ceremonial dress on official occasions.

The earliest record of livery activity is a Royal Charter granted to the Weavers' Company in 1155. Members paid to belong and the word 'guild' is derived from the Saxon 'gildan' meaning 'to pay'. These guilds controlled services and the manufacture and selling of goods and food within the City of London. This prevented unlimited competition and helped to keep wages and working conditions steady. Customers, employers and employees were protected against inferior work that did not meet the guild's standards. Fines and other penalties could be severe – and included expulsion, which meant the loss of livelihood. Disputes were settled by arbitration at the guild's hall, which also served as a meeting place for their particular trade. Many street names within the City of London have trade-derived names, such as Bread Street, Milk Street, Ironmonger Lane and, of course, Cloth Fair. Many of the trades and crafts have now diminished in importance and the modern livery company concentrates its energies on charitable and educational activities.

The first Haberdashers' Hall was built in 1458-61 in Maiden Lane, later re-named Staining Lane, in the City and was destroyed in the Great Fire. The second Hall was built 1667 on the same spot but was destroyed during enemy bombing in World War II and the third was built 1954-56 as part of an office complex. In April 2002 the Company moved to its new bespoke premises here in West Smithfield and which were opened by Her Majesty the Queen.

The West Smithfield façade of the new building is made up of shops and residential units with offices to the rear. The Livery Hall, associated offices and meeting rooms are arranged on two floors around a central courtyard. The Livery Hall, where the official business takes place, has a high vaulted ceiling and oak panelled walls. Designed by architect Michael Hopkins, it has modern stained glass and bespoke furniture by David Linley (the son of the late Princess Margaret). This is a lovely, light, modern, yet classic building. Tours of this building are rare, only four per year at the moment (telephone 020 7246 9988 for further details).

Walking on, past the interestingly named Bishop's Finger pub, cross the road and

⑫ *Smithfield Market*

head for Grand Avenue, which dissects ⑫ **Smithfield Market**. A cattle market was formally established on this site in 1638, and during the early 18th century tales of unruly cattle and even more unruly herdsmen abounded. The beasts were herded into conditions that were totally inadequate and were slaughtered in the market with blood and waste running into the nearby Fleet River. Some of the streets in the area bear witness to this market, such as Cowcross Street.

Sir Horace Jones (1819-87), City architect, was charged with designing a building that would be suitable as the chief meat market for London. The site was enlarged to about ten acres to accommodate Jones's huge building, 631 feet in length and 246 feet wide. Nikolaus Pevsner, said of the building that 'it is of an uncertain style', but without any architectural precedent, finding a suitable 'style' must have been problematic. Jones used red brick with Portland stone decorations and cast iron – lots of it. As you stand in the Grand Avenue note the cast-iron railings, gates and decorations. Also of note is the rather touching war memorial. In 2005 the market underwent a £70 million renovation in which all the paintwork was restored to its original colours; these are unexpectedly vibrant-deep blue, red and green with a lavish sprinkling of gold stars. Sir Horace Jones went on to design Leadenhall Market, parts of the Guildhall and Tower Bridge.

Smithfield is the last of the large wholesale markets left operating in Central London, others such as Covent Garden, Billingsgate and Spitalfields have all moved to more spacious, convenient locations. In recent years a much reduced market operation, confining its business to supplying meat to City restaurants, shops and hotels, and only operating between 2am and noon, has had property developers rubbing their hands at the prospect of development opportunities. However public pressure has led to a rejection of any high-rise office building and the announcement in 2016 that Smithfield Is to be the new home of the Museum of London has been met with general approval. Project architects Stanton Williams and Asif Khan, working together with conservation architect Julian Harrap and landscape design consultants J & L Gibbons, plan to deliver 'a new lifted landmark dome which will create a beautiful light-filled entrance to the museum; innovative spiral escalators will transport visitors down to the exhibition galleries in a vast excavated underground chamber; flexible spaces are included that can serve as a new meeting place for London'. This exciting new project is due to be completed in 2022.

If you are leaving the area by train or underground, you may well want to make your way to the Eastern Ticket Hall of Farringdon Station at the corner of Long Lane and Lindsey Street. This is one of the ten new stations built as part of the multi-billion pound Cross-rail project, bringing the 'Elizabeth Line' from Reading and Heathrow Airport in the west, through new tunnels under central London to Shenfield and Abbey Wood in the east. Note how the Station's architecture, designed by Aedas, resonates with the Barbican Centre, just a short walk away.

In order to see Smithfield Meat Market in full working mode one has to get up very early as the trading 'day' finishes by noon. Some pubs in the area have a 6am licence, the only place in London where this is so. Obviously it must be thirsty work.

When the market is at rest, the many cafés, bars and restaurants in the area come alive, and a lovely view of St Paul's, illuminated at night can be enjoyed from many of the establishments.

More Information:

St Bartholomew the Great
6 Kinghorn Street,
West Smithfield, EC1A 7HW
Tel: 020 7606 5171
www.greatstbarts.com
Transport: Barbican LU,
Farringdon LU, St Paul's LU

14 on the Green
14 Charterhouse Square, EC1M 6AX
Tel: 020 3817 4178
www.14green.cafe
Transport: Barbican LU, Farringdon LU
Open: Mo-Fri

St Bartholomew the Less
Smithfield Gate,
West Smithfield, EC1A 7BE
Tel: 020 7601 8066
www.stbartstheless.org.uk
Transport: Barbican LU,
Farringdon LU, St Paul's LU

St Bartholomew's Hospital Museum
West Smithfield, EC1A 7BE
Tel: 020 3465 5798
www.bartshealth.nhs.uk
Transport: Barbican LU,
Farringdon LU, St Paul's LU

Fleet Street & Beyond Walk

1. **St Bride's Church**
2. **Reuters Building**
3. **St Bride Library**
4. **Daily Express Building**
5. **Daily Telegraph Building (now Peterborough Court)**
6. **The Cheshire Cheese (public house)**
7. **Dr Johnson's House**
8. **Whitefriars Monastery**
9. **Hoare's Bank**
10. **St Dunstan in the West**
11. **Prince Henry's Room**
12. **Temple Church**
13. **Inner Temple**
14. **Middle Temple**
15. **Middle Temple Hall**
16. **Temple Bar**

We start our walk at the Ludgate Circus end of Fleet Street. The street is named after the River Fleet which once flowed down what is now Farringdon Street and New Bridge Street and on into the Thames. What is left of the river today trickles through pipes under the road.

Our first stop is Sir Christopher Wren's beautiful church of ❶ **St Bride** – note the magnificent steeple (see p.71 for more information). As you leave St Bride and rejoin Fleet Street note the building to your left, the ❷ **Reuters Building** (85 Fleet Street). This is the former Headquarters of Reuters and The Press Association and was designed by Sir Edwin Lutyens in 1935. One may be forgiven for thinking the three-storey 'pavilion' was an afterthought, but it was very much part of Lutyens' plan. The building is no longer occupied by Reuters, whose departure from the area in 2005 marked the end of the newspaper publishing era in Fleet Street. Since the time of Wynkyn de Worde, about 1500, the street and the surrounding alleyways have had an association with the printed word. During its early days the Crown and the Church viewed the printed word with suspicion and strict censorship prevailed and an unsuspecting printer could find himself in prison.

If you are particularly interested in the printed word there is a superb little library, ❸ **St Bride Printing Library** tucked away behind St Bride church. This is a good source of books and periodicals relating to the history and

techniques of printing (for details see p.297). The first London newspaper, *The Daily Courant*, was published on 11 March 1702 and others followed such as *The Morning Chronicle* and *The Diary*, all published in Fleet Street. Until recently Fleet Street, and the surrounding area, was primarily concerned with the publication of daily national and provincial newspapers. Even now people of a certain age refer to the press as 'Fleet Street', long after the newspapers had decamped to more convenient premises in Canary Wharf.

However, the departing newspaper industry has left behind a couple of fabulous buildings, the first of which you will see now. Having crossed Fleet Street opposite the Reuters Building you should now be on the corner of Shoe Lane, and in front of you will be the gleaming, unmistakable rounded form of the former ❹ **Daily Express Building**. Designed by Sir Owen Williams and built 1930-33, this was the first curtain walled building in London, with distinctive banding in glass and black Vitrolite set in chromium strips. The printing of the newspaper took place in the basement and at the rear of the building (this part was demolished in 1990). As it is now a private office there is no public access, but by pressing your nose against the reception door you will be able to see into the fabulous Reception Hall; note the ceiling and the concealed lighting arrangement – pure Art Deco. The building is usually part of the 'Open House' scheme (see p.403 for more details).

Just a few paces on is the former ❺ **Daily Telegraph Building** (now Peterborough Court), built 1928-31 by Elcock and Sutcliffe. This massive stone building with six vast columns from the third storey and stepped-back roofline exudes confidence and self-importance, but must have felt old-fashioned within just a couple of years of the opening of the Daily Express building. The huge projecting Art Deco clock is something of a landmark. This building is now a private office and there is no public access.

Now we can take a diversion from Fleet Street. Stay on the north side of the road and you will soon find yourself at a narrow alley way called Wine Office Court and, on entering, you will see to your right ❻ **Ye Olde Cheshire Cheese public house**. Parts of this building date back to 1667, the original pub having perished in the Great Fire of 1666. This very atmospheric building still has its 17th-century room arrangement intact, so there are lots of cosy corners to hide in. This was the haunt of Dr Johnson and his circle, which in turn made it a focus of pilgrimage for later writers such as Mark Twain and Charles Dickens.

Further on along Wine Office Court and to the left is Gough Square. One of the first things you will see is a small statue of a cat called 'Hodge', the companion of Dr Samuel Johnson who lived in the Square for a number of years. Johnson's House, number 17, is his only surviving home and is particularly significant in that it was here, in the attic, he wrote his *Dictionary of the English Language*. ❼ **Dr Johnson's House** is open to the public and gives a good flavour of 18th-century London and the life of the great man of letters (see p.297 for details).

Make your way back to Fleet Street and cross to the south side into Bouverie Street and then left into Magpie Alley; this will bring you to the rear of the offices of the prestigious City law firm Freshfields. Have a look over the railings into the glass-clad basement where you will see the preserved remains of a tiny fraction of ❽ **Whitefriars Monastery**. The Whitefriars were so called because they wore a white mantle over a brown habit, but were really Carmelites, named for Mount Carmel where their mother church was located. A priory had been built for them in this area in the mid 13th century. On the dissolution of the monasteries all the buildings were confiscated, the hall being made into a playhouse.

Back to Fleet Street, turn left and walk on until you arrive at number 37, ❾ **Hoare's Bank**. One of the last remaining private banks in London, it has been in business for over 400 years and is therefore older than the Bank of England. Hoare's has occupied this building since 1830. The bank took the then unusual decision to trade from a bespoke building rather than a converted house, as was the custom. However this building has accommodation to enable the Director of the bank to be always in residence.

The building is made from Bath stone with a wrought-iron balcony, a 1930s addition. The Banking Hall has a circular bronze stove at the centre and polished wood counters.

Just a few yards along Fleet Street, on the opposite side (north) of the road is the church of ❿ **St Dunstan in the West**. Not surprisingly there is another St Dunstan in the City, to the east. The foundation of St Dunstan in the West can be traced back to the 13th century but this present building dates from 1830-33. The plan of the church is a Gothic octagon, unusual for such a late building. The number of interesting external features go some way to compensate for very restricted public access opportunities. To the right of the church, as you are viewing it, is a statue of Elizabeth I, dating from 1586.

As she died in 1603, this statue was made in her lifetime and the question arises whether it is an accurate likeness? It was made to stand at Ludgate (demolished in 1760) as were the statues of King Lud and his sons, which are inside the church. The Northcliffe monument on the exterior of the church commemorates the life of Alfred Harmsworth, 1st Viscount Northcliffe, the journalist and newspaper magnate. He started his career by editing his school magazine and went on to found such publications as *Comic Cuts* (1890), the *Daily Mail* (1896) and the *Daily Mirror* (1903). The huge clock dates from 1671 with two figures, sporting gold loincloths, who strike the quarter-hours with their clubs; they could well be Gog and Magog, the giants of legend who roamed the City.

Proceed along the south side of Fleet Street, until you arrive at the alleyway named Inner Temple Gate. There you will find the building known as ⓫ **Prince Henry's Room** (not open to the public). One of the last remaining timber-framed houses in London, it dates back to at least 1610 and therefore survived the Great Fire of 1666 which ended its path of destruction only a few yards further down the road. The building also survived the threat of demolition in the late 19th century and the Blitz of 1940-41. The building contains interesting interior wooden panelling contemporary with the building and further 18th-century panelling and fireplace. There is also a historically important plaster ceiling decorated with motifs including the Prince of Wales's feathers. The building however probably takes its name from its time as a tavern rather than from any royal associations. Walk down Inner Temple Lane and you will arrive at the west end of one of the most exquisite churches to be found anywhere. This is the ⓬ **Temple Church** (see p.52).

When you exit the Temple church, look around at the buildings in the immediate vicinity. These buildings make up the ⓭ **Inner Temple** and the ⓮ **Middle Temple**, which represent two of the four Inns of Court of London – the others being Gray's Inn (entrance in Gray's Inn Road, telephone 020 7458 7800 for information) and Lincoln's Inn (accessed from Lincoln's Inn Fields, telephone 020 7405 1393 for information).

The four Inns, or Honourable Societies of Barristers, each fulfil the same function but have different traditions, rather like collegiate universities. According to custom, which dates back many hundreds of years, any law student training to be a barrister in England must join one of the Inns of Court and dine there at least 24 times, as well as passing written exams, before becoming officially qualified.

The maze of courtyards and buildings that make up the Inner and Middle Temples seem like something from another era, especially in the evening when the area is still lit by gas light. With your back to the Temple Church make your way right towards ⓯ **Middle Temple Hall**. Built between 1562-73 this Hall saw the first performance of 'Twelfth Night' in February 1602 and it is thought its author,

Temple Bar

William Shakespeare, acted a small part in it. Of note is the magnificent hammerbeam ceiling and the 29 foot table, made from a single oak tree from Windsor forest and presented as a gift by Elizabeth I. (Guided tours of Middle Temple are available and must be pre-booked through the Events Department on 020 7427 4820).

Follow Middle Temple Lane back out to Fleet Street and look for the ⓰ **Temple Bar** (see opposite) in the road. This marks the boundary between the City of London and London in general. Until its removal in 1878, the old Temple Bar was a stone tri-arched affair thought to have been designed by Wren. It had to be taken down and something a little more modest put in its place to ease the flow of the ever-increasing traffic. It is now on display in Paternoster Square, next to St Paul's Cathedral. Since its placement in the 1670s the Temple Bar had seen a lot of activity, not least the custom of displaying the heads of executed traitors on it, the last being that of Francis Townley the Jacobite, in 1746.

The present Temple Bar is made of granite and coloured stone with statues of Queen Victoria and the future Edward VII, topped by a fierce looking griffin rampant. Sir Horace Jones, City architect, who was also responsible for Leadenhall Market, Smithfield and Tower Bridge, designed the Bar in 1880.

This is where the City and this particular walk ends. If you are feeling energetic you could carry on with the Strand walk which, quite conveniently, starts right here (see p.336).

More Information:

St Bride Library
*St Bride's Institute, Bride Lane,
EC4Y 8EQ
Tel: 020 7353 460
www.sbf.org.uk
Transport: City Thameslink Rail
& Blackfriars LU/Rail*

Dr Johnson's House
*17 Gough Square, EC4A 3DE
Tel: 020 7353 3745
www.drjohnsonshouse.org
Transport: Chancery Lane LU,
Blackfriars LU/Rail*

Ye Olde Cheshire Cheese
*145 Fleet Streets, EC4A 2BU
Tel: 020 7353 6170
Transport: City Thameslink Rail
& Blackfriars LU/Rail*

St Dunstan in the West
*Bride Lane, EC4A 2HR
Tel: 020 7405 1929
www.stdunstansinthewest.org
Transport: Blackfriars LU/Rail
Admission free*

Inner Temple
*Middle Temple Lane,
EC4Y 7HL
Tel: 020 7797 8250
www.innertemple.org.uk
Transport: Temple LU*

Middle Temple
*Middle Temple Lane, EC4Y 9BT
Tel: 020 7427 4800
www.middletemple.org.uk
Transport: Temple LU*

Temple Church
*Temple, EC4Y 7BB
Tel: 020 7353 3470
www.templechurch.com
Transport: Temple LU*

Prince Henry's Room
*17 Fleet Street, EC4Y 1AA
Tel: 020 7953 4522
www.cityoflondon.gov.uk
Transport: Temple LU
Not open to the public*

Temple Bar, detail

A UNESCO World Heritage Site since 1997, Greenwich is graced with a variety of interesting buildings, many of which are free of charge to visit, set in beautiful parkland and easily accessed by public transport. River Bus 1 from Battersea Power Station Pier to Woolwich Arsenal Pier stops at Greenwich Pier; the Emirates Air Line, London's only cable car, crosses the Thames from the Royal Docks to the Greenwich Peninsula, just a few minutes by foot from the start of our walk and the area is well served by buses and trains (see www.tfl.gov.uk for details). One option is to arrive by Docklands Light Railway Cutty Sark station to start the walk or alight a stop earlier, at Island Gardens station and take the ❶ **Greenwich Foot Tunnel** and have the unique experience of walking under the Thames.

This tunnel is 1,217 feet in length and built exclusively for pedestrians. Opened in 1902 the tunnel replaced the ferry which had been in operation since the mid 17th century, enabling workers from south London to walk to the West India and Millwall Docks on the north bank of the Thames. At each end of the tunnel there are circular shafts with domed glass roofs that house stairs and lifts (for more details see p.307)

On arrival at Greenwich the first thing we see is the extraordinary sight of the ❷ **Cutty Sark**, the world's only surviving tea clipper from the 19th century. Built by Scott and Linton in Dumbarton, Scotland, she was launched in 1869 and won the prestigious clippers'

Shanghai to London race in 1871. She last sailed commercially in 1938 when she took on the role as a cadet training vessel, but has been here in dry dock since 1957. The Cutty Sark Trust had already embarked on a programme of extensive repairs to save the structurally unsound ship, when in 2007 fire gutted the whole vessel. Miraculously, most of her historic parts had already been removed and were in storage awaiting renovation. Grimshaw Architects, appointed to oversee this project and came up with the brilliant idea of suspending the ship three metres higher than its former position within the dry berth. Cradled by a supporting structure, visitors can now not only view the copper-clad hull, but also walk under it and, if you are tall enough, touch it. Visits to the ship's fully-restored original interior can also be made. A glazed canopy encloses the Cutty Sark up to the ship's waterline and provides visitor amenities.

❸ **St Alfege Church**, at the junction of Church Street and Greenwich High Road, is a splendid Georgian church, named after the Archbishop of Canterbury who was murdered near this spot by Danish invaders in 1012. It replaces a much earlier church in which the future King Henry VIII was baptized in 1491, sadly destroyed by a storm in 1710.

Designed by Nicholas Hawksmoor and built between 1712-18, this was the first church to be built under the Fifty New Churches Act of 1711, funded from a coal tax. The east façade, which faces Greenwich High Road, has a shallow apse, behind which rises the main portico with four Doric pilasters at the sides and two massive columns in the middle supporting a pediment surmounted by three huge urns. The south and north sides carry giant pilasters and on the west end sits the tower. Designed in the manner of James Gibbs, the tower and steeple were in fact added by John James in 1730.

The church suffered extensive damage in the Second World War, restoration of which was carried out by the eminent, if somewhat eccentric, architect Sir Albert Richardson, who faithfully reproduced Hawksmoor's work. The beautifully coffered ceiling of the apse is in fact a trompe l'oeil, a style of painting which uses perspective and shade to make a flat, two-dimensional surface appear three-dimensional.

Thomas Tallis, the 16th-century composer, was buried in the previous church on the site where he had been the organist and is commemorated in a south aisle window. The church is open to the public at varying times, see p.307 for details.

On leaving the church head for Stockwell Street, which forms a three-way junction with Greenwich High Road and Church Street. Walk the length of Stockwell Street which becomes Croom's Hill and at the end of which take the left-hand fork to arrive at Chesterfield Walk. Half way along Chesterfield Walk is ❹ **Ranger's House**. This is one of three houses built in the 1680s by Andrew Snape, the King's Sergeant Farrier, as a speculative venture. One of the houses was demolished in 1815 but the third of this trio, Macartney House you would have passed at the start of Chesterfield Walk, to which additions were made in 1802 by Sir John Soane. It was converted into flats in 1925.

Ranger's House has been the subject of additions over the years to form a very substantial domestic dwelling, one of its owners being Philip, 4th Earl of Chesterfield (1694-1773). The house is seven bays wide of red brick with a stone centre frontispiece, in which sits the main doorway flanked by Ionic columns with a Venetian window above. The wings of the house are in yellow brick, the south wing having a gallery added in 1750. The house has recently been refurbished by English Heritage and now houses the Wernher Collection, an eclectic assortment of more than 700 works of art purchased by mining magnate Sir Julius Wernher 1850-1912 (for more information see p.307).

After Ranger's House make your way across into Greenwich Park and head for the ❺ **Royal Observatory** with its distinctive dome. Greenwich Park itself consists of 163 acres set on a hill between Blackheath and the River Thames. King Henry VI enclosed the park in 1433 and the land is still owned by the Crown. Directly across from Ranger's House and situated towards the top of the park in the far corner is a thirteen-acre enclosure known as 'The Wilderness' in which deer roam – having first been introduced to the park in 1515 for the purpose of hunting.

The name Greenwich is derived from the Anglo-Saxon 'green port' and Saxon remains have been found in the area. From the top of the hill one can take in the splendid views across the Thames towards the skyscrapers of Canary Wharf. If the weather is pleasant you may wish to wander in the park or just sit by the pond, a haven for wildfowl. You may also be lucky enough to be serenaded by music from the decorative cast-iron bandstand that dates from 1880. The park is open to pedestrians every day from 6am to dusk.

King Charles II founded the Royal Observatory at the instigation of the influential Royal Society. Before an official observatory was established, John Flamsteed was appointed first Astronomer Royal in March 1675 and given access to the Tower of London, one of the tallest buildings in the City. Flamsteed used the North East turret of the White Tower as a temporary observatory for around half a year. The original part of the Observatory dates from 1675 and was designed by Christopher Wren and Robert Hooke, both of whom were active members of the Royal Society. This was the first purpose-built scientific research establishment in Britain. ❻ **Flamsteed House**, as the more 'domestic' part of the Observatory is known, is named after the first Astronomer Royal who lived and worked here.

Built from red brick with some nice exterior detailing that Wren called 'a little for pompe', Flamsteed House has one of the best-preserved Wren interiors, particularly the

splendid Octagon Room. Flamsteed lived in the four rooms of the ground floor and worked in the Octagon room above until his death in 1719. The house now contains displays telling the story of time and astronomy. The 28-inch Refracting Telescope in the onion-shaped dome is the largest in Britain and is still used for occasional night viewing. The whole project cost the Crown only £500, but there appears to have been a little 'scratching around' for materials and, splendid as the building is, it does not compare with Perrault's very grand Observatoire in Paris, which Greenwich was trying to emulate.

In 1948 it was decided that the lights of London were too bright and interfering with accurate readings, so the astronomers moved to Sussex and today the Astronomer Royal is based in Cambridge.

The Greenwich meridian, Longitude 0°, an imaginary line joining the north and south Poles, passes through the dead centre of a specialised telescope installed at the Observatory in 1851. A line in the ground marks the position of the meridian. It is a famous feature in the courtyard and it is from where all time zones around the world are measured since an international agreement in 1884. This is your opportunity to stand with one foot in each hemisphere of the East and West – everyone does it!

Above Wren's Octagon Room, on one of the two turrets, is a ball on a rod. This Time Ball has risen at 12.55pm and dropped at 1pm every day since 1833 enabling passing sailors to set their clocks by it (for more details see p.307).

A more recent addition to this area is the ❼ **Peter Harrison Planetarium**, designed by architects Allies and Morrison and opened in 2007 as part of a £16 million re-development. The Planetarium is enclosed by a truncated 45 ton bronze cone, tilted to 51.5° (the latitude of Greenwich), with a gully running across the roof representing the prime meridian (longitude 0°) and a gully on the south elevation pointing directly to the Pole Star. The 120-seat Planetarium is accessed from the 19th-century banded brick and Doulton terracotta South Building, designed by William Crisp in a vaguely Italian Renaissance style. Crisp was also responsible for the nearby Altazimuth Pavillion, named for the type of telescope it housed, a neat little building constructed of brick with terracotta door surrounds and a weather vane atop its dome representing the 1910 sighting of Halley's Comet.

From the Observatory, walk on down the hill towards Inigo Jones's splendid ❽ **Queen's House** (see p.44). Flanking the Queen's House, attached by colonnades, are the long rooms, added during the 19th century and now forming the ❾ **National Maritime Museum**.

The National Maritime Museum was formally established by Act of Parliament in 1934 and was opened to the public in 1937. The museum has displays of boats, real as well as models, and the largest collection of marine art in the world. There is also a permanent exhibition entitled 'Maritime London' using prints and video installations to present the history of the capital's shipping industry.

At the heart of the museum is Neptune Court, a glass-roofed courtyard which now houses large display items. It is claimed that this is Europe's largest free-span glazed roof and it is certainly impressive. British architect Rick Mather masterminded the project between 1996-99, together with a general overhaul of the museum and its facilities, funded by the National Lottery (for more details see p.307).

After leaving the museum we can now walk down to the buildings of the ❿ **Royal Naval College**, crossing the busy Romney Road directly in front of the Queen's House. Enter the gates immediately in front and you will have arrived at the group of four buildings known as the former Royal Naval College. The College moved from Portsmouth to occupy these buildings in 1873. Built from 1696 to 1751 on the site of the demolished Tudor palace of Placentia to a plan by Sir Christopher Wren it was initially used as the Royal Hospital for Seamen.

Greenwich Hospital, as it was universally known, was the naval equivalent of the Royal Hospital Chelsea (see p.93) – a home for needy veterans of the service. The idea was originally mooted by King James II, himself a one-time naval officer, although the development of this site initially began when King Charles II expressed a desire to live at Greenwich. The eastern half of the ⓫ **King Charles Block**, the building nearest to the river towards Greenwich pier, was the only part of his planned 'King's House' to be realised. It was built in 1664-69 to the design of John Webb, pupil and son-in-law of Inigo Jones. Economic factors prevented further building, the money ran out and the project was abandoned.

❾ *Royal Naval College*

Queen Mary, fulfilling her father's, James II, wishes, rededicated the unfinished palace as a hospital and Wren was asked to devise a plan that would accommodate her desire to preserve the King's and Queen's Houses. This he did in his usual brilliant manner in what has been called 'the most stately procession of buildings we possess'. From 1703 he was assisted by a series of outstanding architects including Sir John Vanbrugh and Nicholas Hawksmoor.

After 125 years of residence in these splendid buildings the Royal Navy vacated the site in 1998 and they now house the University of Greenwich. There are two areas of the College open to the public and both are a treat to visit. ⓬ **The Painted Hall**, completed to Wren's design in 1707, was decorated by Sir James Thornhill between 1708 and 1727. For nineteen years he worked for a flat rate of pay, £3 per square yard of ceiling, £1 per square yard of wall. His subject matter ranged from the triumph of the sovereigns William and Mary, who are portrayed surrounded by the four cardinal virtues, to portraits of the great and good such as John Flamsteed, the first Astronomer Royal.

The other area available to visit is the ⓭ **Chapel in the Queen Mary block**, which is diagonally across the courtyard from the King Charles block. The original chapel interior was burnt out in 1779 and the present one is the work of James 'Athenian' Stuart. The domed tower sits over the chapel entrance and a run of double pillars is reminiscent of Perrault's colonnades at the Louvre in Paris. Light floods into the building from the three tiers of windows on the east wall.

The Thames Path, a national footpath passes in front of these buildings. The path runs from the Thames Flood Barrier at Woolwich, just over four miles from here, to Kemble in Gloucestershire one hundred and seventy miles to the west.

Standing on the Path, with your back to Wren's buildings you can gaze across the river to the wonders of ⓮ **Canary Wharf**. During the 1980s financial boom Canary Wharf was conceived as a major new location to complete the golden triangle of world-class financial centres along with New York and Tokyo. It was felt that the buildings of London's traditional financial centre, the City, would not be able to cope with the rush of new technology that was going to be needed to compete in the new age money market.

Canary Wharf, built in 1880, had been one of the largest and busiest docks in Europe, but just 100 years later it lay abandoned. The area then became the focus of the government's London Docklands Development Corporation (LDDC) and the marriage of business and property developers was blessed. Originally conceived by the American developer G.Ware Travelstead in the early 1980s, the whole area still retains a flavour of Chicago and New York from an architectural point of view. Indeed, American architects dominated the whole project.

The first building to be completed at Canary Wharf was **⓯ No1 Canada Square** by César Pelli (1926-), an Argentine-born American, who had been responsible for the huge skyscraper and plaza at the World Financial Centre in New York. No1 Canada Square, a steel-clad building is a true landmark, and is readily identifiable looking east from many parts of London by the flashing red light on its pyramidal top. The light is not for decoration but because the Wharf is under the flight path of aeroplanes using the City Airport. Pelli's obelisk-like building sets the tone of what was to follow: tall, slim and with framed windows rather than strip glass.

Transport links, once the subject of much frustration, have almost been solved by the services of the Docklands Light Railway, the Jubilee Line extension and the new Crossrail 'Elizabeth Line', all with stations designed by Norman Foster. A shopping mall, a plethora of bars and restaurants, summer open air concerts and an impressive display of public art, gardens and a fabulous sheltered public park on the roof of the Crossrail Station go some way to providing a quality environment for those who work, live and visit the area. The Museum of London Docklands, housed in a 19th century warehouse at West India Quay, is particularly interesting (see opposite for more info).

Still, with your back to Wren's building, turn to your right and walk along a little and you will see Greenwich Peninsula and the structure which is now called the **⓰ O2 Arena** but which was commissioned to mark the beginning of the new millennium. The Millennium Dome was intended as a celebratory structure offering a vast, flexible space for exhibitions, displays and events to which over six million people came during the year 2000.

Designed by eminent architect Richard Rogers the structure is 365 metres in diameter, with a circumference of 1 kilometre and a maximum height of 50 metres providing 2.2 million cubic metres of enclosed space. The Dome is suspended from a series of twelve 100 metres steel masts, held in place by more than 70 kilometres of high-strength steel cable, which in turn support the Teflon-coated glass fibre roof.

In 2002 the 'Dome' became the '02 Arena', a 20,000 seat venue with some 25 restaurants, bars and cafés, and an exhibition centre, which has succeeded in attracting top acts thereby ensuring its reputation as the British equivalent of New York's Madison Square Gardens.

If you are travelling from here to Central London you may like to consider taking the Riverbus from Greenwich pier close to where you are standing. The views from the boat are wonderful.

More Information:

Greenwich Foot Tunnel
Greenwich Pier, SE10 9HT
Isle of Dogs, E14 3UX
Transport: Island Gardens
or Cutty Sark DLR
Public access: Open all day, lifts
in operation daily 7am-7pm

The Cutty Sark
King William Walk,
Greenwich, SE10 9HT
Tel: 020 8312 6608
www.rmg.co.uk/cutty-sark
Transport: Greenwich & Maze
Hill Rail

St Alfege Church
Greenwich Church Street,
SE10 9BJ
Tel: 020 8853 0687
www.st-alfege.org
Transport: Cutty Sark DLR,
Greenwich & Maze Hill Rail

Royal Observatory
Greenwich Park, SE10 8XJ
Tel: 020 8858 4422
www.rmg.co.uk
Transport: Cutty Sark DLR,
Greenwich & Maze Hill Rail

Flamsteed House
Greenwich Park, SE10 8XJ
Tel: 020 8858 4422
www.rmg.co.uk
Transport: Cutty Sark DLR,
Greenwich & Maze Hill Rail

Queen's House
Greenwich Park, SE10 9NF
Tel: 020 8858 4422
www.nmm.ac.uk
Transport: Cutty Sark DLR,
Greenwich & Maze Hill Rail
Admission free

National Maritime Museum
Romney Road, SE10 9NF
Tel: 020 8858 4422
www.rmg.co.uk
Transport: Cutty Sark DLR,
Greenwich & Maze Hill Rail
Admission free

Painted Hall & Chapel of the former Royal Naval College
King William Walk, SE10 9NN
Tel: 020 8858 2608
www.oldroyalnavalcollege.org
Transport: Cutty Sark DLR,
Greenwich & Maze Hill Rail
Admission free

Ranger's House
Chesterfield Walk, SE10 8QX
Tel: 020 8853 0035
www.english-heritage.org.uk
Transport: Greenwich &
Blackhill Rail
Wheelchair access

Canary Wharf
Isle of Dogs, E14 5NY
Transport: Canary Wharf LU
& DLR
For information about events
see www.mycanarywharf.com

Museum of London Docklands
West India Quay,
Canary Wharf, E14 4AL
Transport: Canary Wharf LU
Tel: 020 7001 9844
www.museumoflondon.org.uk
Admission free

02 Arena
Peninsula Square,
SE10 0DX
Tel: 0844 856 0202
www.theo2.co.uk
Transport: North Greenwich LU

John Nash and the Via Triumphalis –
from Regent's Park to Buckingham Palace

❶ Gloucester Lodge & Gloucester Gate
❷ Cumberland Terrace
❸ Chester Terrace
❹ Chester Gate
❺ The Royal College of Physicians
❻ London Central Mosque
❼ Hanover Gate
❽ Hanover Terrace
❾ Sussex Place
❿ Cornwall Terrace
⓫ York Terrace
⓬ Marylebone Parish Church

- ⑬ RAM
- ⑭ Ulster Place
- ⑮ Park Crescent
- ⑯ Portland Place
- ⑰ RIBA
- ⑱ numbers 17, 21 & 23
- ⑲ numbers 27-47
- ⑳ Langham Hotel
- ㉑ BBC Broadcasting House
- ㉒ All Souls Church
- ㉓ Piccadilly Circus
- ㉔ Waterloo Place
- ㉕ The Institute of Directors Building
- ㉖ Athenaeum
- ㉗ Carlton House Terrace
- ㉘ Duke of York's Column
- ㉙ Buckingham Palace
- ㉚ Buckingham Palace Ticket Office

08 John Nash Walk

309

John Nash Walk

This route takes you from the edge of Regent's Park down through the heart of the West End to the monarch's London residence, Buckingham Palace. The time taken to cover will depend very much on the temptations the walker gives into en route, such as the Royal Institute of British Architects' bookshop, fashion stores, cafés and restaurants.

The 550 acres of Regent's Park at one time formed a small part of a huge forest and was the property of the Abbess of Barking until the dissolution of the monasteries in the 16th century when the land was appropriated by the Crown and used as a hunting ground; Elizabeth I entertained the Duke of Anjou here in 1582. Following the execution of Charles I in 1649 the land was sold, only to be handed back to the Crown at the Restoration in 1660. Gradually most of the 16,000 trees were felled to make way for the farms that would flourish here for the next 200 or so years. This bucolic scene lasted until 1811 when the farm leases became due for renewal and it was seen that the land could be developed for prestigious housing, enhancing the area and adding to the royal coffers.

Architect John Nash (1752-1835), already a favourite of the Prince Regent, oversaw the whole project, which included a 'triumphal way' connecting the Regent's Palace, Canton House, near The Mall to Regent's Park over a mile away to the north. However, the grand scheme, which saw the creation of new roads and junctions such as Regent Street and Oxford Circus, was not fully realised as money and effort were diverted into the enlargement of Buckingham Palace when the Regent became monarch in 1820.

Before Nash suggested a change of name to honour the Prince Regent, the area had been called Marylebone Park, that is 'place by St Mary's stream' ('bone' being a corruption of 'burna' meaning stream or water). At the top of the park, on the north edge, is the world famous Zoological Gardens (Regent's Park Zoo).

We start this walk at ❶ **Gloucester Lodge and Gloucester Gate** on the Outer Circle, our first encounter with the architecture of John Nash. The Lodge is a pleasingly symmetrical house with a large portico and fluted Ionic half columns. Gloucester Gate, the most northerly of Nash's 11 terraces, sports huge Ionic pilasters (these are the flat representations of a classical column usually placed against a wall). Both buildings date from 1827.

From the outset we can see that Nash was only building for the upper echelons of society, his scheme envisaged 'a boundary and complete separation between Streets and Squares occupied by the Nobility and Gentry, and the narrow Streets and meaner houses occupied by mechanics and the trading part of the community'.

We now come to perhaps the grandest and the most flamboyant of all Nash's terraces, ❷

❷ *Cumberland Terrace*

③ *Chester Terrace*

Cumberland Terrace. Built 1826-27 it is 800 feet long, an essay in symmetry with the centre portion projecting forward and having ten great Ionic columns and an enormous pediment adorned with sculptured figures by J G Bubb. Indeed the central pediment was much noted at the time as being the second largest in England after that on St Paul's Cathedral. Cumberland Terrace looks every inch a palace rather than a set of apartments. If you only have time to look at one of Nash's buildings, this is probably the best example.

Further on is ❸ **Chester Terrace**, again by Nash, dating from 1825. This building has the longest unbroken terrace of all, with 99 bays in a complicated but symmetrical system of division around a central section of seven bays and with a similar number of bays at each end (interspersed with the odd huge Corinthian column for decoration). Contemporary complaints were that Nash's workmanship was shoddy and rumours of rubble behind the stucco and other slapdash practices prevailed. Indeed this building was in such a bad state of repair that demolition was seriously contemplated after World War II. ❹ **Chester Gate** is the two storey building here, again by Nash and with Doric detailing.

We are now going to cross this lower portion of the park to view more Nash terraces (if you wish to miss these out make your way to Park Crescent (see ⑮) to continue the walk. You will pass ❺ **The Royal College of Physicians** in the Outer Circle, a splendid Modernist building designed by Denys Lasdun (see p.321).

From Chester Gate follow any of the footpaths to the Inner Circle and Queen Mary's Garden. Keeping to the south of the gardens look for sign posts to the Long Bridge where we cross the lake. Keeping the lake to your left we cross the Hanover Bridge and ahead you will see the unmistakable outline of the ❻ **London Central Mosque and Islamic Cultural Centre**. Designed by Sir Frederick Gibberd and Partners, 1972-78, this building is an exciting one, if only because it lends a certain exoticism to the Nash terraces with its gleaming copper dome and minaret. The main hall of the mosque is designed to accommodate 1,800 people (for more information see p.321).

In the shadow of the Mosque sits ❼ **Hanover Gate**, a small octagonal lodge house with a pitched roof and a sweet central chimney stack, which forms a traffic island and marks the western entrance to the park. Designed by Nash 1822-23 it had additions made by Lutyens in 1909.

Slightly further south is ❽ **Hanover Terrace**. Again by Nash and built 1822-23, the Terrace is 460 feet in length with four Doric columns at each end and six at the centre. The central pediment has a group of 13 white allegorical figures with a painted blue background reminiscent of a Wedgwood design.

Further south is ❾ **Sussex Place** and here Nash adds to a grand terrace of some 650 feet in length, steep-sided octagonal domes – which, Pevsner notes, are most 'unclassical'.

The next terrace we come to is ❿ **Cornwall Terrace**, the first to be built in 1821. Although attributed to Nash and Decimus Burton, the design was probably more the latter's work.

After Cornwall Terrace we follow the Outer Circle round to ⓫ **York Terrace**, designed by Nash and built 1824-26. It is a very long pair of terraces, providing a vista between them of Marylebone Parish Church, which had been built only a few years earlier. York Terrace has a Doric colonnade, giant Ionic columns at the ends and a central portico without any decorative sculpture.

Make your way down York Gate, towards ⓬ **Marylebone Parish Church**. The church was built 1813-17 and designed by Thomas Hardwick on land donated by the Duke of Portland.

On the corner of York Gate and the busy Marylebone Road is the ⓭ **Royal Academy of Music Museum**, known as the York Gate Collection, which is housed in a John Nash building. Visitors are welcome to view the rare musical instruments, original manuscripts, archives, images and other artefacts. It is also a wonderful opportunity to see the inside of the Grade I listed Nash building (see p.321). The main RAM building dates from 1911 and was designed by Sir Ernest George Yates in brick with stone decorative trimmings. Within the courtyard between the RAM and York Gate is a bold barrel-vaulted concert hall and recording studios inserted in 2001, and connecting to both buildings.

Making our way along Marylebone Road to the ⑭ **Ulster Place** exit of Regent's Park, this terrace, named for George IV's younger brother, Frederick, Earl of Ulster and Duke of York, is an unusual Nash design in that it is devoid of columns and pilasters. However, each of the two end bays has bay windows for emphasis.

Cross the Marylebone Road and we arrive at ⑮ **Park Crescent** – Nash designed this to be a circus, which would have made it the largest in Europe, but only the southern half was realised. Nevertheless, the crescent makes an impressive statement and it is probably more recognisably 'Nash' than any of the Outer Circle terraces. A single storey colonnade runs the length of each of these curving terraces which makes for simply elegant architecture. The generally pristine exterior decoration and stucco work are the result of a total renovation in the early 1960s when many of the somewhat shabby houses were turned into offices.

Between the two terraces of Park Crescent is the start of ⑯ **Portland Place**. Originally laid out by the Adam brothers in 1773 as a speculative building venture, the street was the widest in London at the time and the scheme was intended for grand, detached mansions. However, the financial crisis brought about by the American War of Independence resulted in houses of rather less ambition.

Nash did not need to make any changes to this arrangement as it suited his Via Triumphalis project beautifully. However, the Victorians were less respectful of Regency grandure with one of the finest Adam houses in London, Foley House, built in 1758, demolished in 1864 to make way for the huge Langham Hotel. This marked the beginning of the end - for little evidence now remains of Adam's work in Portland Place.

On the east side of Portland Place, at the corner with Weymouth Street, is the ⑰ **Royal Institute of British Architects**, built 1932-34 by Grey Wornum. Designed in total sympathy with the Adam remains, it is no taller than any of the 18th-century houses yet it is instantly recognisable as a modern piece of architecture. Made from Portland stone, everything about the outside of this building is crisply cut with square or rectangular windows and the huge bronze entrance doors, flat roof and corner plot exaggerate this. There are also interesting bas-relief sculptures by Edward Bainbridge Copnall (1903-73); the figure above the main door is entitled 'Architectural Inspiration'.

What has survived can be seen on the exterior of ⑱ **numbers 17, 21** (with Ionic pilasters and pediment), number 23 and, best of all, ⑲ **numbers 27-47** (the centre of which was unfortunately lost to World War II enemy bombing). Number 48, thought to have been designed solely by James Adam has an interesting double door. Most of these buildings are now in commercial rather than residential use.

At the end Portland Place, ahead of you, is the huge aforementioned ⑳ **Langham Hotel**. Built in the 1860s by architects Giles

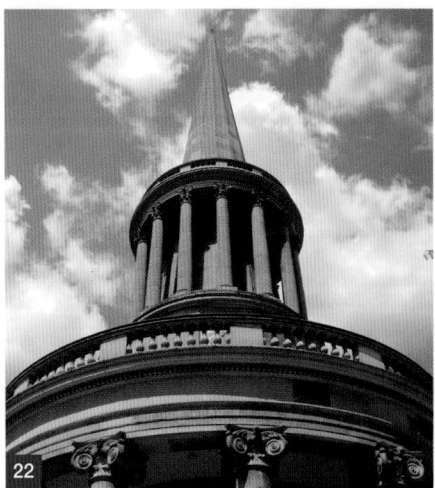

and Murray, at a time when the railways and colonialism had brought greater mobility to the populace, the Langham was an outstanding example of the rash of hotels under construction at the time.

Across Portland Place, on the east side is ㉑ **BBC Broadcasting House**. This is one of those buildings which provokes strong feelings – people either love it or loathe it. Likened to a huge ship, the Tower of Babel and hated by the doyen of architectural writers, Nicholas Pevsner, Broadcasting House was designed by G Val Myers and completed in 1931. The site is an extremely awkward one and the technical requirements of broadcasting made this an unenviable project. The superb sculptures on the exterior of the building are by Eric Gill; of particular note is 'Prospero and Ariel' placed above the main entrance. The demolition of some earlier extensions made way for a new headquarters complex in 2006, which, at 80,000 square metres (860,000 square feet), makes it one of the world's largest and most technically advanced broadcasting facilities. This new building wraps itself behind the heavy mass of Broadcasting House and provides an outdoor performance space close to All Souls Church. However, the saga of this scheme was a rather a bitter and protracted one with the original architect, Sir Richard MacCormac, leaving the project at an early stage.

John Nash cleverly placed the church of All Souls in Langham Place at a point where his Via Triumphalis needed to change direction at the top of Regent Street from Portland Place. He did this at the other end of Regent Street too, by gently taking one's gaze onto another vista. Nash, being the first architect to apply 'town-planning' on such a massive scale in London, is often compared with Haussmann, the man who re-organised so much of Paris in the late 1840s. Nash, however was able to create his little tricks on the eye with twists and turns accommodating any awkwardness in the lay of the land, unlike Haussmann, who had to build in straight lines for purposes of security in post-revolution Paris.

Nash designed ㉒ **All Souls Church** in 1822-24 with a large, circular portico and pillars of the Ionic order with the roundness softening the corner into Langham Place. Atop the portico is a rather curious smaller version of itself from which rises a pointed spire. The inside is light and airy with galleries carried on Corinthian columns. The church is often used for services and concerts broadcast by the BBC. There are, additionally, occasional free lunchtime concerts (for more details see p.321). All Souls Church is the only Nash-building intact on this route, although it received extensive damage from enemy bombing during World War II.

Walking from Langham Place, down Regent Street towards Oxford Circus, we come to the junction of two of the busiest shopping streets in the world – Oxford Street and Regent Street.

Oxford Circus was subject to a two-year project, completed at the end of 2009 at a cost of over £5 million, to relieve some of the serious traffic congestion in the area. A new pedestrian crossing modelled on the famously frantic junction adjoining Shibuya station in central Tokyo was installed and the jumble of street signs and railings have been swept away to make negotiating the area a much more pleasant experience.

Cross Oxford Circus and carry on walking down Regent Street.

Although we are still following the route of the Via Triumphalis, there is nothing left of

Above: Bust of John Nash by Cecil Thomas in portico of All Souls Church. For more information on Nash see p.120

Nash's much acclaimed architecture on Regent Street that had been completed by 1825. The buildings were similar to those we saw at Park Crescent and almost immediately became the focus of the fashionable London social scene. In 1848 the distinctive colonnades were removed; it was rumoured they harboured prostitutes and other unsavoury characters and by the end of the century these premises were deemed too small for the purpose of modern retailing.

Regent Street now hosts many 'flagship' shops such as the Apple Store at number 235 (on your right, just after Oxford Circus).

We arrive now at ㉓ **Piccadilly Circus**, formed when Nash needed to curve his Via Triumphalis into Piccadilly from Regent's Street. It is quite difficult to imagine – standing in the hubbub of people, traffic, and flashing advertisement hoardings – that this was once an elegant oasis of calm! Nash had placed a circle of stuccoed buildings here, not unlike Park Crescent. Unfortunately in the 1880s this arrangement was spoilt by the demolition of the north east quarter of the circle to accommodate the formation of Shaftesbury Avenue. By 1910 the trend for bright, electrically lit advertisements had been started by Bovril and Schweppes and a decade later even larger ones were in place and had become a successful tourist attraction.

The last stretch of Regent Street culminates in ㉔ **Waterloo Place**, named after the then recent battle against Napoleon. This is where Nash's Via Triumphalis was to terminate, at the entrance of Carlton House, the home of the Prince Regent. It was mooted that the most appropriate buildings for this area should be gentlemen's clubs and that their façades should be identical; this latter stipulation was unpopular and not enforced. For The United Services Club of 1826-28, on the east side of Waterloo Place, south of Pall Mall, now ㉕ **The Institute of Directors Building**, John Nash designed a masculine building with just more than a hint of Rome, with a broad two-storey portico consisting of double Doric columns at the lower level and Corinthian columns above.

However attractive this building is, it really does not compare with Decimus Burton's ㉖ **Athenaeum**, also in Waterloo Place, on the west side, and also south of Pall Mall. Built in 1827-30 it is much more of a coherent whole with a very fine Doric frieze running on three sides, carved by John Henning junior. Above the entrance is a large gilt copy of the Pallas Athene of Velletri by E H Baily.

Heading straight on to Carlton House Terrace, we come to the beginning, or end, depending on which way the Prince was travelling, of Nash's 'Triumphant Route'. This street is named for the very large house that once stood on the spot, built originally in 1709, which then became the residence of Henry Boyle, the first Lord Carlton. Remodelled by Sir William Chambers, the house became the residence of the Prince of Wales, the future Prince Regent in 1772.

The Prince was noted for his extreme extravagance in all matters, so it is perhaps no surprise that he engaged the eminent architect Henry Holland to turn Carlton House into a sort of 'Golden House of Nero'. The Prince also employed an army of French decorators and his painted rooms were the talk of the town, as was the debt he was running up: a cool £640,000 by 1795. Even so, the Prince was unstoppable, adding a Gothic conservatory with cast iron fan vaults. The employment of the services of John Nash in 1813, initially to design a Gothic dining room for the Prince, was the beginning of a long association and friendship.

By 1820 the Prince Regent had become King George IV, and having no further use for Carlton House ordered its demolition.

㉗ Carlton House Terrace was designed by John Nash 1827-33 and the whole is pleasing to the eye – offering its best side perhaps to the view from St James's Park. The two long ranges, nine houses in each, are reminiscent of his work around Regent's Park and were the last of Nash's grand designs as he was to die not long after their completion in 1835. Although built as terraces, each individual house is different and Nash was perfectly happy to allow other architects to embellish his basic work here. Numbers 7-9, until World War II, made up the German Embassy with the interior having been remodelled by Albert Speer, Hitler's favourite architect. This is the only example of Speer's work in London (this building is not open to the public).

At number 10 is the British Academy, an organisation that champions and supports the humanities and social sciences and the building is often open for small exhibitions. Next door is the Institute of Contemporary Arts (ICA); a dedicated space for new, experimental and independent arts practice and ideas. On site are two galleries, two cinemas, a theatre, a reading room, bookshop and a super café/bar.

The terraces form a rather good frame for the **㉘ Duke of York's Column** and the powerful granite flight of steps down to St James's Park. The Column is in honour of Prince Frederick Augustus, Duke of York and Albany (1763-1827), the second son of King George III and the Prince Regent's brother. The Column was erected 1831-34 and is loosely modelled on Trajan's Column in Rome. The drum and dome at the top are based on Hooke/Wren's Monument in the City. Designed by B D Wyatt the whole column stands at 137 feet tall, including the bronze statue of the Duke dressed in his Garter robes.

Although Nash's Via Triumphalis finished at the Duke of York's Column we can take in one more London gem, ㉙ **Buckingham Palace**, a project in which John Nash became heavily involved. Go down the steps into The Mall, turn right and walk along to the Palace. There has been a house on the site since at least the mid 17th century, and it was John Sheffield, 1st Duke of Buckingham and Normanby who built his country house here in 1702-05, partly on land owned by himself and partly on Crown land. In 1762 George III purchased the house. The official residence of the monarch was St James's but the young King found the rambling and ramshackle apartments unsuitable for his new wife. Indeed the royal couple, who had fifteen children, were very content with Buckingham House. It was still, however, very much a house and not yet a palace.

It was on the succession of George IV that things changed dramatically. Against advice, he employed his trusted architect friend John Nash and spent colossal amounts of money remodelling the building. Within three years, 1825-28, the exterior alterations had been completed.

When the King died suddenly in 1830, Nash was immediately sacked from his post. The thrifty, reliable architect Edward Blore was given the task of completing the work which was to take many years yet. Indeed George IV's successor, his brother William IV, died in 1837 without ever living at the Palace. The first reigning monarch to do so was Queen Victoria, who she was said to have been 'most happy' there and it has been the London residence of the royal family ever since.

The last major alteration to the building took place in 1913 when Sir Aston Webb added the east wing façade. This is the 'side' of the Palace which is most familiar, made from Portland stone in a neo-classic style but which has received much criticism, most usually because the façade is seen as predictable and boring.

During the summer months of August and September, when the royal family are on holiday elsewhere, the state rooms of the Palace are open to the public; a scheme that was started in the early 1990s to help raise funds to repair fire damage at Windsor Castle. Eighteen state rooms are usually available for viewing during the period of opening. Visitors enter through the Ambassador's Court and take the grand staircase to the set of rooms created by Nash, which, despite all the past controversy, are the highlight of most people's visit.

㉚ **The Buckingham Palace Ticket Office** itself is a little gem designed by Michael Hopkins and Partners. The small timber cabin has a tensile fabric canopy which covers the whole structure and which is erected at the beginning of the tourist season and taken down at the end of it.

More Information:

**London Central Mosque
& Islamic Cultural Centre**
146 Park Road, NW8 7RG
Tel: 020 7724 3363
www.iccuk.org
Transport: Baker Street LU
See website for details
Note: All visitors must remove
their shoes before entering
the building and women
must cover their heads

**Royal Academy
of Music Museum**
Marylebone Road, NW1 5HT
Tel: 020 7873 7373
www.ram.ac.uk/museum

**Royal Institute of British
Architects (RIBA)**
66 Portland Place, W1B 1AD
Tel: 020 7580 5533
www.architecture.com
Transport: Regent's Park or
Great Portland Street LU

All Souls Church
Langham Place, W1B 3DA
Tel: 020 7580 3522
www.allsouls.org
Transport: Oxford Circus LU

Buckingham Palace
The Mall, SW1A 1AA
Tel: 020 7799 2331www.
the-royal-collection.org.uk
Transport: St James's Park LU
See website for opening
times & entrance charges

South Bank Walk

1. Tower Bridge
2. The Bridge Theatre
3. City Hall
4. The Scoop
5. HMS Belfast
6. Hay's Wharf / Galleria
7. Cottons Centre
8. St Olaf House
9. No 1 London Bridge
10. London Bridge
11. Obelisk
12. Southwark Cathedral
13. Borough Market
14. George Inn
15. Golden Hinde
16. Winchester House
17. The Market Porter
18. Clink Museum
19. The Anchor
20. Southwark Bridge
21. Globe Theatre
22. Millennium Bridge
23. Tate Modern
24. Bankside Lofts
25. Blackfriars (road) Bridge
26. 1 Blackfriars (The Boomerang)
27. Oxo Tower
28. Gabriel's Wharf
29. National Theatre
30. Rambert Dance Company

South Bank Walk

Walking along the south bank of the River Thames and taking in the variety of architecture and stunning views of the City over the water is one of the most pleasurable things to do in London today. However, this area hasn't always been so pleasant, for Bankside was once notorious for its lowlife which included 'stews', a sort of combined bathhouse and brothel, bear baiting, unsavoury taverns and stinking prisons. These coexisted with lively theatres showing plays by Shakespeare and his contemporaries; indeed we shall encounter the Bard in a few of the buildings on this walk. During the 18th century much of the area was given over to docks and industrial use and it has been only in the last 20 or so years that the south bank has become a place of leisure and pleasure again.

It is perfectly possible to do this walk at any time of the day or evening, depending if you specifically want to see the interior of any of the buildings en route. Please refer to the list at the end of the walk for details of the individual places of interest, p.335. There are plenty of places to stop for a drink or a meal throughout the walk.

We are going to start this walk at the south end of ❶ **Tower Bridge**, details of which can be found on p.395. The Bridge is always worth viewing at close-quarters, even if you think you know the structure well and it offers one of the best views in London.

Walking west along the Thames Path, with the river to your right we come to Potters Field Park, a small grassy area beloved by children and tired tourists alike. To your left is One Tower Bridge, a low rise residential block containing The Ivy Tower Bridge restaurant and ❷ **The Bridge Theatre**. The building was designed by the prolific, if unsung, London-based architectural practice Squires and Partners, with the theatre by architects Haworth Tomkins, whose previous work includes the 2014 Stirling Prize winning Liverpool Everyman Theatre. The highly flexible space, with a seating capacity for an audience at least 900, opened in 2017 and is the first theatre to be built in London for over four decades. The attractive and comfortable foyer is open daily from morning coffee until late. It's worth going just to see the five hundred bespoke copper light fittings, designed by Haworth Tomkins, that illuminate this public space.

Continuing west along the Thames Path, still with the river to your right, we arrive at the distinctive form of ❸ **City Hall**, which is described on p.242. In conventional terms, the building has no front or back. Its elegant shape is derived from a geometrically modified sphere, designed to minimise the surface area exposed to direct sunlight. The north facade, which receives minimal direct solar heat gain, has un-shaded glazing whereas the south facade inclines so that each floor shades the offices below. There is a visitor centre and a flexible exhibition and function space at the higher levels with a public viewing gallery at the top, all which are open during the week and sometimes at the weekend, see p.335 for more details. The assembly chamber is definitely worth seeing; a transparent and open space looking out over the river to the City and reminiscent of Foster's Reichstag project in Berlin.

As we walk on along the Thames we pass ④ **The Scoop**, to the right of City Hall, an 800 seat sunken amphitheatre which hosts free events throughout the summer months. City Hall and the Scoop are part of More London, a 13 acre development that stretches from Tower Bridge almost to London Bridge. The development includes a hotel, shops, cafés and office space for almost 20,000 people within a pedestrian area incorporating some interesting public sculpture and water features. Norman Foster and Partners were responsible for the master plan of the project.

Continuing west one comes to ⑤ **HMS Belfast** a 11,500 ton battlecruiser launched in 1938 and which could accommodate a crew of 950 men. It has been a floating museum since 1971. Details of visiting times can be found below.

Walking on we arrive at ⑥ **Hay's Wharf**, originally built in 1651 and London's oldest and largest dock. The present warehouse was designed by Thomas Cubitt in 1856 and was used for storing the vast amounts of butter and cheese imported from New Zealand so the building was nicknamed 'London's Larder'. In 1988 the building was restored and given a glazed roof, modelled on Milan's Galleria Vittorio Emanuele and is now a mix of offices, shops, bars and cafés, and home to a huge sculpture by David Kemp titled 'The Navigators'. Constructed in 1987 it pays homage to the area's shipping heritage. Hay's Wharf is certainly worth having a walk through, as too is its neighbour the ⑦ **Cottons Centre**. The Cottons Centre is an office complex with an impressive landscaped atrium housing a number of works of sculpture and where there is often an interesting art exhibition to view. Designed by the London-based architectural practice Twigg Brown, the development reflects how much thought has been given to the riverside exterior landscaping with its welcoming seating area.

There are good information boards along this stretch of the walk illustrating the history of the 'Pool of London', as the river between Tower Bridge and London Bridge is known, and which constituted the farthest reach that could be navigated by a tall-masted vessel. The banks of the river were crammed with wharfs and ships vied with each other for space, as goods, especially coal, were brought to the capital to sustain its ever-growing population. It is said that by the late 18th century the Pool was so congested with ships it was possible to walk from one side of the river to the other just by stepping from one vessel to another. The abrupt collapse of commercial traffic in the Thames, due to the introduction of shipping containers and coastal deep-water ports, such as Harwich, in the 1960s emptied the Pool and led to all of the wharves being closed down, and many being demolished. The area was extensively redeveloped in the 1980s and 1990s to create the new residential and commercial neighbourhoods we see today.

Walking towards London Bridge we walk past London Bridge Hospital (originally built as a warehouse in the 1860s) and pause at the next building along, **❽ St Olaf House**. Built in 1931 as the offices for Hay's Wharf it now serves as an administration block for the hospital next door. This riverside frontage is adorned with Doulton faience panels by Frank Dobson (1886-1963), showing dock life and the unloading of goods titled 'Capital, Labour and Commerce'. It is well worth taking a short diversion into St Olaf Stairs, a passageway between St Olaf House and the pink granite building next door, in order to have a look at the front of the building. You will find further detail about this building on p.196.

The site of St Olaf House had been occupied for many centuries by St Olave's Church, which was the parish church for the area and which remained through all the changes to the district right up to the late 1920s. The church tower had been a landmark in the area since medieval times.

Heading towards London Bridge, passing the cool presence of **❾ No 1 London Bridge**, which consists of two office blocks, one thirteen-storey, one ten-storey and both clad in soft pink granite and linked by a glass atrium. The eastern block, nearest to the bridge, has a dramatic overhang supported by a column clad in polished stainless steel; the window frames of the building are of the same material. Designed by the John S Bonnington Partnership this building really catches the light and must surely cheer the throng of workers as they stream over **❿ London Bridge** between the railway station and the City.

There has been some sort of bridge over this part of the Thames since Roman times. Indeed being able to cross the river here with relative ease is the very reason settlers stopped here and why what we now call 'London' was born. A succession of bridges has served this area throughout history – the medieval bridge was lined with houses and shops although these were removed when it was widened in the middle of the 18th century. In 1824 a new stone bridge was built consisting of five arches, designed by the eminent engineer John Rennie. In 1924 it was found that not only was the unprecedented increase in traffic a problem, but also one side of the bridge was sinking, albeit very slowly, and so the new present bridge was commissioned.

Imagine the surprise of the City of London authorities when an American developer, Robert P McCulloch, on hearing of the imminent disposal of Rennie's bridge, offered to buy it from them. Apparently it was just what he wanted for his leisure park being built near Havasu City, Arizona and so the 10,000 or so pieces of the bridge were dismantled and numbered before being shipped to the United States for rebuilding on dry land before water was diverted under it. What replaced it in London is a somewhat utilitarian prestressed concrete bridge by Mott, Hay and Anderson engineers with architect Lord William Holford.

You may wish to take the steps up to London Bridge itself, turn left and make your way to The Shard Quarter, and the tallest building in the United Kingdom. After approximately 50 metres, on your left you will see the 16 metre tall ⓫ **Obelisk**, made from 25 blocks of Portland stone and designed by architect Eric Parry to mark the boundary between two of the oldest London Boroughs, Southwark, and the City. In place by 1999, this tilting monument surely foresaw the coming of the Shard many years later. See Chapter 7 for more information on The Shard's architect Renzo Piano.

Passing under London Bridge, past the Mudlark pub, a 'mudlark' being someone who made a living scavenging for items of value in the river mud, and after a few more steps we have ⓬ **Southwark Cathedral** on our left side, see p.33 for a brief description.

There is much to look at inside the Cathedral, especially the Shakespeare Monument and Window; the Harvard Chapel in celebration of John Harvard, the founder of the American university who was baptised here, and within that chapel the splendid, tall gilded tabernacle designed by A W N Pugin.

Once you have completed your visit to the Cathedral there is an opportunity for a digression or two. Almost next to Southwark Cathedral is the ⓭ **Borough Market**, a 'foodie's paradise, but only open for trade on certain days of the week. There has been a market on this spot since approximately 1014.

If it is liquid you require at this point, rather than food, then there are plenty of options in this area. One of the best, The George Inn, is about five minutes walk away, but is worth the detour, being one of the most interesting pubs in London. To get there walk along the street between Southwark Cathedral and Borough Market, away from the river; this is 'Cathedral Street', but it becomes 'Bedales Street'. This will bring you to the busy Borough High Street; cross at the traffic lights and carry on walking on under a grey bridge until you arrive at The George Inn at number 77. ⓮ **The George Inn** is London's only surviving galleried coaching inn, more details about which can be found on p.364. When you have finished retrace your steps back to the Cathedral and Market.

Walk towards the river down Cathedral Street, with a new-build office block to your right and Pickford's Wharf, an early 19th-century storage building to your left but which is now rather smart apartments with retail space at its ground floor. Here we see a full scale replica of ⓯ **The Golden Hinde**, the Tudor warship in which Sir Francis Drake circumnavigated the globe between 1577 and 1580. Tours can be made of the vessel and it can be hired for parties, see p.335 for more details.

Take the narrow street at the north of Picksford's Wharf building, the side away from the river. This is Clink Street and here we find the remains of ⓰ **Winchester House**, the

London residence of the Bishops of Winchester from the 12th to the 17th century and which would have been not too dissimilar to Lambeth Palace further along the Thames. The grounds of the House would have extended down to the river where the successive bishops came and went by barge. Nothing is left of the original 12th-century building but what remains dates from the early 14th century: just part of two walls of the Great Hall with a few doorways. However, perhaps of greatest interest is the remains of a rose window which was restored in 1972. Seeing it in its skeletal form one wonders if it could have looked any more beautiful with coloured glass. The site is a 'Scheduled Ancient Monument' and enjoys the same protection as Stonehenge. In recent years Edward Cullinan Architects have sensitively incorporated these remains with restaurants and retail areas at ground level with residential and offices above.

If you are fond of diversions, particularly to public houses, here is another one for you. As you pass the building which incorporates the remains of Winchester House, turn left into Stoney Street and keep walking past the old warehouse buildings and shops, with Borough Market now on your left, until you come to a pub on the corner with Park Street. This is the **⓱ Market Porter** bar and restaurant and a good example of the once ubiquitous Victorian corner public house with its warm, inviting interior. The building was transformed into the 'Third Hand Book Emporium' in the film 'Harry Potter and the Prisoner of Azkaban', and was situated next to 'The Leaky Cauldron'!

Retrace your steps back along Stoney Street to Clink Street. It is the tall, gloomy building standing proud of its neighbours on your left, which gives the street its name, for this is the site of The Clink, a notorious prison which functioned from the 12th century until it was burnt down in 1780 and originally owned by the Bishops of Winchester. The **⓲ Clink Prison Museum** is housed in the basement of the warehouse that was built over the site, details of which are below.

At the end of Clink Street, turning right into Bankside we will find another historic pub ⓳ **The Anchor** which has at its core a mid-17th century building and is certainly a pleasant place to stop and contemplate the fantastic view across the river. It is said that it was from here that Samuel Pepys watched the destruction of the City in the Great Fire of 1666. Samuel Johnson, lexicographer and writer, frequently drank here and a copy of his groundbreaking dictionary of 1755 is on display here.

With the river to our right we carry on walking along Bankside, past blocks of flats and the shiny black glass head office of the *Financial Times*, through the pedestrian underpass of ⓴ **Southwark Bridge**. This underpass is rather a joy with the relatively recent addition of five Westmorland green slate panels, engraved by London artist Richard Kindersley, depicting scenes from the Frost Fairs that were held

⓴ *Southwark Bridge*

whenever the Thames froze over. The Fairs were held on the Thames during the 15th to the 19th century when the British winter was more severe than now, and the river was wider and slower. The bridge itself is the second to have been constructed at this point on the Thames. The first was opened in 1819 to a design by John Rennie, a beautifully simple iron bridge of only three spans, a considerable feat of contemporary engineering, built to relieve the terrible traffic congestion that choked London Bridge. However, Rennie's bridge was deemed too narrow to be useful and a new one was commissioned in 1912, but not completed until 1921 having suffered delays in building during the First World War. The Southwark Bridge under which you pass, was designed by architect Sir Ernest George and Mott and Hay engineers in granite-faced steel with rather strange light coloured stone pier-headings with little 'windows'.

Out of the bridge tunnel and with the river and the Bankside Jetty on our right, where one gets a great view of the City, just ahead of us is one of the most exciting additions to London in recent years the ㉑ **Globe Theatre**. Built just metres away from the original theatre that Shakespeare was familiar with, this new Globe was the brainchild of American actor and director Sam Wanamaker who founded what was to become the Shakespeare's Globe Trust in 1970 and some twenty years later work on the theatre got underway.

It is uncertain what the original theatre actually looked like, but with the aid of modern scholarship and an adherence to Elizabethan building methods a wonderful building has been constructed. Architect Theo Crosby, who gave Wanamaker's dream architectural expression, insisted on using only natural materials and high-quality craftsmanship. Mass-produced materials were banned from the site. Handmade Tudor-sized bricks, 36,000 of them, were fashioned especially for the project and these required 90 tons of lime putty. Green oak laths and staves were used for both sides of the walls and 180 tons of lime plaster was required to cover the outer walls, beautifully crafted by Peter McCurdy and his company. The roof is made from 6,000 bundles of water reed from Norfolk and the Globe was the first building since the Great Fire of London in 1666 to be granted permission for a thatched roof.

Plays are performed regularly throughout the summer season and tours of the building are available, please see p.335 for details.

A recent addition to the Globe Complex is the Sam Wanamaker Playhouse, a recreated 17th-century indoor theatre that opened in 2014. Designed by Jon Greenfield this intimate, candlelit theatre seats an audience of 340 and is based on a design by John Webb, a pupil of Inigo Jones.

Walking on along Bankside we see on our left a cluster of houses. Number 49 is a three-storey early 18th-century building, numbers 50-52 Bankside are a century older and were the Provost's Lodging for the Dean of Southwark Cathedral. In between the houses is Cardinal Cap Alley, which once led to a tavern, drinking house or brothel called the Cardinal's Hat.

Now it is difficult on what to focus first, the gloriously large expanse that is Tate Modern or the exquisite ㉒ **Millennium Bridge**. Bridge first then. Unfortunately, this will always be known as the 'wobbly bridge' since its unfortunate swaying episodes at its opening. The problems were quickly solved, and the bridge is now perfectly stable. This wonderful bridge, also known as 'the blade of light' is the result of collaboration between architect Norman Foster, Arup engineers and sculptor Anthony Caro, and provides a useful link between Bankside and St Paul's Cathedral and the City beyond. There is a splendid view up and down the river from the centre of the bridge.

㉓ **Tate Modern** started life as the Bankside Power Station, generating electricity for London from 1952 to 1981 and was designed by Giles Gilbert Scott, designer of, amongst other things, the red K3-6 telephone box. The redundant building was threatened with demolition until in 1994 the Tate Gallery came up with the genius idea of turning it into a space for displaying international modern art. After a £135 million conversion by Jacques Herzog and Pierre de Meuron, who fashioned galleries from its steel and brick industrial architecture, Tate Modern opened on 12 May 2000. In its first decade an estimated 45 million visitors have been awed by this fabulous building, some may even have come to look at the pictures! See Chapter 7 for further details of this building.

If you exit Tate Modern from the Turbine Hall you will see ahead of you a tall, yellow building which is part of the **㉔ Bankside Lofts** development, a combination of converted and new buildings set around a new raised garden. A red-brick Italianate ex-cocoa mill is at the centre of the group. To its north is a 1950s building of similar height curving round the street line which has been extended upwards and sideways to form a snail plan spiral tower of stepping terraces with large steel windows in an orange/yellow rendered frame. Both buildings have enviable single and double height lofts on the upper floors with commercial floors at ground and basement. To the south are Nell Gwynne's House (number 67 Hopton Street), a restored 17th-century cottage, which at one time was the home of the cocoa mill owner, and a five-storey brick new-build office building which also has a stepped section. To its east, and south of the garden, is the final element, a newly built loft building which is angled to gain good views of the City across the river. This project was designed by CZWG Architects for the Manhattan Loft Corporation and was completed in 1998. There is no public access to the site.

Walking on, again with the river to our right, first we pass under the Blackfriars Railway Bridge, rather grim at this level, then into the pedestrian underpass of **㉕ Blackfriars (road) Bridge**. Dating from the 1860s and designed by Joseph Cubitt, Blackfriars Bridge is a wide, noisy thoroughfare for traffic and is named for the abbey on the other side of the river, which housed an order of Dominican monks who wore black robes. For our delight, the pedestrian underpass has illustrations of the construction of the bridge on its tiled walls.

Pausing in front of the Doggetts Coat and Badge public house, with your back to the river, it is possible to catch a glimpse of one of the newest, shiniest additions to the London skyline, built just behind this pub. At 50 storeys, and measuring 170 metres in height, this is one of the tallest residential blocks in Europe. Designed by Ian Simpson for the Berkeley Group the block contains the now familiar mix of residential apartments, hotel, restaurants and public spaces. Its official address is 'One Blackfriars' but, because of its rather distinctive shape, it is known as **㉖ 'The Boomerang'**.

Moving on, with low-rise apartment blocks, the Mondrian Hotel and offices on our left and with the river still to our right, the path takes a very small left kink and here we have the **㉗ Oxo Tower**, which has been a riverside landmark since it was built in 1928 as an Art Deco addition to a meat manufacturer's London base. At that time there was a ban on any form of neon-lit advertising in the area, however someone hit upon the idea of picking out the name OXO in coloured glass windows at the top of the tower and placing a strong light behind it and the name shone out into the London night. However, by the 1970s it had fallen into disrepair and was largely derelict.

In the 1980's the Tower was taken under the wing of the Coin Street Community Builders (CSCB), a social enterprise and development trust which seeks to make London's South Bank a better place in which to live, work and visit. They have transformed a formerly derelict thirteen acre site into a thriving mixed use neighbourhood by creating new cooperative 'affordable' homes, a park, riverside walkway, sports facilities, cafés, bars, restaurants, galleries and shops. They also organise festivals and events and make this area of London a lively and diverse place. On the eighth floor of the Oxo Tower is a viewing platform, which can be accessed by lift.

Walking on we pass ㉘ **Gabriel's Wharf**, its name hinting at its working past. This area was a derelict wasteland for a number of years until the 1980s when old garages on the site were given shop frontages and became the focus of craft workshops, boutiques and cafés and a lovely place to stroll around.

Passing more office blocks we come to the ㉙ **National Theatre** building designed by Sir Denys Lasdun, who was also responsible for the IBM office block, almost adjacent to the theatre, which we have just passed. More

㉙ *National Theatre*

properly named the Royal National Theatre, this building, a permanent home for the company formed in the early 1960s, was a long time coming, and its doors finally opened here on the South Bank in 1976.

The building actually contains three theatres – the largest is the Olivier, named for the great actor and the National's first artistic director Laurence Olivier, who did so much to make the dream of such an establishment became a reality. The Olivier has an open stage, audience seating for 1,160 and fans out in two tiers. The two other theatres are the Lyttleton, named for the National's first chairman of the Board of Governors, with a 890 capacity and a more conventional proscenium-arch stage; the smallest theatre is the Dorfman, a flexible studio space that can seat up to 300, depending on the production. The building is wrapped by interlocking terraces accommodating outdoor seating and viewing areas overlooking the Thames, with splendid views up and down the river.

A ticket to see a play is not necessary to enjoy the building, as it is open for most of the day and evening, Monday to Saturday, with cafés, bars, a well-stocked bookshop and exhibition space. For further Information about this building and its architect, please see Chapter 7.

Directly behind the National Theatre is the ㉚ **Rambert Dance Company** building. Leave the theatre by its main entrance, bear left then walk along Theatre Avenue where the roadway Upper Ground will be in front of you - across this road you will see a low rise building 'The Green Room', and to its left as we view it, you will see the Rambert. This seven-storey dance studio complex, created by architects Allies and Morrison, references its Brutalist neighbours with its pre-cast concrete façade. There are several double-height rehearsal spaces and associated changing facilities and offices. One of the latest additions to the South Bank cluster of cultural amenities, the Rambert received a RIBA National Award in 2014 as one of the best new buildings of the year. Although there is no public access to the Rambert it is an interesting project to contemplate, and to ponder our apparent love-hate relationship with concrete as a building material.

If you are still in the mood for some more architecture you could return to the front of the National Theatre, carry on walking in the same direction from where you came, going under Waterloo Bridge, where you will find the South Bank complex which includes the Royal Festival Hall (see p.217). Further along and you will arrive at the 'London Eye', see 'Architecture with a View', and the former County Hall (see p.186). Alternatively, make your way up to Waterloo Bridge (see Architecture with a View on p.395), cross to the other side of the Thames, turn left and follow the 'Strand Walk' or turn right and do the 'Fleet Street and Beyond Walk' in reverse.

More information:

Greater London Authority
City Hall,
The Queen's Walk, SE1 2AA
Tel: 020 7983 4000
www.london.gov.uk
Transport: London Bridge LU/Rail

HMS Belfast
The Queen's Walk, SE1 2JH
Tel: 020 7940 6300
www.hmsbelfast.iwm.org.uk
Transport: London Bridge LU/Rail

Hay's Galleria
Battle Bridge Lane, SE1 2HD
Tel: 020 7940 7770
Transport: London Bridge LU/Rail

Southwark Cathedral
London Bridge, SE1 9DA
Tel: 020 7367 6700
www.cathedral.southwark.
anglican.org
Transport: London Bridge LU/Rail

Borough Market
8 Southwark Street, SE1 1TL
Tel: 020 7407 1002
www.boroughmarket.org.uk
Transport: London Bridge LU/Rail
Open throughout week, check
website for details

George Inn
The George Inn Yard,
77 Borough High Street, SE1 1NH
Tel: 020 7407 2056
www.nationaltrust.org.uk
Transport: London Bridge LU/Rail

Golden Hinde
St Mary Overie Dock,
Cathedral Street, SE1 9DE
Tel: 020 7403 0123
www.goldenhinde.com
Transport: London Bridge LU/Rail

The Market Porter
The Market Porter,
9 Stoney Street, SE1 9AA
Tel: 020 7407 2495
www.markettaverns.co.uk
Transport: London Bridge LU/Rail

Clink Prison Museum
Clink Street, SE1 9DG
Tel: 020 7403 0900
www.clink.co.uk
Transport: London Bridge LU/Rail

The Anchor Public House
34 Park Street, SE1 9EF
Tel: 020 7407 1577
Transport: London Bridge LU/Rail

Globe Theatre
21 New Globe Walk, SE1 9DT
Tel: 020 7902 1400
www.shakespeares-globe.org
Transport: Southwark LU
See website for details of tours
& theatre tickets

Tate Modern
53 Bankside, SE1 9TG
Tel: 020 7887 8752
www.tate.org.uk
Transport: Southwark LU
Admission free (except for major
exhibitions)

Oxo Tower
& Gabriel's Wharf
South Bank, SE1 9PH
Tel: 020 7021 1600
www.coinstreet.org
Transport: Southwark LU

National Theatre
South Bank, SE1 9PX
Tel: 020 7452 3000
www.nationaltheatre.org.uk
Transport: Waterloo LU/Rail

Strand Walk

1. Royal Courts of Justice
2. St Clement Danes
3. 'Roman Bath'
4. St Mary-le-Strand
5. Somerset House
   Courtauld Institute of Art
   Courtauld Institute Gallery
6. King's College London
7. Australia House
8. Bush House
9. India House
10. ME London
11. Savoy Chapel
12. 6-10 Adam Street
13. Royal Society of Arts

This is a particularly good walk on a wet day as there are plenty of buildings to disappear into. We start this walk where the Fleet Street Walk finished, at the Temple Bar. We are now out of the City of London and Fleet Street has become the Strand. The street is so named because until the 19th century and the embankment of the river Thames, the Strand was very close to the river. The first building we stop at is the **❶ Royal Courts of Justice** on the north side of the road (stand with your back to the Temple Bar – the monument with the griffin on the top – and the building will be on your right).

The Royal Courts of Justice, often referred to as the 'Law Courts', stand on a seven acre site which was cleared of its festering slum dwellings in the mid 19th century to make way for a new Court of Justice. The Courts deal largely with civil cases such as family law and bankruptcy but some aspects of criminal law are dealt with here although jury trials are held at the Old Bailey (see p.182).

The Royal Courts of Justice were conceived in the wake of the success of the Parliament building in Westminster, with the consequence that every submitting architect put forward plans in the Gothic Revival style. The design of George Edward Street (1824-81) was chosen and work began in 1871. Street had previously built many churches and looking at the Royal Courts of Justice one could be forgiven for thinking the building was actually a cathedral! By the time the construction was

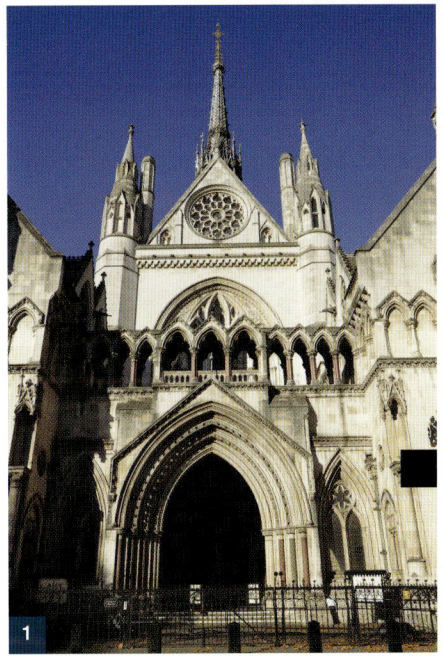

underway Gothic Revival was going out of fashion and, on its completion, the reception the building received was cool to say the least. This is particularly sad given that the architect died the year before it was finished – the stress of the project being said to have been a large contributory factor in Street's relatively early death.

The façade, so familiar as the background to reports from the Courts on television news programmes, is complicated: bay after bay of free design with pinnacles and towers stretching up and a rose window over the main entrance. The whole is brick built, an estimated 35 million were used, faced in Portland stone, and contains 1,000 separate rooms, 88 of them court rooms, served by an estimated 3.5 miles of corridors. Immense care was taken over detailing, such as the metal work on the exterior, and this attention to detail extends to the interior.

The public is allowed into the court rooms to watch proceedings, and there is a small exhibition of legal costumes. A good diversion from the walk is just to wander in and admire the splendour of Street's work (see p.343 for more details).

We now walk on to the church whose rear can be seen as we leave the Court. This is ❷ **St Clement Danes**, one of the two small churches which sit on islands in the middle of the Strand's heavy traffic, and whose name derives from the Danish settlers who came to the area in the 9th century.

The present church was built by Sir Christopher Wren in 1680-82, with additions to the tower and the provision of a spire by James Gibbs in 1719, but extensive restoration work was carried out in 1955 by Anthony Lloyd, who faithfully reproduced Wren's beautiful interior, following extensive bomb damage in the Blitz.

If the church is open and you have time, do go in and look at the plasterwork, particularly that on the barrel-vaulted ceiling and at the east end of the church. There is also a very good dark stained wooden gallery. This is the place to contemplate the immense task of the renovator, Anthony Lloyd, who studied photographs and drawings to re-create Wren's church and his work here is considered to be his most successful. In 1958 the church was adopted by the Royal Air Force, hence the proliferation of RAF badges and rolls of honour.

On leaving St Clement Danes cross to the south side of the Strand and proceed west. Make your way to Surrey Street, just off the Strand, and look for the entrance to the ❸ **Roman Bath**, which has a National Trust sign pointing you in the right direction.

Although known as a 'Roman Bath', there is certainly nothing to suggest that it is anything of the sort; the bricks are not Roman and there is no evidence of Roman settlement in the area. However, this was the site of a grand house owned by Thomas Howard, Lord Arundel (1586-1646). He had a passion for paintings, antiquities and travel and had been in Rome during the excavation of the Forum, so it is quite feasible that he would have returned with the idea of a Roman bath, perhaps with genuine decorations. The surrounding street names, Arundel and Surrey (he was also Earl of Surrey) commemorate the site's history. Dickens mentions this bath in his *David Copperfield*. The 'Roman Bath' can be viewed through the window from the pathway at any time.

Back to the Strand and we can now cross the road to the other church that sits in the middle of the road. This is the church of ❹ **St Mary-le-Strand**, details of which can be found on p.106

Return once more to the south side of the Strand to ❺ **Somerset House**. This was the site of a palace built 1547-52 by Edward Seymour, Duke of Somerset who foolishly fell out with his monarch Henry VIII, was duly executed in 1552 and his building passed into royal hands. The palace was the domain of the monarch's consort until the reign of George III and Queen Charlotte, who preferred Buckingham House. The buildings were demolished in 1775 and the architect William Chambers set about designing one of the first purpose-built office blocks in Europe. The offices were used by the Navy Board, the newly-formed Royal Academy of Arts and the Society of Antiquaries. Over the subsequent years the buildings also housed the Registry of Births, Marriages and Deaths and the head office of the Inland Revenue.

Completed first were the buildings we come to first, those that face the Strand. As you pass through the entrance arch the building to your left is the Courtauld Institute of Art and, except for those attending lectures or wishing to use one of the two art libraries, is not open to the public. The building to your right is the Courtauld Institute Gallery.

The Courtauld Gallery moved to Somerset House in 1990 and occupies rooms which were once home to the Royal Academy of Arts. Here is one of the best collections of art anywhere in Europe, with major works by the Impressionists and Post-Impressionists – including Degas, Cézanne, Manet, Renoir, Gauguin, and Van Gogh. Other periods are well represented in the collection, particularly early Flemish and Italian painting (for more details see p.343).

After the Gallery continue further into the courtyard of Somerset House – looking to your left through a gap in the buildings you will see the rear of ❻ **King's College London** and the building designed by Robert Smirke in 1829. So much better than the unfortunate 1960s front of the College which faces the Strand.

The courtyard of Somerset House used to be a car park for the Inland Revenue but is now a new space for cultural events. Known as Fountain Court, its new name is not misleading as there is indeed a charming group of fountains which magically turn into a skating rink during the winter months.

Somerset House holds a programme of temporary exhibitions in its Embankment Galleries which focus on contemporary fashion, architecture, photography and design. It is possible to walk through the south buildings of Somerset House and out onto the River Terrace, where you can take coffee, lunch, afternoon tea or supper during the summer months. A steel and glass walkway connects to Waterloo Bridge from here.

It is interesting to remember that until the 19th century and the embankment of the Thames, the river lapped against the terrace immediately below the building. The Water Gate, where boats would have sailed into the basement of Somerset House, is still visible.

After looking around William Chamber's magnificent neo-classical complex, we rejoin the Strand. Next stop on our walk is three of the buildings that languish between the Strand and Aldwych and are so often passed by when travelling by car or bus. All three buildings are of the early 20th century and were built as part of a town-planning scheme by the London County Council, rather in the mood of Nash and his Regent Street plan, but not nearly so ambitious. Slum dwellings were cleared and the tenants re-housed in blocks of flats on Drury Lane. Aldwych was to be the culmination of the widening and re-building of Kingsway and the architecture had to be fairly monumental. Unfortunately, as a group, the buildings look rather over-the-top, some might even say vulgar. It is most likely you will not be able to enter the buildings for security reasons, but the exteriors of Australia House and Bush House are worth looking at and are best viewed from the north side.

The first building of the group is ❼ **Australia House** and is on the extreme right of the group when you are looking at them with your back to Somerset House. Australia House is the oldest of the trio, built 1913-18 and designed by Marshall Mackenzie and was the first in a series of large buildings in London associated with Commonwealth countries, such as India House nearby and South Africa House in Trafalgar Square (see Whitehall Walk p.344). Fittingly for a High Commission the building is very grand in a Beaux Arts design.

Some excellent sculpture is incorporated within, as with all the buildings in this group. To the left and right of the main entrance are the monumentally-sized 'Awakening of Australia' and 'Prosperity of Australia' by Harold Parker, a British born, Australian trained sculptor of note. Above and central to the entrance is a sculpture in a heroic vein, a bronze male nude wearing just a cloak and crown with four horses entitled 'Phoebus Driving the Horses of the Sun' by Australian-born Bertram Mackennal. All the sculpture dates from the early 20th century.

The centre building, ❽ **Bush House**, designed by the New York architects Helme and Corbett in 1920-23, was named for its first owner Irving T Bush, an American. His vision was that the building would be a large, grand showcase for manufactured goods and the interior decoration reflects this, with ample application of marble. Alas the economic climate changed and the luxury goods market on which Bush had set his sights faltered, so the building was bought by the Church of Wales. In 1940 Bush House was leased to the British Broadcasting Corporation when it became the home of the BBC's World Service., Since 2012 Bush House has been part of the Strand Campus of King's College London.

The building is big and bold with two huge columns and two male figures, both twelve feet tall, representing England and America, each with an outstretched hand holding a torch between them in the arched area above. Bush House looks very impressive from Kingsway during the evening when the façade is illuminated.

❾ India House, by Sir Herbert Baker and Alexander Scott, was built in 1928-30 and its rather forgettable exterior belies its wonderful interior, mainly executed by Indian artists. If you are ever fortunate enough to be invited to tea by the Indian High Commissioner, do accept and take in the lovely carved jali-type open work decoration.

To the west of this trio of buildings, overlooking the busy junction of Aldwych, the Strand and Waterloo Bridge, is the white Portland stone façade of the Norman Foster designed **❿ ME London**, part of the international Melia hotels group. Once the site of the Edwardian Gaiety Theatre, rebuilt as offices in the late 1950s and subsequently demolished, in 2005, to make way for the hotel which opened in December 2012, Foster has produced a 157 bed hotel, with a minimalist interior in greys and whites, guest terraces and a rooftop garden and bar, from which there is a wonderful view to Westminster and beyond. Externally, the elliptical tower is a contemporary nod to its past and a glass canopy marks the entrance at street level. The overall project also incorporated the shell of the adjacent Marconi House, originally built in 1906 as the Gaiety Restaurant, with elevations by eminent architect Norman Shaw; this now houses 87 apartments.

Cross back over the road to the south (Somerset House) side and negotiate the traffic at Lancaster Place to continue along the Strand. On your right you will find Savoy Street and from there you will find Savoy Hill which is the location of the **⓫ Savoy Chapel**, or to give the building its full title, The Queen's Chapel of the Savoy.

This very simple chapel dates back to the Savoy Palace of John of Gaunt, Gaunt being the younger son of Henry III and born in Ghent, (hence 'Gaunt'). The palace was razed to the ground during the Peasants' Revolt of 1381.

The present building dates back to the early 16th century but a fire in the 18th century destroyed much of the original decoration, which has since been reconstructed. Note the nice heraldic details. In 1936 it became the chapel of the Royal Victorian Order and is now a private chapel of the present Queen. Visitors are most welcome to this relatively unknown little gem.

Further west along the Strand you will come across Adam Street which has several excellent examples of Robert Adam's work at ⓬ **numbers 6-10**. Another good example of his work is to be found just around the corner at the ⓭ **Royal Society of Arts** in John Adam Street (see p.118 for further details).

Walking on along to the end of John Adam Street, which runs parallel with The Strand, you will see before you an excellent example of Post-Modern architecture in Terry Farrell's Embankment Place, details of which can be found on p.256. Turn right into Villiers Street and walk on where you will rejoin The Strand.

This concludes our walk but if you would like to look at some more architecture, and you have the energy, you could continue west along the Strand to Trafalgar Square which is easy to find with Nelson's Column at its centre. Now you are ready to start the 'Whitehall Walk' (see p.344).

More Information:

Royal Courts of Justice
Strand, WC2A 2LL
Tel: 020 7947 6000
www.hmcourts-service.gov.uk
Transport: Temple LU
See website for opening times

St Clement Danes
Strand, WC2R 1DH
Tel: 020 7242 8282
www.raf.mod.uk/
stclementdanes
Transport: Temple LU
See website for tours,
opening times & events

St Mary-le-Strand
Strand, WC2R 1ES
0207 836 3126
www.stmarylestrand.org
Transport: Temple LU
See website for opening times

Somerset House
Somerset House, Strand,
WC2R 1LA
Tel: 020 7845 4600
www.somersethouse.org.uk
Transport: Temple or Covent Garden LU

The Courtauld Gallery
Somerset House, Strand,
WC2R 0RN
Tel: 020 7872 0220
www.courtauld.ac.uk/gallery
Transport: Temple or Covent Garden LU

The Savoy Chapel
Savoy Hill, Strand,
WC2R 0DA
Tel: 020 7836 7221
Open daily except Monday

Whitehall Walk

1. Trafalgar Square
2. Nelson's Column
3. National Gallery
4. Canada House
5. St Martin-in-the-Fields
6. South Africa House
7. Admiralty Arch
8. Admiralty House
9. Admiralty Screen
10. DEFRA
11. Old War Office
12. Horse Guards & Horse Guards Parade
13. Citadel
14. Whitehall Court
15. Ministry of Defence
16. Banqueting House
17. Downing Street
18. Privy Council Chambers
19. Foreign & Commonwealth Office
20. Cenotaph
21. National Monument to the Women of World War II
22. New Government Offices
23. Portcullis House
24. Houses of Parliament
25. Scotland Yard
26. Westminster Underground
27. Supreme Court
28. Westminster Abbey
29. St Margaret's Church

This walk starts and finishes at two world famous landmarks, Nelson's Column and the Houses of Parliament respectively and takes in fine examples of work by some of the best architects that Britain has produced. If started early enough in the day, the walk could culminate in a visit to Westminster Abbey. Refreshments can be obtained at the café and restaurant in the National Gallery, the crypt café at St Martin-in-the-Fields, the café in the Supreme Court building (Parliament Square) and the café at the Methodist Central Hall (see p.184). Whitehall enjoys easy access to St James's Park where you will find St James's Café (see p.372) by entering the park through Horse Guards Parade.

The 2003 re-routing of traffic from the north side of ❶ **Trafalgar Square** has given London an impressive new public space with a new café and plenty of places to sit and contemplate the surrounding buildings. The most famous landmark at the heart of the square is ❷ **Nelson's Column** (see right) and this monument together with the naming of the square, commemorates the British naval victory over the French at the Battle of Trafalgar on 21 October 1805. However, it was forty years after the event before it was decided to build some sort of memorial to the occasion and the man.

The site on which Trafalgar Square now stands has a long history of use. From at least the early 13th century it had been the Royal Mews; mews being a corruption of the French verb 'muer' meaning to moult, being the place where

❷ *Nelson's Column*

royal hawks were confined whilst moulting their feathers. During the 14th century the area was part of a pleasure garden and from the time of Elizabeth I it was the home of the royal stables. William Kent (1685-1748), architect responsible for Horse Guards Parade, built the Crown Stables here in 1732. The plot became vacant when the stables were re-located to Buckingham Palace, since when it has been a public area.

The first square on this site had been designed and built by John Nash in the 1820s, but this was remodelled in the 1840s by Charles Barry when it was decided to honour Nelson and his victory. The memorial to Nelson is probably better appreciated from a distance, being 185 feet in the air, but is nonetheless impressive from any angle. The statue itself stands at 17 feet, weighs 18 tons, was designed by E H Baily and executed in Craigleith stone from Edinburgh. The fluted Corinthian column on which the statue stands is of Devonshire granite from Foggin Tor carved by William Railton and the bronze Corinthian capital was inspired by examples from the Temple of Ultor, Rome. The bronze lions who lie at the bottom of the column were designed by Sir Edwin Landseer, who was one of Queen Victoria's favourite artists. The whole project was completed in 1868.

To the north of the Square stands the ❸ **National Gallery** built by William Wilkins between 1832-38, and to which the pedestrianised north terrace provides direct access. Built to house the nation's blossoming collection of publicly-owned art, it now ranks alongside the Louvre, the Prado and the Uffizi as one of the world's great art collections. Much criticism has been levelled at Wilkins' design, which aimed to produce a crowning effect for the square, but the building was felt to lack impact. Wilkins favoured, whenever possible, keeping his design 'pure' in the classical sense and perhaps lacked the ability to assimilate and to synthesise. The architect's decision to place a dome over the portico, with its eight Ionic columns from King George IV's newly demolished Carlton House in Pall Mall and turrets over the outer wings, attracted much derision. One critic likened the effect to a clock and two vases on a mantelpiece – but of less use! Wilkins also designed University College, in Gower Street, in a similar classical fashion.

As the gallery's collection grew so the building has been extended, three times during the 19th century, twice in the early 20th, and a further addition at the rear of the building added in the 1970s. The latest extension is the very substantial 'Sainsbury Wing', designed by the architectural partnership of Venturi, Rauch and Scott Brown, built between 1987-91. The rather sober exterior, incorporates echoes of Wilkins' Corinthian orders but takes nothing away from the main building's façade. The rather restrained and muted galleries inside are the perfect foil for the highly coloured collection of Italian and Northern European early Renaissance paintings displayed here.

Standing in Trafalgar Square with your back to the National Gallery you will find to your right ❹ **Canada House**, built by Robert Smirke between 1822-25 (see also the entry for British Museum p.125). This building was originally shared between the Royal College of Physicians and the Union Club. Smirke was a dedicated Greek Revivalist and this style is reflected in the unified Grecian Ionic order of this building. In 1924 the interior and some of the exterior was remodelled for the Canadian High Commission.

Still with your back to the National Gallery, to your left is the unmistakable frontage of James Gibbs' church of ❺ **St Martin-in-the-Fields**.

Completed in 1726, Gibbs' church would have been surrounded by squat, squalid medieval buildings which were eventually cleared away in Nash's rethinking of the space in the early 19th century, leaving St Martin in the Fields as exposed as we see it today. The interior was altered in 1887 by architect Sir Arthur Blomfield, with a somewhat lurid colour scheme, apparently sponsored by Harrods, added in 1904. Despite a shrinking congregation, the church and its associated buildings have been in constant, heavy use and in 2009 Eric Parry Architects completed a £36 million project to refurbish and refigure the whole complex. The result is outstanding. The exterior of the church has been cleaned and the interior space has been returned to the elegant, Baroque clarity that Gibbs envisaged; achieved by consulting his original model and drawings and a painting by Hogarth. The barrel vault ceiling has been returned to white and the gilding renewed. The hand-blown glass windows lend an air of calm, as does the beautiful, thought-provoking east window, specially commissioned by Iranian artist Shirazeh Houshiary.

Below the church itself, is the brick barrel-vaulted crypt accommodating the excellent café, accessed via a granite based pavilion to the north side of the church. The new space houses a large shop, information point and ticket office, a double-height church hall lined with smoked oak wood and a plain glass clerestory, and a music rehearsal room lined with light maple. Much of the space is lit by a two-story light well, particularly the 'Dick Sheppard Chapel', dedicated to the memory of the incumbent vicar of the same name who later became Dean of Canterbury Cathedral. Whilst at St Martin's he opened the crypt as a retreat

for homeless soldiers returning from the 1914-18 war and thereafter for anyone homeless. The church is still associated with those in need in the community. Lunchtime and evening concerts are held regularly.

Still to your left, but further down from St Martin is ❻ **South Africa House** (1935) by Sir Herbert Baker. Designed to be in keeping with the National Gallery and St Martin, its porticoes have been placed at the same level as Gibbs' church.

Walk down through Trafalgar Square, taking in the wonderful view stretching away down Whitehall towards the Houses of Parliament as you do so, and on reaching Whitehall to your right you will see ❼ **Admiralty Arch** designed by the respected architect Sir Aston Webb in 1908-11. The arch is part of a memorial to Queen Victoria, the other being her statue outside Buckingham Palace. The building is in fact three archways, all of equal height, with offices on either side, and makes a pleasing entrance to the Mall.

Continue along on the right hand side of Whitehall and you will find yourself outside ❽ **Admiralty House** built 1786-88 by S P Cockerell. Two and a half storeys tall, its most redeeming feature is its interior – which is sadly not open to the public. The house has been home to the First Lord of the Admiralty, of whom Earl Grey (1806) of tea fame and Winston Churchill (1911-15 and 1939-40) are but two. Built as an extension to the Admiralty (built 1722-6 by Thomas Ripley) next door, the rear of this whole complex can be viewed from Horse Guards Parade slightly further down Whitehall. In front of these buildings, facing Whitehall, is Robert Adam's ❾ **Admiralty Screen** made in 1760-61 when Whitehall was subject to a road-widening scheme. This is the first work Adam completed in London on his return from an extensive trip to Rome. The row of ten Tuscan columns against a blank wall hides the rather dour buildings behind and give a glimpse of Adam's blossoming genius.

Staying on this side but looking across the street to the white building that stands between Great Scotland Yard and Whitehall Place is ❿ **Department for the Environment, Food and Rural Affairs (DEFRA)**. The rather splendid 'front' onto Whitehall is actually the side of the building and was designed by J W Murray in 1906-9 in a Classical style in keeping with its neighbours, especially the Banqueting House, see p.47. DEFRA's immediate neighbour the ⓫ **Old War Office**, designed by Scottish architect William Young in 1898, and completed by his son Clyde Young, is a typical example of Edwardian Baroque.

Walking a little further down Whitehall you will come to two finely-dressed mounted guards, members of the Household Cavalry, who are usually surrounded by picture-snapping tourists. You have arrived at ⓬ **Horse Guards Parade**. This was at one time the site of the tiltyard of Whitehall Palace, where in 1540 Henry VIII presided over a huge tournament with knights journeying from all parts of Europe to attend. In 1650 a guardhouse was erected but after much enlargement and re-building, finally fell into decay. It was decided the whole building needed re-designing and this was done by William Kent in 1748. Construction was undertaken after Kent's death and was finished in 1760.

The result is not only one of the best and most accessible buildings in Whitehall, but perhaps one of the finest examples of Georgian architecture in Britain. In contrast to Inigo Jones's flat-fronted Banqueting House (see below), Kent manages to create a quite dramatic Palladian-inspired building, using projection and recession and without a single column in sight. The building is surmounted by a cupola containing a clock, to which the 18th-century Londoner looked for the correct time. Note the black circle around the Roman numeral II (two o'clock), which is probably a reference to the time at which King Charles I was executed just across the street, outside the Banqueting House some 100 years earlier in 1649.

Walking through the arches of the building you will arrive at the Horse Guards parade ground, which leads on to the Mall and St James's Park. It is in this parade ground that the Trooping the Colour takes place every year in celebration of the Queen's official birthday on 10 June. The rather curious, creeper-clad building at the north-west corner of the parade ground is the ❽ **Citadel**. Built in 1939 from blocks of compressed pebble and flint, it is the entrance to a series of deep underground shelters designed to house the country's political leaders during the air raids of the Second World War. It seems far too modern for its surroundings and yet it is a strangely attractive building and one of the few remaining examples of its type.

Return to Whitehall, and with your back to William Kent's magnificent building, almost directly opposite is Horse Guards Avenue. This short thoroughfare leads to ❾ **Whitehall Court** which, built by Archer and Green and completed in 1887, is an eight-storey block of very superior flats, faced with Portland stone in an almost French Renaissance style.

Another interesting building in this Avenue is the massive ❿ **Ministry of Defence** offices. Originally planned at the beginning of the 20th century, actual construction did not commence until 1938, with the project being delayed further by the outbreak of World War Two. Indeed the building took another 20 years to be completed. Designed by Vincent Harris, who had been responsible for several large public buildings, such as Sheffield City Hall, Leeds Civic Hall and Manchester Central Library, this huge building is entirely faced in Portland stone and has sculptures representing 'Earth' and 'Water' by Sir Charles Wheeler over the entrance. Perhaps the most exciting feature of this building, hidden within its basement and unable to be seen by the general public are the preserved remains of the wine cellar of the former Whitehall Palace, which used to occupy the space, and a fine example of a Tudor brick-vaulted roof some 70 feet long and 30 feet wide. The area now serves as the focus for Ministerial social gatherings.

Back on Whitehall stands the magnificent ⓰ **Banqueting House**. This building formed just a small part of the former Whitehall Palace, from which the road and indeed the whole area, takes its name. The story of Whitehall starts in 1514 when Cardinal Wolsey, then Archbishop of York, rebuilt the existing London house of the Archbishopric known as York Place. He built York Place in the grandest manner and in the latest fashion, but later fell foul of Henry VIII, being dismissed in 1529. Henry lost no time in occupying York Place. The building was renamed Whitehall Palace and became the monarch's principal London residence until William III (1650-1702). Henry acquired the land round about (what is now Horse Guards Parade) and had a tiltyard, four tennis courts and a cockpit built – truly a 16th-century leisure complex!

Banqueting House, Inigo Jones's addition to Whitehall Palace, was finished in 1622 in the reign of James I and may have been the intended start of an improvement plan for the whole site, but nothing further was built. Whatever architectural merit the building exudes (see p.47 for further details), its popular fame rests on its association with the execution of Charles I.

On the morning of Saturday 27th January 1649 in Westminster Hall, the clerk of the court read to the King his fate that 'this court doth adjudge that he the said Charles Stuart…shall be put to death by severing his head from his body'. The King was not allowed to speak but taken back to Whitehall and later the same day transferred to St James's Palace. Over the next two days workmen were busy setting up the scaffold against the walls of the north side of the Banqueting House facing Whitehall, and the building which epitomised the spirit of the Stuarts, with flamboyant masques and sumptuously painted ceiling, was now to be the backdrop for the dynasty's darkest hour.

The King was executed at two o'clock on 30th January, having been led from the private chambers through the hall of the Banqueting House and on to the scaffold via one of the large windows, which had been removed for the purpose. Charles won sympathy for his display of dignity at his trial and execution.

On 5th January 1698 Whitehall succumbed to a terrible fire which destroyed practically all of the Palace, although the Banqueting Hall miraculously escaped. The Court moved to St James's (see p.42) and Whitehall was never re-built.

Proceed south along Whitehall and on the same side of the road as Horse Guards Parade we arrive at the security gates that prevent entry to ⓱ **Downing Street**, the official London residence and office of the Prime Minister (Number 10) and of the Chancellor of the Exchequer (Number 11). If you are able to stop and peer through the gate note the modest Georgian façade of number 10, which is misleading, as the original house now connects with a much larger and grander house looking onto the Horse Guards parade ground. Downing Street dates from the late 17th century when it was developed by Sir George Downing, a speculative builder, after whom the street was named. Between 1766 and 1774 many alterations were made, but the street's façade has changed little since then. Number 10 was gifted to the country's first Prime Minister Sir Robert Walpole, by King George II in 1732.

In Whitehall on either side of Downing Street are government offices dating from the 19th century. To the north, that is the side closest to Trafalgar Square, stand the ⓲ **Privy Council Chambers** designed by Sir Charles Barry and built between 1844-5. On the south of Downing Street is the ⓳ **Foreign and Commonwealth Office**, designed by Sir George Gilbert Scott and constructed between 1862-75. The conception and birth of this building is steeped in controversy, an episode in the history of London architecture known as 'the Battle of the Styles'. Changes in government during the planning meant Gilbert Scott had to modify his plans for a Gothic construction to something more Italian. The final result, as we can see, is every inch a neo-Renaissance palace that would not look out of place in Florence.

The Foreign and Commonwealth Office is a huge complex; in reality four separately functioning blocks, each arranged around its own courtyard and linked by a large quadrangle at the centre. The India Office and the Foreign Office are at the rear, overlooking St James's Park and The Home Office and the Commonwealth Office face Whitehall. The interior of this whole building is particularly sumptuous, with grand reception rooms, dining rooms, suites of conference rooms and a domed State Staircase of marble, mosaic and gilding. This building is usually open to the public during 'Open House' weekend in September, see p.403 for further details.

In the centre of the busy Whitehall roadway there are statues and memorials, two of particular note being in the immediate vicinity. The first is the ⓴ **Cenotaph**, a word that means 'empty tomb'. This is the national memorial to those who lost their lives in both World Wars and all conflicts involving Commonwealth armed forces. Originally a simple wooden affair used as the focus of the 1919 victory parade, the Portland stone Cenotaph we see now was designed by the architect Edwin Lutyens and was in place by 1920. Slightly further back along the road is the ㉑ **National Monument to the Women of World War II**. The sculpture stands 22 feet high, 16 feet long and 6 feet wide and the lettering on the side replicates the typeface used on war time ration books. There are 17 individual sets of clothing and uniforms around the sides, symbolising the hundreds of different jobs women undertook in World War Two and then relinquished to the homecoming men at the end of the war. Designed by sculptor John Mills, it was unveiled by the Queen in July 2005.

Continuing towards Parliament Square, the very last building on this side of Whitehall is the **㉒ New Government Offices**, which primarily house HM Treasury. Designed in 1898 by J M Brydon in a Neo-Baroque style these were finally completed in 1915. The basement of this building contains the Cabinet War Rooms used by Winston Churchill during the 1939-45 war. These once top secret rooms have been preserved in their original state since 1948 and are now open to the public (for more details see p.355).

In our journey down Whitehall we have arrived at Bridge Street and if you look to your left you will see **㉓ Portcullis House**. Completed in 2001 this building is the outcome of a long, drawn-out process to consider development of the area. Michael Hopkins and Partners were commissioned to design office and committee room accommodation for Parliament in 1989, the same year it was mooted that an extension of the Jubilee line of the London Underground should be routed to include a station at Westminster. The need for total security of the Houses of Parliament ruled out the station being placed below Parliament, so it was incorporated into Michael Hopkins and Partners brief for the office site; work on which started in early 1994. Portcullis House not only had to fit in with the Gothicised-Classicism of the **㉔ Houses of Parliament** over the road (see p.143), but also Norman Shaw's much admired **㉕ Scotland Yard** building next door. Indeed the new building strongly echoes the sloping roof and tall chimneys of Shaw's building.

㉔ *Houses of Parliament*

Portcullis House, and Scotland Yard House, which is also used as Parliamentary offices, can accommodate 450 Members of Parliament and their administrative staff. Within the new building there are seven Select Committee rooms, two TV interview studios, a post office, café and eight meeting rooms arranged on seven floors around a central courtyard. The building is highly efficient and uses only approximately one third of the fuel of conventionally air-conditioned offices, being heated by recycled exhaust heat from the system and cooled by groundwater from deep bore holes. The cost of the building was a 'cool' £231 million.

㉖ Westminster Underground station below Portcullis House is a modern miracle of engineering. Its design had to take into consideration the existing District and Circle lines, which had to remain open and fully operational during the building work; care had to be taken with regard to the foundations of the nearby Houses of Parliament and Westminster Bridge; provision had to be made for the six massive column foundations of Portcullis House above. The result is a bold statement which celebrates these engineering feats – a 130 feet deep, 72 feet wide space which contains a series of intersecting escalators capped with a glass roof. The decoration is subdued, granite grey and steel. A fantastic piece of architecture.

The patch of green between Portcullis House and Westminster Abbey is Parliament Square. The area was cleared of small properties and roadways in the early 19th century to give a more appropriate setting for the meeting of Whitehall, the Houses of Parliament, and Westminster Abbey. The Square often became congested with horse-drawn vehicles and it was here that London's first traffic signals were employed in 1868 but the present layout was designed by architect George Gray Wornum in 1950. On the west side of the Square, opposite the Houses of Parliament sits The Supreme Court, the highest law court in the United Kingdom. Originally built in 1913 by Scottish architect James Gibson (1864-1951), as the Middlesex Guildhall, it has been serving as **㉗ The Supreme Court** since 2009. Constructed in Portland stone with an internal steel frame, it is fully conscious of its historic neighbours in design, being roughly neo-Gothic meets Arts and Crafts, and polite in size; no taller than nearby St Margaret's Church. Of note are the wonderful stone sculptures on the external walls, mostly by Henry Charles Fehr. Guided tours of the building are available and recommended, please see www.supremecourt.uk. A café in the basement is open to the public.

The walk can end here but if time permits the delights of **㉘ Westminster Abbey** can be explored (p.27), passing **㉙ St Margaret's Church** (see p.41) and the Houses of Parliament on the way. Note the bust of Charles I placed on the exterior of St Margaret's from where he gazes over towards the Houses of Parliament, and its statue of Oliver Cromwell, depicted head bowed in thought-or shame.

More information:

National Gallery
Trafalgar Square, WC2N 5DN
Tel: 020 7747 2885
www.nationalgallery.org.uk
Transport: Charing Cross LU/Rail
Admission free

St Martin-in-the-Fields
Trafalgar Square, WC2N 4JJ
Tel: 020 7766 1100
www.stmartin-in-the-fields.org
Transport: Charing Cross LU/Rail

Household Cavalry Museum
Horse Guards, Whitehall,
SW1A 2AX
Tel: 020 7930 3070
www.householdcavalry
museum.co.uk
Transport: Charing Cross
LU/Rail, Westminster and
Embankment LU

Banqueting House
Whitehall, SW1A 2ER
Tel: 0844 482 7777
www.hrp.org.uk
Transport: Charing Cross
LU/Rail, Westminster and
Embankment LU

Houses of Parliament
Houses of Parliament,
SW1A 0AA
www.parliament.uk
Transport: Charing Cross
LU/Rail, Westminster and
Embankment LU
See website for opening times
and entrance charges

Westminster Abbey
20 Dean's Yard, SW1P 3PA
Tel: 020 7222 5152
www.westminster-abbey.org
Transport: Westminster
and St James's Park LU

Church of St Margaret
20 Dean's Yard, SW1P 3JX
Tel: 020 7222 5152
www.westminster-abbey.org/
st-margarets
Transport: Westminster
and St James's Park LU
Admission free

Cabinet War Rooms
Clive Steps, King Charles
Street, SW1A 2AQ
www.cwr.iwm.org.uk
Transport: Charing Cross
LU/Rail, Westminster and
Embankment LU

St James's Café
St James's Park
(west of Horse Guards Parade),
SW1A 2BJ
Tel 020 7451 9999
www.innthepark.com
Transport: Green Park and St
James's Park LU

Skylon, see p.376

09

EAT & DRINK ARCHITECTURE

No matter whether it is fine dining or just a cup of tea, the following offer an opportunity to take refreshment in some of London's most interesting buildings.

Bibendum Oyster Bar & Restaurant
François Espinasse, 1909-11

Bibendum, Michelin House, 81 Fulham Road, SW3 6RD • Tel 020 7581 5817 • www.bibendum.co.uk • Nearest transport South Kensington LU

The style of this building hovers between Art Nouveau and Art Deco – with colourful decorations and motifs playing on the theme of wheels and tyres as befitting the former British Head Office of the Michelin Tyre Company. Built 1909-11, this is a very early example of what could be achieved with reinforced concrete. Michelin sold the building in 1985 to Terence Conran and Paul Hamlyn who began an extensive programme of renovation and reinvention. The result is a stylish café, restaurant and oyster bar, with a ground floor crustacean stall should you wish to buy something fresh to take home.

'Bibendum' is the name of the Michelin man, (who is surely Bertie Bassett's Gallic uncle), hence the name of this fashionable establishment.

The Black Friar
H Fuller Clark, c1905

The Black Friar, 174 Queen Victoria Street, EC4V 4EG • Tel 020 7236 5650 • www.nicholsonspubs.co.uk • Nearest transport Blackfriars LU & Rail

First built in 1873, this is a typical London-pub-on-the-corner wedge shaped building. Of earlier pedigree than those of the 1890s pub boom, the Black Friar was given a new ground floor sometime at the turn of the last century. The interior was completely redecorated by Herbert Fuller Clark and his colleague artist Henry Poole and what was accomplished needs to be seen to be believed. The entire bar area is decorated with red and green marble depicting the activities of the monks who lived on the site when the land belonged to the Dominican, or Black Friars, monastery. The whole work was executed in an Arts and Crafts manner and it is a truly unique experience to come and sip a beer in this pub.
Area Map p.8, A:2

The Black Friar

British Library Coffee Shop
Colin St John Wilson & Partners, 1997

The British Library, 96 Euston Road, NW1 2DB • Tel 020 7412 7332 • www.bl.uk • Nearest transport Euston LU & Rail and King's Cross/St Pancras LU & Rail

The impetus to form the British Library came from the donation of his father's book collection by George IV to the British Museum. The library moved from the British Museum to new premises in 1999 and the King's Library is now attractively displayed in the Tower of Books which can be seen by all in the entrance hall, but which can be contemplated more closely from the comfort of the Coffee Shop.

Open to the public in general as well as library users and exhibition visitors, the self-service coffee shop offers coffee, pastries, light lunches and afternoon teas.
Area Map p.2-3, B:2

Café Below
c1087+

St Mary-le-Bow, Cheapside, EC2V 6AU • Tel 020 7329 0789 • www.cafebelow.co.uk • Nearest transport St Paul's and Bank LU

The City offers many eye-wateringly expensive restaurants and ubiquitous high street chain cafés, however the Café Below not only offers delicious, wholesome food and drink, but also the chance to sit amongst and admire some exquisite Norman architecture.

Café Below operates in the crypt of Sir Christopher Wren's St Mary-le-Bow (see p.79 for a description of this church) constructed on the site of the church of circa 1087 which was destroyed in the Great Fire of 1666. Wren chose to preserve the Norman columns, piers and vaulting, some of which were made from re-used Roman brick, as far as he could.

Chiswick House Café
Caruso St John Architects, 2010

Chiswick House Café, Chiswick House & Gardens, Burlington Lane, W4 2QN • Tel 0208 995 6356 • www.chiswickhouseandgardens.org.uk • Nearest transport Turnham Green LU, Chiswick Rail

This café building was constructed as part of the major landscaping project carried out between 2006 and 2010 at one of London's most exquisite properties, Chiswick House (see p.108 for further details) and was named RIBA London Building of the Year 2011.

Created by the ever innovative architectural practice of Caruso St John, this little building is no neo-Palladian pastiche, but rather its elevation recalls the arcaded facades of the stable wings of country villas in the Veneto, such as Palladio's Villa Angarano. This is particularly fitting as the café is built on the site of the old stables, to the east of the house. The smooth stone colonnade provides covered exterior seating around the main room of the café, from where visitors have a superb view south of the surrounding lawns and mature trees.

Open most days of the year, the café is available to visitors to the house as well as those using the park.

Chucs Café at the Serpentine Sackler Gallery
Zaha Hadid, 2013

West Carriage Drive, W2 2AR • Tel 207 298 7552 • www.chucsrestaurants.com/serpentine • Nearest transport Lancaster Gate, Queensway or Marble Arch LU •

Where Kensington Gardens meets Hyde Park at the north end of the Serpentine Bridge sits the old Powder Magazine, a low brick building with a neoclassical porticoed front and colonnade of Doric columns. It was built around 1805 as a store for gunpowder for use in military drills in the park when fear of a Napoleonic invasion of Britain was at its peak. The building was later used as a general storeroom, eventually falling into disuse, but this rare example of its type, the only one in London, ensured a Grade I listing in the 1970s.

In 2013 the building was given a new lease of life when it became the Serpentine Sackler Gallery and Restaurant. Developed in two distinct parts, the 19th-century Magazine is now an airy gallery space and a glass-walled eating area under an undulating fabric roof, a tensile structure which curves down to meet the ground at three points around the periphery and penetrated by curvaceous columns reaching down from oval skylights. This exciting conversion was designed by Zaha Hadid. The Restaurant is now run as part of the Chucs group, and offers all-day refreshment and dining.

Duck and Waffle
& SUSHISAMBA
Kohn Pedersen Fox 2008

110 Bishopsgate, EC2N 4AY •
www.duckandwaffle.com • Tel 0203 640
7310 • www.sushisamba.com •
Tel 0203 640 7330 • Nearest transport
Liverpool Street LU

This floating "culinary village" is set in a crystalline three-storey volume at the top of Salesforce Tower (formerly Heron Tower), currently the tallest building in the City of London. The space is home to both SUSHISAMBA London, the renowned Brazilian/Peruvian/Japanese restaurant, and Duck & Waffle, a unique '24/7' restaurant that is inspired by British artistic and culinary traditions. Emerge from one of the two dedicated glazed lifts, which hug the outside of the building, and one is met with a sweeping sculptural orange glass and metal staircase connecting all three levels and walls decorated with street art. The interior is the work of one of the coolest design companies on the planet – CetraRuddy of New York.

Salesforce Tower represents a new generation of office structure containing highly flexible space organized around a series of office "villages" with a triple-height atrium at the heart of each, allowing natural light to penetrate throughout. The design of the building provides good public areas at ground level, with cafés and planting adding interest at this busy area. *Area Map p.8, C:3*

Foyer Bar & Reading Room, Claridge's
Oswald Milne, 1931

Claridge's, 49 Brook Street, W1K 4HR •
Tel 020 7629 8860 • www.claridges.co.uk
• See website for opening times

The epitome of glamour and with a reputation for impeccable, professional service, Claridge's is one of London's most iconic hotels. In business since the very early 19th century and noted for its late 1920s Art Deco makeover by architect Oswald Milne the hotel has not rested on its considerable laurels.

In 1999 Claridge's embarked on the first major designer restoration since the 1930s when New York-based designer Thierry Despont was brought in to revitalize the Foyer area. He used archive photographs of the Ballroom Extension of early the 1930s as inspiration and the space was completely made over in a modern Art Deco style, with a magnificent silver-white light sculpture by artist Dale Chihuly as its centrepiece. Created from more than 800 individually hand-blown glass pieces, it hangs from the Foyer's 18 feet high ceiling.

The Foyer is open every day from breakfast through to the evening, with live music to accompany the sumptuous afternoon teas.

George Inn
C1676+

George Inn Yard, 77 Borough High Street, Southwark, SE1 1NH • Tel 020 7407 2056
• www.greeneking-pubs.co.uk • Nearest transport London Bridge LU & Rail

Tucked away in a cobbled courtyard just off Borough High Street, the George Inn is a unique survivor – the last galleried inn left in London. Coaching inns were once commonplace and here the Old Bar was once the waiting room for coachmen and passengers. The coming of the railway to the area in 1899 resulted in the demolition of the north wing and centre of the original inn, so we are left with just one third of the original. Charles Dickens was a regular visitor and liked to frequent the Coffee Room, now the Middle Bar, and he mentions this inn in *Little Dorrit* (1857).

Inns have occupied this site since medieval times; this building dates from about 1676 and the wealth of oak beams and lattice windows make the building highly atmospheric. *Area Map p.8, B:1*

The German Gymnasium
Edward Gruning, 1865

26 Pancras Road, N1C 2TB • Tel 020 7287 8000 • www.germangymnasium.com • Nearest transport King's Cross & St Pancras LU & Rail

The German Gymnasium or Turnhalle, thought to be the first purpose-built gymnasium in Britain, was designed by Edward Gruning as part of a terrace of shops on the Pancras Road constructed in 1865. The following year the gym hosted the indoor events of the first National Olympian Games, an annual event until the first modern Olympic Games were held at White City in 1908. After this date the building was sold to the Great Northern Railway who added flooring at the gallery level to maximise the space for office use. Since that time the building has had a variety of uses: art depot, gallery, dance venue although its survival was in doubt until 1976 when it was given a Grade II listing.

The recent redevelopment of the area has seen its neighbours felled and the gym is now a freestanding structure with a new skin of brickwork, made to mirror the original decorative detailing. Despite its Grade II status the Gymnasium has in recent years sacrificed its western end to make way for the St Pancras International terminus.

Previously used as the marketing suite for the asset management team for the King's Cross development, the building is now open for business as a restaurant, grand café and bar, with some outdoor seating, weather permitting.

The Ned
Edwin Lutyens 1924-39

27 Poultry, EC2R 8AJ • Tel 020 3828 2000 • www.thened.com • Nearest transport Bank LU and DLR

Originally constructed as the Midland Bank Headquarters, this huge, steel-framed building weathered the financial catastrophes of the 1930s to re-emerge, phoenix-like, as the apogee of luxurious living today.

Nick Jones, founder of the Soho House stable, took on the project, turning this Lutyens temple of finance into the latest, coolest hotel, private members' club, spa and collection of restaurants and bars in London. It must have been a brave decision, no doubt borne out of love and admiration for this wonderful building, a short walk from St Paul's, around the corner from the Bank of England, across the road from the Royal Exchange and opposite Stirling's No1 Poultry.

The Ned, named for its architect Edwin 'Ned' Lutyens, is just the latest chic private members' club to open in London in the last few years – notable among them are The Wine Lovers' Club, housed in another Lutyens building, the former Hambros Bank at 67 Pall Mall and The Devonshire Club which has opened in a transformed 18th-century East India Company warehouse and an adjacent Georgian townhouse near trendy Spitalfields.

Despite the almost cathedral-like proportions of the Banking Hall, Lutyens' eye for detail is everywhere in evidence – white marble walls act as a foil for the forest of beautiful green African verdite square Corinthian columns; the lovely old, wooden tellers' cabins have been transformed into seating in some of the eight restaurants in the Hall. However, this is no hideous 'food court', each of the eateries has its own ambience; there is something for everyone here. The Banking Hall is very much a space for non-residents and non-members, so feel free to experience this wonderful place.

Hotel residents and Club members can enjoy the rest of this brilliant conversion – the rooftop pool; the basement spa; comfortable bedrooms, all walnut and good taste with twelve categories to choose from and 250 rooms in total. However, the pièce de résistance is reserved for Club members only - access to the Vault Room, located two floors underground. The original 20-tonne door remains, along with 3,000 original silver safety deposit boxes which line the walls. The vault, one of only two made by the Chatwood Safe Company, was used in the 1964 James Bond film 'Goldfinger' – now it is a stylish all-hours cocktail bar. *Area Map p.8, C:3*

Oxo Tower
Albert W Moore, 1928

Oxo Tower Wharf, Barge House Street, SE1 9PH • Tel 020 7803 3888 • www.oxotowerrestraunt.com • Nearest transport Blackfriars LU & Rail

The Oxo Tower was built in 1928 as an Art Deco addition to a meat manufacturer's London base. At this time there was a ban on any form of neon lit advertising in the area, so one bright spark thought of picking out the name OXO in coloured glass windows at the top of the tower and placing a strong light behind it which shone out into the London night.

The Tower, which sits equidistant between Blackfriars Bridge and Waterloo Bridge and long abandoned by its originators, is now part of the Coin Street Housing Association. Shops, galleries and small workshops occupy the first three floors and the next five floors consist of affordable housing, while the top floor is devoted to the restaurant, brasserie and bar.

Both the restaurant and brasserie are modern and spacious and lack any form of cosiness, but the views over the Thames are spectacular, especially in the evening.

Pizza Express, Alban Gate
Terry Farrell, 1988-92

Pizza Express, 125 London Wall, Alban Gate, EC2Y 5AJ • Tel 020 7600 8880 • www.pizzaexpress.com • Nearest transport Moorgate LU/Rail, St Paul's LU

The Pizza Express chain has always, wherever possible, sited its restaurants in architecturally interesting places and this property provides an opportunity to eat lunch or supper inside a piece of very modern architecture. The Alban Gate complex spans the busy London Wall roadway at Wood Street and Terry Farrell, its architect, likens it to a gigantic gatehouse. Completed in 1992 Alban Gate provides 8.6 acres of office space in granite of differing colours and glass.

There are in fact two Pizza Express restaurants here, almost side by side and mirror images of each other. Although it's almost impossible to see out of the windows whilst dining, it is fun to contemplate the glass and steel and wonder what is holding it all up!

This restaurant is situated near the Museum of London and the delights of the City.
Area Map p.8, B:3

Portrait Restaurant & Bar, National Portrait Gallery
Dixon and Jones, 1994-2000

National Portrait Gallery, St Martin's Place, WC2H 0HE • Tel 020 7312 2490 (Restaurant), 020 7306 0055 (Gallery) • www.npg.org.uk • Nearest transport Charing Cross LU/Rail or Embankment LU • Table reservations are essential for the restaurant

On its completion in 1896 this was the world's first purpose-built portrait gallery. The architect chosen for this most prestigious project was Ewan Christian (1814-95), a man more associated with church restoration. However, the much-travelled Mr Christian gave London a Florentine Renaissance palazzo with an entrance porch at its north-west end that resembles the little oratory of Santa Spirito in Bologna.

As the Gallery's collection grew, the 19th century interior felt somewhat cramped and fusty, with few visitors venturing through its revolving door. During the 1990s architects Jeremy Dixon and Edward Jones were tasked with creating space for additional galleries and public areas, to be known as the Ondaatje Wing. Miraculously a three-storey atrium was created from an old, narrow service yard, resulting in a stunning light and airy interior and now possessing the cultural pull of late-night openings where wine and music can be enjoyed along with the block-busting exhibitions.

Provision was also made for a public restaurant and at ninety-two feet above ground level on the fifth floor of the Ondaatje Wing, it has spectacular views facing south over Nelson's Column, down Whitehall and on to the Houses of Parliament. The restaurant and bar are open seven days a week for brunch, lunch and afternoon tea, and for dinner on Thursday, Friday and Saturday. It is advisable to book well in advance and do specify that you would like a window table, although there are good views from most.

An increase in visitor numbers means the NPG's revolving door has never been so busy. Indeed, in 2018 architect Jamie Fobert, together with heritage specialists Purcell, were appointed to give the gallery a major overhaul for the 21st century. The project, due to be completed in the early 2020s, will increase the gallery space by almost twenty percent and include a complete re-interpretation of the gallery's collection across forty refurbished spaces, provide a new learning centre and, by making a new access on the north side of the building, create a spacious, welcoming entrance to the gallery and a new public space outside. The lovely exterior of the gallery, along with its eighteen original stone busts, will remain intact. *Area Map p.6, B:3*

Rex Whistler Restaurant, Tate Britain
Sidney R J Smith et al, 1893+

Tate Britain, Millbank, SW1P 4JU • Tel 020 7887 8000 (reservations 020 7887 8825) • www.tate.org.uk • Nearest transport Pimlico or Westminster LU

Although a visit to Tate Britain is always a treat, discovering new works of art and revisiting favourites, the architecture is of interest in itself. The main building was built with money donated by the sugar tycoon Sir Henry Tate on the boggy site of a miserable prison known as Millbank Penitentiary. A large projecting portico and fairly shallow dome give this building a classical air, but with a little Victorian over-enthusiasm.

The Clore Gallery extension, by the eminent architect the late Sir James Stirling, was added in 1987 to house the Tate's incomparable collection of paintings by J M W Turner. More recent additions include the Linbury Galleries and Manton Street entrance (on Atterbury Street), designed by John Miller & Partners, and a multi-million pound revamp of the Tate's original Grade II listed Millbank building by Caruso St John (opened 2013).

The restaurant at the Tate is a very grand affair, decorated with murals executed by a young Rex Whistler in 1926-27, after whom it has been named. Appropriately he took as his subject 'The Expedition in Pursuit of Rare Meats'. Open daily and booking ahead is almost essential.

The Ritz
Charles Mewes, 1903-06

The Ritz, 55 Piccadilly, W1J 9BR • Tel 020 7493 8181 • www.theritzlondon.com • Nearest transport Green Park LU

Whether taking tea or propping up the bar, do take a closer look at the first steel-framed structure in London. This lovely building looks as though it strayed in from Paris and indeed the architect did design the Paris Ritz in 1899, very wisely repeating all the successful parts here.

If you are unable to venture in to the hotel, through lack of time or shortage of funds, stay outside and admire the ground floor arcade, again very French. The whole building is faced in Norwegian stone at the ground floor with Portland stone above.

Tea at the Palm Court of the Ritz costs in the region of £60 per person, but is truly a treat you will not forget in a hurry. You will need to book at least six weeks ahead. *Area Map p.6, A:2*

Rotunda Bar & Restaurant, King's Place
Dixon-Jones, 2008

King's Place, 90 York Way, N1 9AG • Tel 020 7014 2840 • www.rotundabarandrestaurant.co.uk •
Nearest Transport King's Cross & St Pancras LU/Rail

One of the most exciting new-builds of recent years, designed by architects Dixon-Jones, is 'King's Place' which brings together under one roof a dining venue, a conference and events centre, and office complex. Containing two public concert auditoriums, the larger, with a seating capacity of 450, has an oak veneer interior from a single 500-year old German oak tree. After felling, the wood was cut into 5 metre lengths and boiled at 80°C for one week, then sliced. The tree has produced an acre of superb veneer, covering the wall panels, columns, roof coffers, doors, the back of seats, and the musicians' desks. The other auditorium is a smaller, flexible 250-seat space, which is now the home of the world-renowned Orchestra of the Age of the Enlightenment. There are also two major spaces designed specifically for the display of visual arts, Pangolin London and King's Place Gallery.

The King's Place building itself has an attractive frontage onto York Way with a three-layered undulating glass façade; a free-standing transparent surface made up of hundreds of very slightly curved sheets of glass, produced in a factory near Venice. Enter here and the visitor is led to a magnificent atrium which gives views up to all seven levels as well as bringing light into the central core of the building.

Also visible to the rear is the Battlebridge Basin, one of the larger pools on the Regent's Canal, which opened from Paddington to Camden in 1816 and onward to Limehouse in 1820. The Basin was used for the shipment of goods to and from the canals and was kept busy handling goods such as ice, imported from Norway and used for making such delicacies as ice cream. The former ice warehouse is now the London Canal Museum here in the Basin.

Some of the best views of the waterway can be obtained from the King's Place Rotunda Bar and Restaurant, where al fresco dining is available during the summer months. Customers can sit at the Bar for drinks and lighter meals, with a table service for lunch and dinner. Quality food takes pride of place, with much of the meat served here raised at the restaurant's own farm in Northumberland. Both Bar and Restaurant are open seven days a week.

St James's Café
Michael Hopkins, 2004

St James's Park (west of Horse Guards Parade), SW1A 2BJ • Tel 020 7451 9999 • www.royalparks.co.uk • Nearest transport Green Park and St James's Park LU

Made from Austrian larch wood, which has been left untreated externally so that it gradually weathers over time, this café has been cleverly designed by Michael Hopkins to appear as part of the landscape. Even the surrounding grassy areas continue over the structure's roof and the glass frontage gives diners superb views of the nearby lake. Within its curved walls there is seating for over 100 diners and the same number again on the covered terrace outside.

Open everyday, from breakfast to dinner, this café/diner is managed by Benugo. *Area Map p.6, B:2*

St John's, Smith Square
Thomas Archer, 1713-28

The Footstool Restaurant, St John's, Smith Square, SW1P 3HA • Tel 020 7222 2779 • www.sjss.org.uk • Nearest transport St James's Park LU

St John's is considered to be one of the finest examples of English Baroque architecture to be found anywhere. Built as part of the 'Fifty Churches' scheme during the reign of Queen Anne, to a Greek-cross plan, the north and south 'arms' of the building have enormous Doric columns and these mark the two entrances. The east and west ends each have a large Venetian window and Doric pilasters. However, on first seeing the church, one's eye is immediately drawn to the four corner towers – circular with short Doric columns set diagonally and each topped by a small pineapple ogee lantern.

The church was severely damaged by enemy bombing in 1941 and was restored by Marshall Sisson 1965-69 as a concert hall. With its excellent acoustics and varied programme of classical music, St John's is now a much-valued venue in the heart of Westminster.

However, one does not need to attend a concert to savour the delights of the interior of St John's for in the brick-vaulted crypt there is the superb Footstool restaurant. An à la carte British menu, light buffet, drinks and snacks are available weekday lunch times and from 5.30pm onwards on concert evenings. *Area Map p.6, B:1*

St Pancras Grand Champagne Bar, St Pancras Station
William Barlow, 1868 / Martin Brudnizki Design Studio, 2008

St Pancras Station, Upper Concourse, Euston Road, N1C 4QL • Tel 020 7870 9900 • www.searcys.com • Nearest transport King's Cross & St Pancras LU & Rail

The transformation of this railway station is truly astonishing. For a great many years it was a rather grim place where commuters and visitors would have been hard-pressed to buy a decent coffee or sandwich. Now St Pancras Station is itself a destination, not merely somewhere to pass through, thanks to the addition of shops, bars, cafés and restaurants, as part of the £800 million restoration and extension. Trains run not only to the north of England from here but also to the Continent via Eurostar and the high-speed link to the Channel Tunnel; the centre of Paris is under three hours away.

The most glamorous of all the additions is the Champagne Bar, at 96 metres Europe's longest, situated below the magnificent Barlow Shed and allowing a full appreciation of the amazing architecture of the station. When the station first opened in 1868 William Barlow's train shed was an outstanding feat of Victorian engineering. The roof is 689 feet long and 100 feet high and with a span of 243 feet it held the record for the world's largest enclosed space for many years. During recent restoration work it has been completely reglazed and the paint work returned to its intended pale sky blue.

The Bar's main seating area consists of comfortable booths accommodating six people; each booth has its own adjustable fan heater and a black Art Deco-inspired lamp which dispenses a flattering pool of light. There are also tables for two and plenty of standing room for larger groups. The Bar is open seven days a week for drink and food, including a most sumptuous afternoon tea. For further information about this wonderful building see p.156.

Sky Garden, 20 Fenchurch Street
Rafael Vinoly 2015

Sky Garden, 1 Sky Garden Walk, EC3M 8AF • Tel 0207 337 2344
• www.skygarden.london • Nearest transport Monument LU

Not many nice things are said of 20 Fenchurch Street. Indeed it was presented with the 2015 Carbuncle Prize, an annual award given by Building Digest magazine for the worst UK building. Even before it was finished, the building attracted the nickname of the 'Walkie Talkie' because of its bulbous, top-heavy shape. On completion, some wag said it should have been called 'Walkie Scorchie' when claims were made that the glare from the curvaceous glass façade of the 37-storey tower had caused the paintwork of cars parked below to melt and their bodywork to distort. Since then protective fins have been added to the building's facade in a bid to solve the problem. Complaints of unacceptable levels of wind at pavement level have also been noted. The issue, known as the "downdraught effect", occurs when wind hits a building and is forced downwards. It is most troublesome when the wall faces the prevailing wind, which in Britain is from the south west.

Perhaps Londoners can forgive Uruguayan architect, Rafael Vinoly for this somewhat rude, looming building when they sample the delights of the 'Sky Garden'. The large viewing deck, bar and restaurants are included on the 35th, 36th and 37th floors, which are, with restrictions, open to the public. Views over the capital from all four sides of the building are breath-taking, as is looking down over the Tower of London, dwarfed, as though a toy castle. See the website for dining options. Visits can be made to the Sky Garden free of charge but must be booked in advance. You don't have to eat here but there are several dining options including a relaxed coffee/drinks bar and the Fenchurch Restaurant. Please see the website for details. *Area Map p.8, C:2*

Skylon Restaurant, Grill & Bar
Allies and Morrison 1995

Royal Festival Hall, Belvedere Road, SE1 8XX • Tel 020 7654 7800 • www.skylon-restaurant.co.uk • Nearest transport Waterloo LU & Rail

This cool, contemporary venue sits well within the Modernist host building of the Royal Festival Hall. Clever lighting has, to a large degree, turned the cavernous space of this part of the Grade I listed building into intimate dining areas with wonderful views from the huge plate glass windows over the Thames to the centre of London.

Named in honour of the structure that stood at the heart of the 1951 Festival of Britain and designed by two young architects Hidalgo Moya and Philip Powell in collaboration with structural engineer Felix Samuely, the Skylon stood 105 metres tall. The cigar-shaped steel construction captured the imagination of the nation, its futuristic form pointing to an optimistic period for a war-torn Britain. Despite its popularity, the Skylon was torn down by the incoming government of Winston Churchill later that year. For further details of the Royal Festival Hall please see p.217.

Four Seasons Ten Trinity Square (formerly The Port of London Authority)
Sir Edwin Cooper, 1912

10 Trinity Square, EC3N 4AJ • Tel 020 3297 9200 • www.fourseasons.com • Nearest transport Tower Hill LU

This is one of those rather imposing corner buildings that Edwardian builders seemed to love so much. The building is rather chunky and busy, considering that the obvious influence of the Beaux-Arts is usually expressed in a lighter tone. Six huge Corinthian columns stretch from ground level to the entablature that runs around the whole building. The exterior sculpture includes Father Thames and sea horses and galleons. These were designed by Albert Hodge and worked by C. Doman.

The Port of London Authority occupied the building for many years but with the decline in the docks the Authority moved to smaller offices in St Katharine Dock in 1971. The building was then used as office accommodation for various companies until it was purchased by Chinese investors in 2010 when, following a six-year, multi-million- pound renovation, 'Ten Trinity Square' emerged. Now part of the Four Seasons Hotels stable, with all the luxurious rooms and suites you would expect. Two restaurants, La Dame de Pic London and Mei Ume are complemented by the bar and all-day dining in the Rotunda, where coffee or cocktails can be sipped under the Art Deco, domed ceiling in this most elegant space. *Area Map p.8, C:1*

Vertigo, Tower 42
Seifert and Partners, 1970-81

Vertigo,Tower 42, 25 Old Broad Street, EC2N 1HQ • Tel 0207 877 7842 • www.vertigo42.co.uk • Nearest transport Bank LU

Champagne and seafood bar located 590 feet up the famous Tower 42 (formerly known as the NatWest Tower) in the heart of the City. Built 1970-81 by Seifert and Partners, the building has a stabilising concrete service core with floors cantilevered out from it, and the whole is enclosed in a glass sheath. For ten years this was the tallest building in London, indeed in Britain, until the towers of Canary Wharf sprang up.

The views from this bar are the best in London and the food and drink is outstanding too.
Area Map p.8, C:2

Wesley's Café at the Methodist Central Hall
Lanchester & Rickards, 1905-11

Methodist Central Hall, Storey's Gate, SW1H 9NH • Tel 020 7222 8010 • www.c-h-w.com • Nearest transport St James's Park or Westminster LU

The café in this splendid Edwardian Baroque building is a bit of a secret in this almost café/restaurant-free part of Westminster. Tours of the building are offered every day of the week – enquire at reception. Please see p.184 for a description of this building.

09 Eat & Drink Architecture

Barkers, Kensington High Street see p.380

10

SHOPPING & ARCHITECTURE

As if one needs an excuse to go shopping, here is a short list of some of the architectural gems in London which just happen to be retail outlets too.

Barkers (former)
Bernard George, 1937-38

Barkers, 63-97 Kensington High Street, W8 5SE • Nearest transport Kensington High Street LU • Open daily, usual shop opening hours

It was during the heyday of the department store, that Bernard George was given the brief to remodel the highly successful Barkers store. The building had originally been designed by architect Sir Reginald Blomfield in 1912-13.

Bernard George presented Kensington High Street with an outstanding example of Art Deco. The unmistakable outline of the building owes much to the twin glass towers which soar above neighbouring rooflines. The façade has some remarkable ornamental stonework and exquisite murals celebrating the art of chic shopping.

Alas, Barkers succumbed to the economic downturn of recent decades and is no longer a department store, closing for business in 2006. The building is now occupied by an upmarket wholefood food emporium.

It is interesting to contrast the splendour of Barkers with the nearby building at Nos 99-121 Kensington High Street. This was also designed by Bernard George in a 'Moderne' style for the department store Derry and Toms. The building now houses Marks and Spencer and looks rather subdued in comparison with its more famous neighbour.

Burlington Arcade
Samuel Ware, 1819

51 Piccadilly, W1J 0QJ • www.burlington-arcade.co.uk • Nearest transport Green Park and Piccadilly Circus LU

One of three shopping arcades off Piccadilly, the other two being the Princes and the Piccadilly, both of which are on the opposite, south side of the road. Burlington Arcade was built in 1819 by the architect Samuel Ware (1781-1860) for Lord George Cavendish, who owned Burlington House. The arcade formed the western boundary to Cavendish's property and it is said that the impetus behind its construction was to stop passers-by flinging rubbish into his Lordship's garden, not because he wanted to make money from this piece of speculative building.

The arcade consists of two rows of small, bow-fronted, shops with rooms above, set in a narrow passage, some 585 feet long, which becomes wider and one-storey taller in three places. At every fourth shop a cross arch rests on Ionic pilasters, thereby adding variety and the whole passage is top lit from windows in the roof.

The shops cater for the luxury end of the market; cashmere, perfume, leather goods, pens, and jewellery. Security is provided by the frock-coated, top-hatted Beadles who are instructed to eject anyone running, carrying large parcels, whistling or generally causing a nuisance – you have been warned. *Area Map p.6, A:2*

Fortnum and Mason
Wimperis, Simpson & Guthrie, 1926-29

Fortnum and Mason, 181 Piccadilly Circus, W1A 1ER • Tel 020 7734 8040 • www.fortnumandmason.com • Nearest transport Green Park and Piccadilly Circus LU

This enterprise was started in the 1770s by Charles Fortnum – who, as a former footman in the royal household of George III, knew about service – and his friend John Mason, who owned horses, a yard close-by and who dealt with the deliveries. They made their reputation by importing exotic foods and supplying such to the gentlemen's clubs of London.

In the late 19th century Fortnum and Mason took the radical step of stocking Heinz canned food, becoming one of the first stores in the world to do so but it is still most famous for being the Queen's grocer.

Fortnum and Mason started their business in premises close to their present shop in Piccadilly, which was built in 1926-29 by Wimperis, Simpson and Guthrie who, given the shop's pedigree, chose a Georgian style. The fussy automated clock by Eric Aumonier was made in 1964, but appears to come from an earlier era, and on the hour four foot high mechanical replicas of the original Mr. Fortnum and Mr. Mason emerge and bow to each other.

Harrods
Stevens and Munt, 1901-05

87-135 Brompton Road, Knightsbridge, SW1X 7XL • Tel 020 7730 1234 • www.harrods.com • Nearest transport Knightsbridge LU • See website for opening times

The store's motto is 'omnia, omnibus, ubique' (everything for everyone, everywhere) and Harrods could indeed at one time brag that they could supply anything from a packet of pins to an elephant! Henry Charles Harrod began this retail legend as a tea merchant in the early 19th century at Eastcheap in the City, moving to Knightsbridge in 1849. Harrods stayed a thriving, family-run shop until 1889 when it became a limited company. Its present building was constructed between 1901-05, with additions made until the 1930s.

The building, with its famous terracotta façade, was designed by the architectural practice of Stevens and Munt, and was the largest department store in Europe, occupying a site of some 4.5 acres, with a total retail space of 13.5 acres over five floors. To see the tilework in the magnificent Food Hall on the ground floor is alone well worth the trip to Knightsbridge, as is the Art Deco ladies' restroom on the first floor and the gentlemen's hairdressers in the basement.

Make Architects were shortlisted for the 2017 Word of Interiors 'Interior of the Year' award for their work on the store's dedicated women's luxury fashion floor, 'Superbrands'. Using a palette of Portoro marble, black granite, bronze and brass, Make have presented those in search of a little haute couture with a series of boutique fronts, shops-within-shops, where brands such as Chanel, Prada, Givenchy, and Alexander McQueen display their wares.

The famously comprehensive Toy Department is where A A Milne purchased the original Pooh bear for his son Christopher.

Royal Exchange
Sir William Tite, 1841-44

Royal Exchange, between Threadneedle Street and Cornhill, EC3V 3LR • www.theroyalexchange.com • Nearest transport Bank LU • Grand Café Tel 020 7618 2480 • See website for opening times

This building is often mistaken for the Bank of England, which is just over the road in Threadneedle Street. With its massive portico supported by huge Corinthian columns, the front of the building is much wider, at 175 feet, than the back 119 feet. This is the third Royal Exchange building on the site, the others having burned down in 1666 and 1838; the present building was declared open by Queen Victoria in 1844.

The 'Exchange' was established by Sir Thomas Gresham, a successful merchant and favoured courtier, in 1565. Prior to this City merchants and traders had carried out their business in a fairly informal way, gathering together in the street twice a day, but after visiting the Antwerp Bourse Gresham decided that a more formal setting was needed for business in London. The first building was opened in 1570 by Elizabeth I, who gave it its Royal title and it is from its steps that the new monarch is announced to the City.

The Royal Exchange ceased to be a business institution in 1939 and since then the building has been occupied by various organisations, including the Guardian Royal Exchange Assurance until 1991. Disused and neglected after this time it was decided to breathe new life into the place by turning it into a retail and restaurant complex.

The interior of the Exchange forms a covered quadrangle surmounted by colonnades, with a statue of Queen Victoria by Thornycroft at the centre and a series of paintings around the walls of the courtyard by artists such as Lord Leighton, Frank Brangwyn, and Stanhope Forbes.

The shops within the Exchange are bordering on the luxury end of the market with Lulu Guinness, Tiffany, Montblanc and Jo Malone amongst them, and they are fun to browse. There are four places within the Exchange in which to take refreshment, be it a coffee, cocktail, breakfast, lunch or supper, and enjoy the architecture. *Area Map p.8, C:2*

Leadenhall Market
Sir Horace Jones, 1880-81

Leadenhall Market, Gracechurch Street, EC3V 1LT • www.leadenhallmarket.co.uk • Nearest transport Bank and Monument LU

The name 'Leadenhall' comes from a large medieval house which once stood close by to this site, which apparently had a lead roof, with the market being established on adjoining land. The house, its estate and the market were sold to the City Corporation at the beginning of the 15th century. House and market both perished in the Great Fire of London but were quickly rebuilt on a plan around three courtyards.

The present market, designed by City architect Sir Horace Jones, in 1880-81, is a lovely structure built on the cross-plan of the old street configuration. The main entrance, off Gracechurch Street, has engaged, fluted columns in dark-red and cream paintwork with gilded capitals. These appear to support a stone pediment with carved decorations and a fairly small, simple clock.

The market still sells fresh meat and fish but is mainly given over to fashion, with shops such as Jigsaw and Hobbs doing a brisk trade during the City lunchtime. *Area Map p.8, C:2*

Peter Jones
W Crabtree et al, 1936-38

Peter Jones, Sloane Square, SW1W 8EL • Tel 020 7730 3434 • www.peterjones.co.uk • Nearest transport Sloane Square LU • Wheelchair access • See website for opening times

Peter Jones is part of the John Lewis Partnership chain and one can purchase almost anything in the way of household, electrical, sports goods and fashion. This was one of the first uses of the glass curtain wall in Britain and was heavily influenced by Mendelsohn's designs for the Schoken department stores in Stuttgart and Chemnitz. The concept of curtain walling in modern buildings is a thin subordinate wall, usually made of glass or metal, held between piers or other structural members but which are not load-bearing.

This fine building– which has something of the ocean-going liner about it – has recently been the subject of a £100 million renovation programme adding air conditioning, new restaurants, over 20% extra retail space and a dramatic central atrium in which escalators to all floors are sited.

Right: Leadenhall Market

Selfridges
Daniel Burnham et al, 1906+

Selfridges, 400 Oxford Street, W1A 1AB •
Tel 0800 123 400 • www.selfridges.com •
Nearest transport Bond Street LU

Arguably London's most popular department store since it was first opened in March 1909, Selfridges was the brainchild of its owner, American-born Henry Gordon Selfridge (1858-1947), who learned the business of retail in Chicago. He brought the art of browsing to the London shopper who up until this point was used to simply being shown items selected by the shopkeeper – this was a radical departure.

Selfridge bought the huge plot in 1906 and set about creating a building the likes of which Londoners had not seen before. Massive shop windows separated by short pillars dominate the ground floor, while gigantic Ionic columns stretch up from the first floor to the exquisitely carved attic floor balustrade. Over the central entrance recess is an 11 feet figure named 'Queen of Time' as well as a huge clock, both of which were installed in 1931. The whole project took nearly 30 years to complete and a number of architects were involved, the most prominent being Daniel Burnham of Chicago.

In 2018 Selfridges opened a multi-million pound refurbishment of its Grade II listed store, featuring the creation of a new accessories hall and a triple height entrance by David Chipperfield on Duke Street, linking the 1909 building with a 1930s extension. *Area Map p.4, B:1*

Waterstones (formerly Simpsons of Piccadilly)
Joseph Emberton, 1935-36

Waterstones, 203-206 Piccadilly, W1J 9HD • Tel 0843 290 8549 • www.waterstones.com •
Nearest transport Piccadilly Circus LU • See website for opening times

It is easy to walk by this building and not realise its significance for 20th-century architecture. This was the first shop in Britain to have an uninterrupted curved glass front, made possible by arc-welding the wide-span steel-frame, rather than using bulky bolted joints. The method had been pioneered the year before at the renowned De La Warr Pavilion in Bexhill-on-Sea by Mendelsohn and Chermayeff, who were members of MARS (Modern Architecture Research) set up in 1933. Notable among the group were Walter Gropius, Marcel Breuer, Ove Arup, Hugh Casson, and John Betjeman.

The interior was designed to domestic proportions as a series of rooms with an open-well staircase (there is an apologetic notice explaining why the handrail appears to be a little short for today's customers); note also the original hanging light fitting.

The shop was originally commissioned by Alexander Simpson for his quality menswear store. The move to Piccadilly was prompted by success of the DAKS brand of trousers with their patented self-supporting waistband. During the very early 1970s the writer Jeremy Lloyd was employed as an assistant and it from his short spell at Simpsons that the idea of a television sitcom blossomed into 'Are you Being Served?', which in 1979 was turned into an American version called 'Beanes of Boston'.

In 1999 the shop was sold to Waterstones and is now their flagship store, on the top floor of which is a bar conveniently located next to the 'Art and Architecture' section. From the comfort of the bar there is a wonderful view south, over the rooftops towards the Palace of Westminster. *Area Map p.6, A:2*

View from The London Eye, see p.393

11
ARCHITECTURE WITH A VIEW

There are many places that afford great views across London, below are a few favourite spots in which to enjoy the wonderful mix of buildings that make London and its architecture so unique.

Right: View from Emirates Air Line

Emirates Air Line

Greenwich Peninsular – Emirates Cable Car Terminal, Edmund Halley Way, SE10 0FR • Nearest Transport North Greenwich Royal Docks

Emirates Air Line, 27 Western Gateway, E16 4FA • Nearest transport Victoria Royal Dock • www.emiratesairline.co.uk for ticket prices and information

If climbing over the O2 Arena is not your cup of tea (see p.394) and you prefer to take in the views sitting down, then a trip across the Thames in a cable car may be for you. Board one of the thirty-four cars that connect the O2 arena on the Greenwich Peninsula with the ExCeL centre at the Royal Docks and be whisked ninety metres above the Thames with the one kilometre length journey taking ten minutes, or five minutes during busy periods when things can be speeded up. Better still, purchase a return ticket and try to take in the Air Line's sculpted towers that rise high above the river, formed from a series of steel ribbons and arranged as a tapering spiral. These rather beautiful twisting structures and the glass terminals at either end of the journey were designed by Wilkinson Eyre architects.

Opened in June 2012 the facility is fully accessible. This is the first urban cable car system to be built in Britain and, as well as providing a marvellous view of London, is a quite spectacular project in itself.

Right: The London Eye

The London Eye
Julia Barfield and David Marks, 1993-2000

Jubilee Gardens, Embankment, SE1 7PB • www.londoneye.com • Nearest transport Westminster LU and Waterloo LU/Rail • Booking is highly recommended but it is possible to purchase tickets at County Hall (next to the London Eye) but be prepared to queue • See website for opening times and admission charges

One of the most popular structural projects ever carried out anywhere was conceived at the kitchen table of architects Julia Barfield and David Marks in 1993. This was the year that marked the centenary of the unveiling of the 'Big Wheel' at Chicago's World Columbian Exposition designed by George W Ferris. The Ferris Wheel became the main attraction of the fair – just as the London Eye was to become the 'hit' of millennium celebrations in London when it first took paying passengers in January 2000.

The wheel of the London Eye is the largest of its kind ever built at a height of 450 feet. The foundations consist of 44 concrete piles, 110 feet deep, sunk in 2,200 tonnes of concrete. The holding backstay cables are held in place by 1,200 tonnes of concrete and about 1,700 tonnes of steel was used in the construction – the statistics are mind-boggling.

Each of the 32 capsules gently glide the visitor up into the air above the buildings of London and provide a panorama of up to 25 miles in all directions – with the whole trip taking 30 minutes. This is an experience not to be missed, even if you normally do not like heights, and the ride feels as though you are hardly moving. It is difficult to recommend the best time of day to enjoy the trip but a particular favourite is dusk when the lights are coming on all over London: sheer magic. The whole of the capital city stretches out before you and the higher you rise the smaller and more model village-like it becomes – the perfect way to appreciate London's fabulous architecture.
Area Map p.6, C:2

The Monument
Sir Christopher Wren and Robert Hooke, 1671-76

Monument Street, EC3R 8AH • Tel 0207 626 2717 • www.themonument.info • Nearest transport Monument LU • See website for opening times and admission charges

This work is often attributed to Wren alone and yet it has all the hallmarks of a Robert Hooke project, particularly given that the basement was arranged so that he could carry out his experiments and observations with the aid of the column itself, which he used as a sort of telescope.

Erected as both a memorial to the devastated City of London after the Great Fire of 1666 and as a morale-booster to those who were struggling to put the City back together, the Monument stands at 202 feet, taller than Trajan's Column in Rome, and is still believed to be the tallest isolated stone structure in Europe. There are 311 steps to the observation gallery where a spectacular 360° view of the City and beyond awaits.

Made from Portland stone, this fluted Roman Doric column is topped with a bronze urn with flames licking the sky. Area Map p.8, C:2

O2 Arena Climb
Richard Rogers

O2 Arena, Peninsula Square, SE10 0DX • Tel: 0844 856 0202 • www.theo2.co.uk • Nearest transport North Greenwich LU

Perhaps one of the most exhilarating ways of taking in the sights of the capital, 'Up at the O2' offers a guided expedition of the roof of The O2 via a fabric walkway up and over the structure for almost a quarter of a mile. Suspended two metres above the surface of Richard Rogers' O2 roof, the walkway is fifty-two metres above ground level and at its steepest point has an incline of 28° on the way up and 30° on the way back down. At the summit there is an observation platform where climbers can catch their breath and take in the fantastic views.

Please see the O2 website for details and the 'Greenwich Walk' in Chapter Eight of this book for details of the O2 Arena itself.

Tower Bridge
Sir Horace Jones, 1886-94

The Tower Bridge Exhibition, Tower Bridge, SE1 2UP • Tel 020 7403 3761 • www.towerbridge.org.uk • Nearest transport Tower Hill LU • See website for opening times and admission charges

Architect Sir Horace Jones collaborated with engineer Sir John Wolfe Barry to design this definitive London landmark. Victorian technological wizardry hides behind architecture which was designed to be in keeping with the Tower of London nearby; the architect referred to it as 'a steel skeleton clothed in stone'

At the time of the bridge's construction the Pool of London was used intensively. Goods transited through here involved the movement of thousands of ships crammed into moorings designed for just five hundred. The bascules, a French word meaning 'see saw', of the bridge were raised, by necessity, many times during the working day and pedestrians were able to cross the river by means of a high walkway when ships were passing underneath. However, this was wholly unsuitable for those carrying heavy loads or who suffered from vertigo and indeed the walkway was closed in 1910 through lack of use.

Happily, the walkway has been re-opened, from where panoramic views can be enjoyed and is now accessed by passenger lift from the south bank of the Thames. An 11 metre long glass floor in the walkway gives a remarkable birds-eye view of the comings and goings on the bridge directly below, particularly when the bascules are raised to let the occasional ship through. It should be noted that the glass floor can be avoided if so wished! Tower Bridge also offers interesting exhibitions, 'behind the scenes' tours and visits to the engine room. *Area Map p.8, C:1*

Waterloo Bridge
Rendell, Palmer and Tritton, 1937-42

Waterloo Bridge, approached from Lancaster Place on the north bank or Waterloo Road on the south • Free access

All those of a certain age will remember the song 'Waterloo Sunset' by the Kinks and think of Julie and Terry meeting here. Who could blame them, the views are splendid. The river frontage of Somerset House is particularly interesting; from here you can see the water gate that allowed boats into the complex although it's been land-locked since the embankment of the river.

The bridge was built in 1937-42, with Gilbert Scott acting in an advisory role to the architects. This bridge replaced the much-loved one of 1811 by Rennie, the foundations of which were considered unstable.

The Viewing Platform
Jacques Herzog & Pierre de Meuron, 2016

Blavatnik Building (Switch House), Tate Modern, 53 Bankside, SE1 9TG • Tel: 020 7887 8752 • www.tate.org.uk • Nearest transport Southwark LU • Admission free (except for major exhibitions)

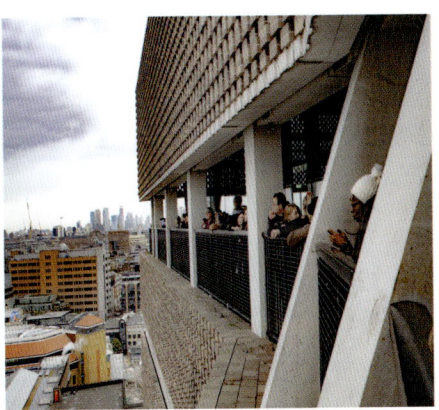

Visitors can linger on the tenth-floor viewing platform for as long as the gallery is open to the public, which means until 10pm on a Friday and Saturday. Although not the tallest of structures in London, this open-air terrace, wrapped around the building, enables visitors to take in some fantastic scenery, particularly towards St Paul's Cathedral and beyond as far as Wembley Stadium. Access is free of charge and the Tate has very thoughtfully provided a refreshment point – should you be unable to tear yourself away.

Please see 'South Bank Walk' in Chapter Eight and the entry for Jacques Herzog and Pierre de Meuron in Chapter Seven for further details about the Tate Modern building.

Please also see 'The Shard', described under 'Renzo Piano' in Chapter Seven. The Shard boasts the highest viewing platform in London with views that stretch forty miles.

Many of the entries in Chapter Nine, Eat and Drink Architecture, feature buildings with distracting views – particularly Oxo Tower and Skylon Restaurant on the Southbank, both with good views across the Thames. In the City, Vertigo at the top of Tower 42; Duck and Waffle at Salesforce Tower (formerly Heron Tower), 110 Bishopsgate and Sky Garden at 20 Fenchurch Street have bars and restaurants worth visiting any time of the day or evening for good news over London. It is advisable to book well in advance at any of these establishments and request a table with a view.
Area Map p.8, A:1

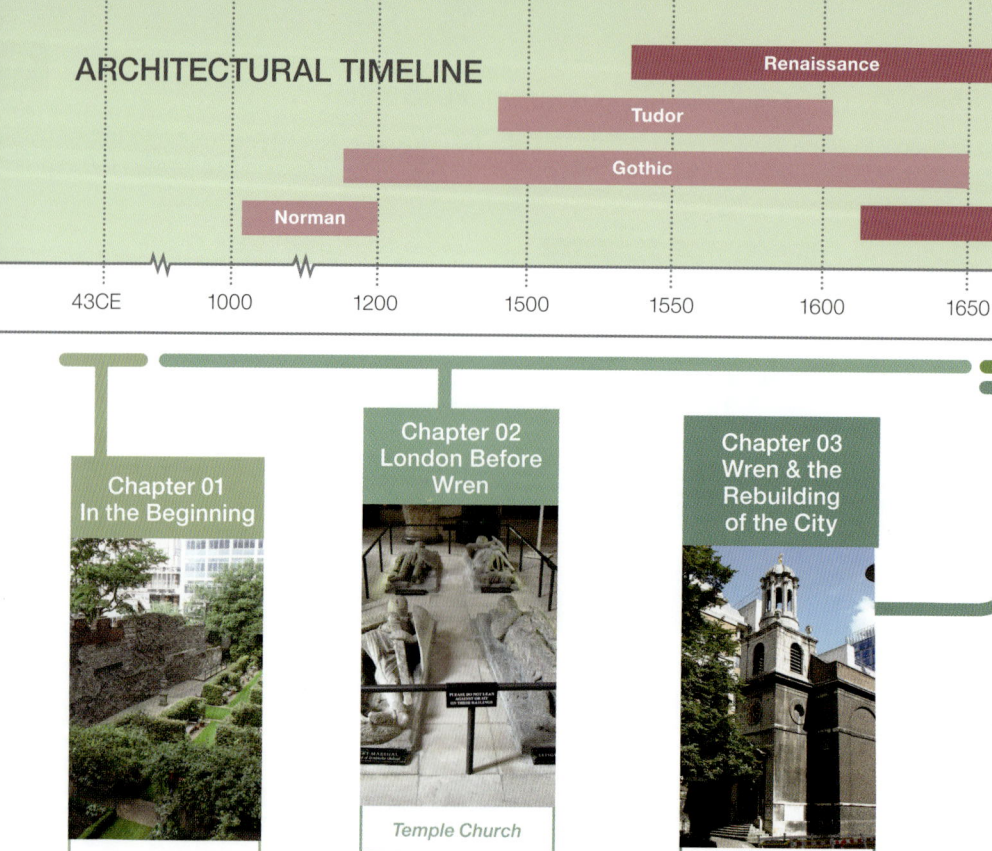

Above (in pink): Architectural Timeline – major periods and styles of British architecture set within their time periods.
Below: See the chapters set within the Architectural Timeline

Baroque							
		Regency				Post-Modernism	
	Neo-Classicism				Modernism		
	Georgian			Art Deco	Brutalism		
Palladian			Arts & Crafts				
1700	1750	1800	1850	1900	1950	2010	

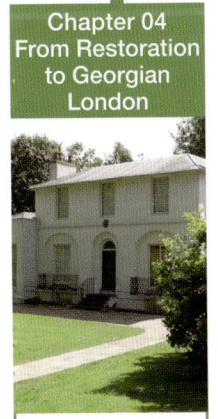

Chapter 04
From Restoration to Georgian London

Keat's House

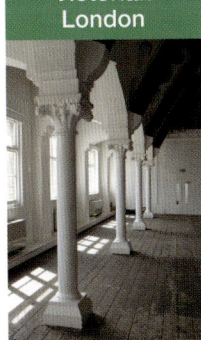

Chapter 05
Victorian London

German Gymnasium

Chapter 06
Edwardian London & the Rise of Modernism

Carreras Cigarette Factory

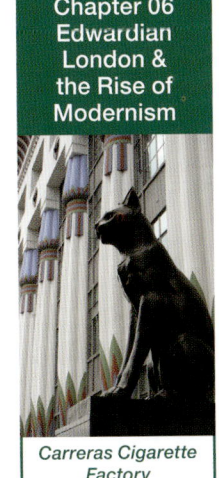

Chapter 07
1945 to the 21st Century

Darwin Centre

Glossary

Abacus: A flat slab (usually of stone or marble) forming the top of a capital.

Ambulatory: A passage (usually at the eastern end of a church) around the sanctuary.

Amphitheatre: An open-air theatre with tiered seating.

Apse: The semicircular end of a Roman basilica (a building used for administrative purposes). The apse was subsequently incorporated into church architecture.

Arcade: Series of arches supported by columns or piers. Also refers to a covered shopping street.

Ashlar: Stone blocks cut into a regular size.

Atrium: A covered court rising through all storeys of a building (especially Roman or 20th century).

Attached or Engaged Column: One that partly merges into the wall and is thus not freestanding.

Bay: Division of an elevation by regular verticals such as arches or windows.

Boss: An ornamented projection usually at the intersection of vault ribs.

Buttress: A wall built at right angles to the main wall to stabilise it or take the thrust of the arch or vault behind. A 'flying buttress' of the Gothic period transmits the thrust to a heavy abutment by means of an arch.

Capital: The head of a classical column.

Caryatids: Female figures supporting an entablature (as seen on the northern exterior of St Pancras New Church, Euston Road, London NW1).

Chancel: Sited towards the eastern end of a church, separated from the nave. Used by officiating clergy and choir.

Clerestory: The wall above the aisles of a church (especially Norman and Gothic) pierced by windows.

Coade Stone: Artificial stone manufactured in London circa 1769-1840.

Concrete: A mixture of cement (ie calcined lime and clay), aggregate (ie small stones or broken brick), sand and water. First used by the Romans but the knowledge of this material was lost at the end of the Roman Empire and only rediscovered during the 15th century. Reinforced concrete contains steel rods for additional support.

Crypt: Underground vaulted chamber, usually at the eastern end of a church, and which sometimes held specific chambers for relics.

Cupola: A dome, and more usually a small dome placed upon a larger one.

Curtain Wall: Non load-bearing external wall (20th-century building); also the wall connecting two towers of a castle or fort.

Dormer: A window projecting from the slope of a roof. 'Dormer' is French for 'to sleep' and often these windows let air and light into roof voids to allow the space to be used as a bedroom.

Eaves: The overhanging edge of a roof.

Entablature: The collective name for the three horizontal members (architrave, frieze and cornice) in classical architecture that is supported by the column.

Fenestration: The arrangement of windows in a building.

Gable: The triangular part of an end wall of a sloping roof.

Hammerbeam: Timber beam projecting from a wall, often elaborately carved.

Hypocaust: Underfloor heating system perfected by the Romans.

Keystone: The top central stone in an arch or vault.

Lancet Window: Long, slim, pointed window.

Lantern: Windowed turret, usually circular, upon a dome.

Lintel: Flat stone or beam above an opening in a wall.

Nave: The central, usually the largest, space in a church.

Pediment: The triangular part above the entablature.

Pilaster: Column, usually square or rectangular, or pillar slightly projecting from a wall.

Rendering: The plastering on the outside wall of a building.

Reredos: Screen, usually painted or carved, behind the altar in a church.

Rood Screen: A partition between the nave and choir of a church – usually carved.

Rotunda: A building or room circular in plan and often with a dome over it.

Rustication: Tooled surface of building stone made to look exaggeratedly rough.

Stucco: A mixture of lime plaster and sand applied to exterior walls – usually to hide inferior brickwork – and often marked to give the impression of stonework.

Vault: Arched stone or brick roof or ceiling.

Bibliography

100 Buildings 100 Years, Twentieth Century Society, various contributors, (Batsford, 2014)
A History of London, *Stephen Inwood* (Macmillan, 1998)
Dictionary of British Architects 1600-1840, *Howard Colvin* (Yale University Press, 1995)
English Architecture, *David Watkins* (Thames & Hudson, 1979)
In Search of London, *H V Morton* (Methuen, 1951)
Liquid History, *Stephen Croad* (Batsford, 2003)
London A-Z, Newer editions have the principal buildings marked (Geographers' A-Z Map Company)
London – Bread and Circuses, *Jonathan Glancey* (Verso, 2001)
London: A Social History, *Roy Porter* (Penguin, 1994)
London's Riverscape – Lost and Found (The London's Found Riverscape Partnership, 2000)
Museums & Galleries of London, *Abigail Willis* (Metro Publications, 2016)
Oxford Dictionary of Architecture, *James Stevens Curl* (Oxford, 1999)
Restoration London, *Lisa Picard* (Phoenix, 2003)
Lisa Picard has also written **Elizabeth's London** and **Dr Johnson's London** (Weidenfeld and Nicholson 2003 and 2000 respectively).
The Buildings of England, *Nikolaus Pevsner* (Founding Editor) (see www.pevsner.co.uk)
The Great Stink of London, *Stephen Halliday* (Sutton Publishing, 1999)

Websites

www.londonopenhouse.org –Open House organises an annual weekend event when hundreds of buildings open their doors to the public
www.architecturelink.org.uk – Provides useful information about architecture, especially buildings in London of the 20th and 21st century.
www.museumoflondon.org.uk – Invaluable information about the history and people of the capital.
www.architecture.com – The website of RIBA (Royal Institute of British Architects).
www.c20society.org.uk – Originally called the Thirties Society the society changed its name to the Twentieth Century Society when good post-war buildings became under threat.
www.london-city-churches.org.uk – A valuable site packed with information and illustrations of the fifty or so churches within the City of London.
www.lookingatbuildings.org.uk – Created by the Pevsner Architectural Guides this is a comprehensive website, with pages on building types, architectural styles and traditions, building materials and methods of construction.
www.newlondonarchitecture.org – NLA is a focus for the debate and discussion of issues facing architecture, planning, development and construction in the capital. Find out about projects that are recently completed, currently under construction or planned.

Index

1-3 Willow Road 175, **213**
1 Blackfriars (The Boomerang) 322, 332
1 London Bridge 327
6-10 Adam St 3, 36
9 Robert Street 118
20 Fenchurch St (Walkie-Talkie) 9, 208, **374**, 397
30 St Mary Axe (Swiss Re HQ) 9, **208**, **244**, 269
38 & 39 Cheyne Walk **181**
44, Berkeley Square, Mayfair **110**
122, Leadenhall St (Cheesegrater) 208, 234

A

Adam, James 112, 314
Adam, Robert 89, 111, **112-119**, 127, 236, 343, 349
Adam Street 7, 118, 343
Adelphi, The 7, **118,** 119
Admiralty The 7, 119, 275, 344, 349,
Aitchison, George 151
All Hallows by the Tower 9, 14, 22, **30**
All Hallows Church 9, 122
Allies and Morrison 217, 303, 334
All Saints (Chelsea Old Church) **54**
All Saints Church 5, **146**
All Souls Church 5, 120, 309, 316-317, 321
Alsop, Will **260**, 272
Apsley House 91, **118**
Aquatics Centre 252, **267**
Archer, Thomas 90, **104-105**, 350, 372
Arnos Grove Underground Station **193**
Art Deco 1, 39, 176, 188-189, 194-196, 282, 292, 332, 358, 364, 368, 373, 380, 382, 399
Art Nouveau 166, 172, 358
Arts & Crafts 141, 165, 172, 175-177, 181, 354, 359
Ashbee, C R 181
Athenaeum, The 7, 309, 318
Australia House 7, 336, 341

B

Baily, E H 318, 346
Baker, Sir Herbert 125, 342, 349
Balfron Tower 212, 215

Banco Commerciale Italiana 9, **145**
Bank of England 9, 124, **125**, 174, 246, 293, 367, 383
Banks, Robert Richardson 271
Bankside Lofts 9, 322, 332
Banqueting House 7, 25, **47,** 88, 91, 110, 344, 349-351, 355
Barbican Estate 9, **230- 231**, 269
Barfield, Julia 393
Barkers 378, **380**
Barlow, W H 156
Baroque 63, 73-74, 88, 98-99, 102-105, 186, 192, 349, 353, 372, 399
Barry, Charles 143, 145, 271, 346, 352
Bazalgette, Sir Joseph 138, 155
BBC Broadcasting House 5, 309, 316
Bedford, Eric **222**
Bentley, John Francis 164, 178
Betjeman, Sir John 29, 159, 165
Bevis Marks 9, 51
Bibendum Oyster Bar 358
Billingsgate Roman House 9, 17
Bishopsgate Institute 140, **165**
Black Friar Public House 9, 359
Blavatnik Building 9, 264, 397
Bloomberg European Headquarters 9, 14, 246
Blore, Edward 28, 55, 320
Bon, Christoph **230**
Borough Market 322, 328-329, 335
Bridge Theatre 9, 322, 324
Britannic House 9, **187**
British Library 2, 3, 129, 241, 360
British Museum 3, 14, 17, 22, 128, **129**, 161-163, 183, 189, 203, 240-241, 347, 360
Brown, Denise Scott 203, 256
Brutalism 219, 230, 399
BT Tower 3, 222, **223**
Buckingham Palace 7, 248, 275, 308-310, 320-321, 346, 349
Burlington, Lord 89, 102, 108, 110
Burlington Arcade 7, 381
Burnet, Sir John 183
Decimus Burton 52, 313, 318

Bush House 7, 336, 341-342
Butterfield, William 73, 146

C

Cabinet War Rooms 7, 353, 355
Cadogan Hall **185**
Café Below **360**
Campbell, Colen 88, 108
Canada House 7, 129, 344, 347
Canary Wharf 198, 206, 272, 291, 298, 301, 305-307, 377
Carlton House Terrace 7, 309, 319
Casson, Hugh 200, 387
Cenotaph 344, 352
Central Criminal Court 9, 182
Central Saint Martins 207
Centre Point 3, **224**
Chamberlin, Peter **230**
Chambers, Sir William 47, 90, 96, **111-112**, 319, 340
Channel 4 Headquarters 7, 234
Charles, Prince 42, 202, 227
Charlton House **43**
Charterhouse House & Square 9, **56**, 281-282
Chester Gate & Terrace 5, 308, 312
Chipperfield, David 1, 239, **270-271**, 386
Chisholm, R F 185
Chiswick House 86, 91, **108-109**, 361
Christ Church, Newgate St 66
Christ Church, Spitalfields **99**
Church Building Commission 127
Church of St Margaret 355
Citadel 344, 350
City Hall 9, **242-243**, 269, 322, 324-325
City of London Information Centre 9, **269**
Claridge's 364
Cloth Fair 9, 281, 282-283, 286
Coliseum Theatre 7, **180**
Cooper, Sir Edwin 235-236, 376
Corbusier 200, 215, 217, 219, 226, 230
Cornwall Terrace 5, 308, 313
Cottons Centre 322, 325
Country Life Offices 7, **181**
County Hall 7, **186**, 334, 393

Courtauld Gallery 340, 343
Courtauld Institute of Art 114, 336, 340
Crabtree, W 384
Crescent, City of London **123**
Crewe, Bertie 193
Crosby Hall **54**
Crossness Pumping Station 138, **155**
Cubitt, Thomas 325
Cumberland Terrace 5, 120, 308, 310-312

D

Daily Express Building 1, 7, 9, 290, 292
Daimler Car Hire Garage 3, 195
Dance the elder 121-122
Dance the Younger 40, 121-124, 128, 133, 187, 284
Darwin Centre 163, 205, 399
Davis, Joseph Gordon 149
de Meuron, Pierre 203, **262-264**, 331, 397
Design Museum, The 6, 220
Dixon and Jones 369, 371
Dockray, Robert 145
Duck and Waffle **363**, 397
Duke of York's Column 7, 309, 319-320
Dulwich Picture Gallery **125**

E

Economist Building, The 7, **232-233**
Edward Cullinan Architects 329
Edward VII Galleries 183
Elcock and Sutcliffe 292
Eltham Palace **39**
Embankment Place 7, 202, 256, 343
Emirates Air Line 299, 390
Eric Parry Architects 208, 282, 347
Euston Fire Station 3, **177**
Evelina London Children's Hospital 7, 249
Exhibition Road Quarter **274-275**

F

Farrell, Terry 202, **256**, 343, 368
Festival of Britain 200, 209, 217, 220, 376
Fielden and Mawson 96, 114
Finsbury Health Centre 210

Fitzrovia Chapel 5, 168
Fitzroy Square 3, 119
Flamsteed House 298, 301, 307
Florin Court 9, 281-282
Foreign and Commonwealth Office 7, 148, 352
Fortnum and Mason 7, 381
Foster, Norman 198, 203-206, 209, 234, **238-247**, 248, 256, 269-271, 306, 325, 331, 342
Fowke, Captain Francis 152, 161
Fox, Kohn Pedersen 194, 363
Frederick Place 9, 119
Freemasons' Hall 3, **189**
Fulham Palace **49**, 237

G

Geffrye Museum **130-131**
Gehry, Frank 200, 237
George, Bernard 380
George, Sir Ernest 313, 330
George Inn 9, 322, 328, 335, **364**
The German Gymnasium **365**
Gherkin 9, 208, **244**, 269
Gibbs, James 90, 106-107, **251**, 277, 285, 300, 338, 347, 349
Gill, Eric 178, 191, 194, 316
Globe Theatre 330, 335
Gloucester Gate & Lodge 5, 308, 310
Goldfinger, Erno 175, 200, **212-213**
Goodhart-Rendel, H S 196
Gothic 23, 28-29, 33, 40-41, 52-53, 55, 62, 67, 72-73, 78, 80, 91, 98, 101-102, 127, 136, 139-140, 143, 146, 148, 157, 172, 178, 184, 293, 319, 337, 352, 354, 398, 400
Graduate Centre, London Metropolitan Uni **259**
Great Court, The British Museum **240-241**
Great Exhibition 96, 140, 148, 152, 161, 200, 275
Great Fire of London 23, 38, 43, 50, 60-63, 66-68, 72-74, 79-81, 83, 283, 286, 293-294, 329, 331, 360, 384, 394
Greenwich Foot Tunnel 298-299, 307
Gribble, Herbert 160
Gibbons, Grinling 30, 48, 77, 92-93
Gropius, Walter 175, 387

Gruning, Edward 365
Guildhall 9, **18**, 22, 40, 74, 121, 231, 288, 354

H

Haberdashers' Hall 9, 248, 281, 285-286
Hackney Empire 174, 180
Hadid, Zaha 209, 237, 252, **266-267**, 276, 362
Handel House & Hendrix Flat 131
Hanover Gate & Terrace 5, 308, 313
Hardwick, Philip 99, 136
Hardwick, Thomas 284, 313
Harrap, Julian 99, 288
Harrods 173, 347, **382**
Hawksmoor, Nicholas 28, 73, 76, 80-90, 95, **98-101**, 300, 305
Hayward Gallery 7, 218-219
Haywood, William 149
Heatherwick Studio 207
Heron (Salesforce) Tower 9, **363**, 397
Herron, Ron 204
Herzog, Jacques **262**, 264, 331, 397
Herzog and de Meuron 203, **262-264**
Highpoint One & Two 210
Hoare's Bank 7, 290, 293
Holden, Charles 176, 183, 191, 193, 197
Holl, Steven **276-277**, 285
Holland, Henry 90, 319
Holy Trinity Church, Marylebone 5, 127
Home House 5, **114**
Hooke, Robert 60, 62, 66, 69-70, 73, 75, 77, 82, 301, 394
Hopkins, Lady Patty 248
Hopkins, Sir Michael **248**, 256, 286, 320, 353, 372
Horniman Museum **166**
Horse Guards Parade 110, 344-346, 349, 351, 355
Houses of Parliament 7, 32, 99, 136, 138, **143**, 184, 344-345, 349, 353-355, 369

I

Imagination 3, 203-204, 236
India House 7, 336, 341-342
Inner Temple 290, 294, 297
Institute of Directors, The 7, 309, 318

J

James, John 28, 192, 300
Jewel Tower 7, 32, **33**, 143
Dr Johnson's House 132, 290, 293, 297
Jones, Edward 369
Jones, Inigo 14, 25, 43-44, 47-48, 61, 70, 88, 91, 105, 108-109, 283, 303-304, 350-351
Jones, Sir Horace 141, 236, 288, 296, 384, 395

K

Kaplicky, Jan 272-273
Keats House **132**
Kensington Palace 94-95
Kent, William 89, 95, 108-**109**, **110**, 114, 270, 346, 350
Kenwood House 116, 209
King's College 7, 129, 336, 340, 342
King's Observatory, Richmond **111**
King William Block 103, 298
Knott, Ralph 186
Kohn Pedersen Fox Associates 194

L

Lambeth Palace 7, 55, 249, 329
Lanchester & Rickards 184, 377
Langham Hotel 5, 309, 314
Lansdowne House **114**, 121
Lasdun, Denys **226**, **227**, 228, 312, 333
Leadenhall Market 9, 141, 236, 288, 296, **384**
Leighton House 150, **151**
Levete, Amanda 1, **272-273**, 275
Lex Garage 7, 174, **192**
Libeskind, Daniel **258-259**
Lloyd's of London 9, 201, **235**
London 2012 Velodrome 252
London Architectural Society 91
London Central Mosque 5, 308, 313, 321
London Eye 7, 186, 245, 334, 388, 392, **393**
London Mithraeum 9, **18-19**, 246
London Oratory Church **160**
London Transport HQ 7, 176, 190, **191**
Mottistone, Lord 30, 284
Lord's Cricket Ground 272, **273**

Lubetkin, Berthold **210**, 226
Lutyens, Edwin 172, 181, 187, 291, 313, 352, 367

M

Mackintosh, Charles Rennie 165, 276
Maggie's Centres 9, **276-277**, 281, 285
Make Architects 252, 382
Mansion House 9, 121, **122**
Marks, David 393
Marlborough House 7, **96**
Martin, Sir Leslie **216**, 217, 220
Marylebone Parish Church 308, 313
Masey, Cyril 193
Matcham, Frank 174, 180, 193
Mather, Rick 125, 224, 304
Matthew, Sir Robert 217, **220-222**
McAslan, John 145
Collins, M E and O H 188
ME London 7, 336, 342
Albert Memorial 139, **148**
Methodist Central Hall 7, 173, **184**, 345, 377
Mewes, Charles 370
Middle Temple 290, 294, 296, 297
Midland Grand Hotel, The 3, **156-159**
Millennium Bridge 9, 83, 203, 269, 322, 331
Milne, Oswald 364
Mithras 9, **18-19**, 246
Modernism 5, 185, 187, 192, 200-201, 230, 399
Moller, C F 161, 163, 205
Monument, The 9, 96, 394
Morris, William 141, 149, 165, 175, 181, 275
Moya, Hidalgo 376
Museum of London 9, 14, 19, 186, 288, 306, 307

N

Nash, John 5, 42, 91, **120**, 173, 222, 228, 248, 280, **308-320**, 341, 346, 347
National Gallery 7, 202, 344-349, 355
National Maritime Museum 44, 298, 303, 307
National Portrait Gallery 7, 369
National Theatre 7, 226, **227**, 322, 333-335
Natural History Museum 152, **161-162**, 205, 276
Ned, The 9, 367

New Government Offices 7, 344
News International headquarters 272
New Zealand House 7, 222
Nicholas Hare Architects 205
No1 Canada Square 298, 306

O
O2 Arena 298, 306-307, 390, **394**
Octagon of Orleans House **107**
Open House 1, 139, 197, 215, 236, 292, 352, **403**
Osterley Park **115**
Oxo Tower 322, 332, 333, 335, **368**, 397

P
Painted Hall 298, 305, 307
Palace of Westminster 7, 27-33, **142-144**, 387
Palestra 9, **260**
Palladian (Palladianism) 44, 47, 88-89, 102, 91, 108-110, **122**, 125, 271, 350, 361
Park Crescent 5, 309, 312, 314, 317-318
Parry, Eric 208, 282, 328, 347
Pawson, John 6, 220
Pearson, John Loughborough 168-169
Peter Jones **384**
Pevsner, Nicholas 20, 49, 105, 160, 183-184, 282, 288, 313, 316, 402-403
Phoenix Theatre 7, **193**
Piano, Renzo 1, 201, 234, 254-255, 328, 397
Piazza, & St Paul's Church 7, **48**
Pizza Express 9, 368
Portcullis House 7, 248, 344, 353-354
Portland Place 5, 309, 314, 316, 321
Port of London Authority 9, 189, 376
Powell, Geoffrey 230
Powell, Philip 376
Prince Henry's Room 7, 290, 294, 297
Privy Council Chambers 7, 344, 352
A W Pugin 143, 164, 328

Q
Queen Elizabeth Hall 7, 219
Queen's House 25, **44-45**, 88, 91, 298, 303-304, 307

R
Rambert Dance Company 322, 334
Ranger's House 298, 300-301, 307
Regent's Park Zoo 5, 310
Rendell, Palmer and Tritton 395
Rennie, John 327, 330
Reuters Building 9, 291
RIBA Stirling Prize 237, 244, 246, 260, 266, 270, 273
Riley, W E 177
Ritz, The 7, 173, 370
Rogers, Richard 17, 201, 203, 208, **234-237**, 238, 254, 256, 270, 272, 306, 394
Rogers Stirk Harbour & Partners 237
Roman Bath 7, 336, 338
Rotunda Bar **371**
Roundhouse, The **145**
Royal Academy of Arts 1, 7, 91, 239, **271**, 340
Royal Albert Hall **152**, 161
Royal Arsenal, Woolwich **103**
Royal College of Physicians 5, **228**, 308, 312, 347
Royal Courts of Justice 7, 336-337, 343
Royal Exchange 9, 62, 367, **383**
Royal Festival Hall 7, 200, **217-219**, 334, 376
Royal Hospital Chelsea **93**, 304
Royal Institute of British Architects (RIBA) 5, 202, 204, 310, 314, 321, 403
Royal Naval College 298, 304, 307
Royal Observatory 96, 298, 301, 307
Royal Opera House 7, 22
Royal Society of Arts 7, **118**, 336, 343
Rudolf Steiner House 5, **192**
Russell House 7, **105**

S
St Alban 9, **67**
St Alfege Church 298, 300, 307
St Andrew by the Wardrobe 9, **68**
St Andrew, Holborn 3, **68**
St Anne and St Agnes **69**
St Anne, Limehouse **99**
St Anne & St Agnes 9, **69**
St Bartholomew's Hospital 9, 34, 277, 281, 283-285, 289

Index

St Bartholomew the Great 9, **34**, 277, 281-284, 289
St Bartholomew the Less 9, 123, 284, 289
St Benet 9, **70**
St Bride 9, **71**, 79, 290-291, 297
St Clement Danes 7, 336, 338, 343
St Clement Eastcheap 9, **72**
St Dunstan in the East 9, **72**
St Dunstan in the West 7, 290, 293, 297
St Edmund the King & Martyr 9, **73**
St Ethelburga's, Bishopsgate 9, **50**
St George's Bloomsbury 3, 100
St Helen's Bishopsgate 9, **38**, 82
St James Garlickhithe 9, **73**
St James's Café 7, 345, **372**
St James's Palace 7, **42**, 351
St James's, Piccadilly 7, **92**
St John, Caruso 361, 370
St John's Priory 9, **36**
St John's, Smith Square 7, 99, **372**
St Lawrence Jewry 9, **74**
St Magnus the Martyr 9, **74**
St Margaret Lothbury **75**
St Margaret Pattens 9, 76
St Margaret's Church 7, **41**, 344, 354
St Martin-in-the-Fields 7, 107, 285, 344-345, 347, 355
St Martin within Ludgate 9, **77**
St Mary Abbots 148
St Mary Abchurch 9, **77**
St Mary Aldermary 9, **78**
St Mary at Hill 9, **79**, 80
St Mary-le-Bow 9, 66, **79**, 360
St Mary-le-Strand 7, 90, **106**, 285, 336, 340, 343
St Mary's Church **164**
St Mary Woolnoth 9, 90, **100**
St Michael Cornhill 9, **80**, 101
St Michael Paternoster Royal 9, **81**
St Nicholas Cole Abbey 9, **83**
St Olaf House 9, **196**, 322, 327
St Pancras Grand Champagne Bar **373**
St Pancras International 159, 365
St Pancras Old Church **37**
St Pancras Station 3, 134, **136**, **156**, 159, 206, 373
St Paul's Cathedral 58, 61, **63-65**, 71, 85, 98, 194, 208-209, 264
St Paul's Church 7, **48**
St Paul's Deptford **105**
St Peter upon Cornhill 9, **82**
St Peter, Vere Street 5, **107**
St Stephen Walbrook 9, 66, **85**, 246
Sackler Galleries **239**
Sadler's Wells 3, 205
Sambourne House, Linley **149**
Savoy Chapel 336, 342, 343
Scotland Yard 7, 344, 349, 353-354
Scott, George Gilbert 28, 37, 40, 41, 52, 80, 139, 148, 156, 159, 193, 263-264, 331, 352, 395
Scott, Giles Gilbert 37, 40, 193, 263, 264, 331
Sedding, J D 165
Seely and Paget 30, 284
Seifert, Richard 224, 377
Selfridges 1, 5, 175, **386**
Senate House 3, 170, 176, 183, **197**
Serpentine Sackler Gallery 266, **362**
Severs' House, Dennis **133**
Shard, The 1, 9, 254, **255**, 328
Shaw, Norman 165, 342, 353
Shuttleworth, Ken 230, **269**
Simpson, J Lomax 194
Soane, Sir John 37, 47, 112, **124-127**, 128, 301
Soane's Museum, Sir John 3, 124, 126, **127**
Sir Paul Pindar's House Façade, **56**
Skidmore, Owings & Merrill 208, 233
Sky Garden **374**, 397
Skylon Restaurant **376**, 397
Smirke, Robert 42, 52, **128**, 129, 183, 241, 340, 347
Smirke, Sidney 52, 129
Smith, Sidney R J 370
Smithfield Market 9, 141, 281, 286, 288
Alison & Peter Smithson **232**
Somerset House 7, 90-91, 111, 114, 239, 336, 340-343, 395
South Africa House 7, 341, 344, 349
South Bank 1, 5, 196, 204, 217-219, 227-238, 242, 280, 322-329, 331-335, 397

Image credits:

p.35 St Bartholomew the Great © Dillif, p.38 © Eltham Palace, p.44 © Queen's House, p.48 © Banqueting House, p.49 © Fulham Palace, p.55, Lambeth Palace © Chris Dorney, p.64 St Paul's © Chris Dorney, p.87 & p.89 © Chiswick House, p.89 © Apsley House, p.90 Somerset House © Marco Beck Peccoz, p.109 © Chiswick House, p.113 © Syon House, p.116 © Kenwood House, p.126 Sir John Soanes Museum © Martin Charles, p.151 © Leighton House, p.153 Royal Albert Hall © VisitBritain, p.163 National History Museum © Derek Adams, p.166 Horniman © Caroline Hughes, p.167 Whitechapel Gallery © Guy Montagu-Pollock, p.178 Westminster Abbey © Chris Dorney, p.179 Westminster Abbey © Dillif, Lloyd's of London © Chris Dorney, p.204 © Imagination, p.212, 213 Willow Road © National Trust, p,216 © Royal Festival Hall, p.221 Design Museum © VisitBritain. P.240 © British Museum, p.247 Bloomberg Offices © Nigel Young/Foster + Partners, p.249 Evelina London Children's Hospital © Paul Tyagi, p.250 Wellcome Trust Gibbs Building © Nick Guttridge, p.253 Velodrome © Hopkins, p.265 Tate Modern © Andy Stagg, p.267 Aquatics Centre © Hufton + Crow, p.269 London Wall Place © Make Architects, p.271 Royal Academy of Arts Extension © Simon Menges, p.275 Exhibition Road Quarter © Hufton + Crow, p.277 Maggie's Barts © Marcela Spadaro and Freya Najade, p.353 Chiswick House Café © Jeff Knowles, p.363 © SUSHISAMBA, p.366 © The Ned, p.375 © Sky Garden, p.385 Leadenhall Market © Chris Dorney, p.387 Waterstones © Mike Massaro

Stephen Millar: p.10, p.20, p.26, p.29, p.37, p.41, p.51, p.52, p.53, p.58, p.69, p.72, p.73, p.78, p.80, p.81, p.84, p.93, p.99, p.101, p.104, p.120, p.134, p.137, p.139, p.141, p.143, p.146, p.161, p.162, p.165, p.170, p.186, p.188, p.190, p.195, p.197, p.198, p.202, p.208, p.223, p.239, p.241, p.243, p.356, p.365, p.373, p.388, p.392

Metro Publications: p.16, p.31, p.37, p.40, p.57, p.63, p.67, p.69, p.70, p.75, p.76, p.82, p.83, p.85, p.94, p.115, p.123, p.128, p.129, p.130, p.154, p.156, p.157, p.158, p.159, p.168, p.169, p.175, p.177, p.182, p.185, p.187, p.196, p.198, p.206, p.207, p.211, p.214, p.218, p.225, p.227, p.228, p.231, p.232, p.254, p.257, p.258, p.254, p.257, p.258, p.,262, p.356, p 362, p.378, p.386, p.391. p.398

Southwark Bridge 322, 329, 330
Southwark Cathedral 9, 33, 322, 328, 331, 335
Spa Green Estate 3, **210**
Staple Inn 3, **43**
Street, George Edward 337
Stuart, James 'Athenian' 89, 305
Supreme Court 7, 344-345, 354
Sussex Place 5, 308, 313
Switch (Blavatnik Building) House 9, 264, **397**
Syon House **113**

T
Tate Britain 370
Tate Modern 9, 203, **262-263**, 322, 331- 332, 335, **397**
Taylor, John 96
Temple Bar 7, 290, 296-297, 337
Temple Church 7, **52-53**, 290, 294, 297, 398,
Terry, Quinlan 38
Tite, Sir William 383
Tower 42 (Nat West Tower) 9, **223**-224, **377**, 397
Tower Bridge 9, 242, 288, 296, 322, 324, **395**
Tower of London 9, **31**, 301, 374, 395
Townsend, Charles Harrison 165-167
Trellick Tower 212, **215**
Two Temple Place 7, **169**

U
Ulster Place 5, 309, 314
Unilever House 9, **194**

V
Vanbrugh, Sir John 85, 88, 91, 96, 98, **102**, 103, 173, 182, 305
Vanbrugh Castle 102
Vauxhall Cross **257**
Venturi, Robert 202, 256
Venturi, Rauch and Scott Brown 347
Vertigo (Tower 42) 9, 377, 397
Holborn Viaduct **149**
Victoria & Albert Museum 1, 258, 272, **275**
Vinoly, Rafael 208, 374
Voysey, C F A 165

W
Walkie-Talkie (20 Fenchurch St) 9, 208, **374**, 397
Wallis Gilbert & Partners 195
Ware, Samuel 381
Waterhouse, Alfred 139, 152, 161, 163, 205
Waterloo Bridge 334, 395
Waterstones 7, **387**
Webb, Aston 34, 186, 275, 320, 349
Webb, John 304
Welcome Collection & Trust 5, **251**
Wesley's House, John **133**
Westminster Abbey 7, 20, 23, 26, **27**, 31-33, **101**, 168, 184, 222, 345, 354, 355
Westminster Cathedral 7, 164, **178-179**
Westminster Hall 7, **32**, 143
Wheeler, Montague 192
Whitechapel Art Gallery **167**
Whitehall Court 344, 350
Wilkins, William 346
Williams, Sir Owen 292
Williams, Stanton 207, 275, 288
Wimperis, Simpson & Guthrie 381
Winchester House 9, 322, 329
Mann, Withrford Watson 167
Wood, Robert 89
Wood, Sancton 145
Wornum, Grey 314
Wren, Sir Christopher 5, 25, 28, **60-97**, 98, 102, 127, 173, 181, 182, 184, 291, 296, 303, 304, 305, 306, 338, 360, 394, 398
Wyatt, James 28, 114, 118

Y
Yates, Sir Ernest George 313
Yevele, Henry 28, 32, 33, 56
Young, William 349

Z
Zimbabwe House 7, 176, **183**